MARY TUDOR

For my family, who give me unconditional support and of course Mary Tudor, Queen of France, without whom this book would not exist.

MARY TUDOR

Queen of France

AMY McELROY

PEN & SWORD
HISTORY

AN IMPRINT OF PEN & SWORD BOOKS LTD.
YORKSHIRE – PHILADELPHIA

First published in Great Britain in 2025 by
PEN AND SWORD HISTORY
An imprint of
Pen & Sword Books Ltd
Yorkshire – Philadelphia

ISBN 978 1 39904 185 0

A CIP catalogue record for this book is available from the British Library.

Typeset in Times New Roman 10.5/13.5 by
SJmagic DESIGN SERVICES, India.
Printed and bound in the UK by CPI Group (UK) Ltd.

The Publisher's authorised representative in the EU for product safety is Authorised Rep Compliance Ltd., Ground Floor, 71 Lower Baggot Street, Dublin D02 P593, Ireland.
www.arccompliance.com

For a complete list of Pen & Sword titles please contact:
PEN & SWORD BOOKS LIMITED
George House, Units 12 & 13, Beevor Street, Off Pontefract Road,
Barnsley, South Yorkshire, S71 1HN, England
E-mail: enquiries@pen-and-sword.co.uk
Website: www.pen-and-sword.co.uk

or

PEN AND SWORD BOOKS
1950 Lawrence Rd, Havertown, PA 19083, USA
E-mail: uspen-and-sword@casematepublishers.com
Website: www.penandswordbooks.com

MIX
Paper | Supporting responsible forestry
FSC® C013604

Contents

Acknowledgements

This is my third book, but my first biography focusing on one individual. It has been a pleasure to research and write about Mary Tudor, a woman who is thoroughly deserving of her own story, not just a cameo in another's story.

Once again, I must thank those at Pen and Sword for giving me this opportunity, in particular Sarah-Beth, Lucy and Laura. A further thank you to the Pen and Sword author family; I have been met with nothing but kindness, in particular thank you to Sarah J. Hodder, Carol Ann Lloyd, Helene Harrison, Caroline Angus and Brigitte Webster for your kindness and support. I owe a huge thank you to Tony Riches. Tony is not only responsible for me making the step onto Twitter (now X) to share my book reviews, and therefore taking the first steps to becoming an author, but also for sharing valuable sources with me, including his own copy of *The French Queen's Letters*, a book that would prove of vital importance to the writing of this. Tony had used the work in his own work on Mary, a book I greatly enjoyed, and can now understand even more the depth of his research when he entertains us with his historical fiction. Tony, your kindness, generosity and support has been wonderful and I hope I can one day return the favour.

Pops, I know history isn't really your genre (other than Dan Jones' *Essex Dogs*) so thank you for all of your support and the updates on your reading progress when reading my work, I love you. Michelle, thank you for the road trips and supporting me since the beginning. I'm not the best at responding quickly but you know how grateful I am for everything you do. Bec, as always you have given me such great advice and support since I started writing, you have kept me grounded when I doubt myself and encouraged me to keep going, one word at a time. An additional thank you for your help with a couple of sources, I am forever grateful and of course, to Jem, for his help. My eternal gratitude to my friend, John Simmons, for all his support and assistance with some tricky sources; I need to also thank you for the laughs and entertainment along the way. Special thanks to Pam, an incredible friend who supports every step I take, always encourages me, keeps my spirits up, and always makes sure I am fully stocked on pens and Snickers. Helen, I can never thank you enough for the support you give me, I am hoping by the time you read this you will have your very own publication news – I believe in you! I also owe my gratitude to Charlotte for listening to my worries and helping me decide on chapter titles when I could not make a decision.

I am very grateful to St Mary's Church, Bury St Edmunds for kindly allowing me to take many photographs and producing a number of them here. St Mary's Church is not only beautiful but is the resting place of Mary Tudor and I could not have been made to feel more welcome. I very much enjoyed chatting about Mary and I do hope you enjoy this book. St Laurence's Church in Ludlow have also been kind in the same way. Along with sharing sources, Tony Riches also provided me with some of the images you will see within and I am so grateful to be able to share them with you all. There is a wealth of kindness within the Tudor community and I have been very fortunate in receiving more than my fair share.

Lastly, as always, a huge thank you to the institutions who permit the use of their images: The National Library of Wales; Wellcome Collection; Rijksmuseum; and the Folger Shakespeare Library. Locating images can be incredibly difficult and their dedication to sharing those images they hold is gratefully received. I would also like to thank Westminster Abbey for making the procurement of images so easy and without having to file for bankruptcy as a result of costs.

List of Illustrations

Notable Persons

* The numbers in brackets following a marriage correlate with brackets after the children to show the issue of each marriage. Not all births are noted here.

Anne Boleyn – Born: *c.*1507, Blickling Hall. Parents: Elizabeth Howard and Thomas Boleyn, 1st Earl of Wiltshire. Coronation: 1 June 1533. Married: Henry VIII (1533). Children: Elizabeth I. Died: 19 May 1536, Tower of London. Buried: Church of St Peter ad Vincula, Tower of London.

Anne Brandon – Born: *c.*1507. Parents: Anne Browne and Charles Brandon. Married: Edward Grey, 3rd Baron Grey of Powys; Randal Haworth. No children. Died: January 1558. Buried: Possibly Westminster Abbey or St Margaret's Church, Westminster.

Arthur, Prince of Wales – Born: 19 or 20 September 1496, Winchester. Parents: Elizabeth of York and Henry VII. Married: Katharine of Aragon on 14 November 1501 at St Paul's Cathedral. Died: 2 April 1502, Ludlow Castle. Buried: Worcester Cathedral; it is believed Arthur's heart is buried in St Lawrence's Church, Ludlow.

Cardinal Thomas Wolsey – Born: *c.*1473, Ipswich. Parents: Joan Daundy and Robert Wolsey. Died: 29 November 1530, Leicester. Buried: Leicester Abbey.

Charles Brandon, Duke of Suffolk – Born: *c.*1484. Parents: Elizabeth Bruyn and Sir William Brandon. Married: Margaret Neville (1); Anne Brown (2); Mary Tudor (3); Katherine Willoughby (4). Children: Anne Brandon, Baroness Grey of Powys (2); Mary Brandon, Baroness Monteagle (2); Henry Brandon (3); Frances Brandon, Duchess of Suffolk (3); Eleanor Brandon, Countess of Cumberland (3); Henry Brandon, 1st Earl of Lincoln (3); Henry Brandon, 2nd Duke of Suffolk (4); Charles Brandon, 3rd Duke of Suffolk (4). Died: 22 August 1545, Guildford. Buried: St George's Chapel, Windsor.

Charles Archduke of Austria, later Charles V, Holy Roman Emperor – Born: 24 February 1500, Prinsenhof of Ghent. Parents: Juana, Queen of Castile and Philip I of Castile. Succeeded as Holy Roman Emperor in 1519. Married: Isabella of Portugal in 1526 (she died 1539). Children: Philip II of Spain; Maria, Holy Roman Empress; Joanna, Princess of Portugal; Margaret, Duchess of Florence and Parma; John of Austria (Illegitimate). Died: 21 September 1588, Monastery of Yuste. Buried: El Escorial.

Claude, Queen of France – Born: 13 October 1499, Romorantin-Lanthenay. Parents: Anne, Duchess of Brittany and Louis XII of France. Coronation: 10 May 1517. Married: Francis d'Angoulême, Duke of Valois (Later Francis I of France) in 1514. Children: Louise; Charlotte; Francis III, Duke of Brittany; Henry II of France; Madeline, Queen of Scots; Charles II, Duke of Orléans; Margaret, Duchess of Savoy. Died: 20 July 1524, Château de Blois. Buried: Basilica of St Denis.

Eleanor Brandon – Born: 1519. Parents: Mary Tudor, Queen of France and Charles Brandon, Duke of Suffolk. Married: Henry Clifford, 2nd Earl of Cumberland in 1535. Children: Margaret Stanley, Countess of Derby; Henry Clifford; Charles Clifford. Died: 27 September 1547, Brougham Castle. Buried: Skipton.

Elizabeth of York – Born: 11 February 1466, Westminster Palace. Parents: Elizabeth Woodville and Edward IV. Married: Henry VII on 18 January 1486. Mother of seven children, four of whom survived infancy: Arthur, Prince of Wales; Margaret Tudor, Queen of Scots; Henry VIII; Mary, Queen of France. Died: 11 February 1503, Tower of London. Buried: Westminster Abbey.

Frances Brandon – Born: 16 July 1517, Hatfield. Parents: Mary Tudor, Queen of France and Charles Brandon, Duke of Suffolk. Married: Henry Grey, 1st Duke of Suffolk (1); Adrian Stokes (2). Children, all with Henry Grey (her children with Adrian Stokes did not survive infancy): Lady Jane Grey; Lady Katherine Grey; Lady Mary Grey. Died: 20 November 1559, London. Buried: Westminster Abbey.

Francis I of France – Born: 12 September 1494, Château de Cognac. Parents: Louise of Savoy and Charles, Count of Angoulême. Coronation: 25 January 1515. Married: Claude, Duchess of Brittany (1514–1524) (1); Eleanor of Austria (1530–1547) (2). Children (all with Claude, Queen of France): Louise; Charlotte; Francis III, Duke of Brittany; Henry II of France; Madeline, Queen of Scots;

Charles II, Duke of Orléans; Margaret, Duchess of Savoy. Died: 31 March 1547, Château de Rambouillet. Buried: Basilica of St Denis.

Henry Brandon – Born: 1516. Parents: Mary Tudor, Queen of France and Charles Brandon, Duke of Suffolk. First son of Mary Tudor and Charles Brandon. Died: 1522.

Henry Brandon, 1st Earl of Lincoln – Born: 1523. Parents: Mary Tudor, Queen of France and Charles Brandon, Duke of Suffolk. Second son of Mary Tudor and Charles Brandon. Their first son, also named Henry, died 1522. Created 1st Earl of Lincoln by his uncle, Henry VIII, in 1525. He was originally intended to marry Katherine Willoughby but his father married her instead. Died: 1 March 1534, Southwark.

Henry VII – Born: 28 January 1457, Pembroke Castle. Parents: Lady Margaret Beaufort, Countess of Richmond and Edmund Tudor, 1st Earl of Richmond. Coronation: 30 October 1485. Married: Elizabeth of York on 18 January 1486 at Westminster Abbey. Seven children, four of whom survived infancy: Arthur, Prince of Wales; Margaret Tudor, Queen of Scots; Henry VIII; Mary, Queen of France. Died: 21 April 1509, Richmond Palace. Buried: Westminster Abbey.

Henry VIII – Born: 28 June 1491, Palace of Placentia (Greenwich). Parents: Elizabeth of York and Henry VII. Married: Katharine of Aragon in 1509 (divorced 1533) (1); Anne Boleyn in 1533 (beheaded 1536) (2); Jane Seymour in 1536 (died 1537) (3); Anne of Cleves in 1540 (annulled 1540); Catherine Howard in 1540 (beheaded 1542); Kateryn Parr in 1543. Children: Mary I of England (1); Elizabeth I of England (2); Edward VI (3); Henry Fitzroy (Illegitimate). Died: 28 January 1547, Palace of Whitehall. Buried: St George's Chapel, Windsor.

Jane Grey – Born: *c.*1537, possibly Bradgate Park. Parents: Frances Brandon, Duchess of Suffolk and Henry Grey, 1st Duke of Suffolk. Married: Lord Guildford Dudley in 1553. Died: 12 February 1554, Tower of London. Buried: Church of St Peter ad Vincula, Tower of London.

Joan Vaux, Lady Guildford – Born: *c.*1463. Parents: Katherine Penyston and Sir William Vaux. Married: Sir Richard Guildford (1); Sir Anthony Poyntz (2). Only one child, Henry Guildford, with her first husband. Died: 4 September 1438. Buried: Convent of Blackfriars.

Katharine of Aragon – Born: 16 December 1485, Archiepiscopal Palace, Castile. Parents: Isabella I of Castile and Ferdinand of Aragon. Married: Arthur, Prince of Wales in 1501 (1); Henry VIII in 1509 (2). Children: Mary I (2). Died: 7 January 1536, Kimbolton Castle. Buried: Peterborough Cathedral.

Katherine Grey – Born: 25 August 1540, Bradgate Park. Parents: Frances Brandon, Duchess of Suffolk and Henry Grey, 1st Duke of Suffolk. Married: Henry Herbert, Lord Herbert in 1553 (annulled 1554) (1); Edward Seymour, 1st Earl of Hertford in 1560 (2). Children, both with Edward Seymour: Edward Seymour, Lord Beauchamp; Thomas Seymour. Died: 26 January 1568, Cockfield Hall. Buried: Salisbury Cathedral.

Katherine Willoughby – Born: 22 March 1519, Parham Old Hall. Parents: Lady Maria de Salinas and William Willoughby, 11th Baron Willoughby de Eresby. Married: Charles Brandon, Duke of Suffolk (1); Richard Bertie (2). Children: Henry Brandon, 2nd Duke of Suffolk (1); Charles Brandon, 3rd Duke of Suffolk (1); Susan Bertie, Countess of Kent (2); Peregrine Bertie, 13th Baron Willoughby de Eresby (2). Died: 19 September 1580, Grimsthorpe Castle. Buried: Spilsbury Church, Lincolnshire.

Louis XII of France – Born: 27 June 1462, Château de Blois, France. Parents: Marie of Cleves and Charles, Duke of Orléans. Coronation: 27 May 1498. Married: Joan of France in 1476 (annulled 1498) (1); Anne, Duchess of Brittany in 1499 (she died 1514) (2); Mary Tudor in 1514 (3). Children: Claude, Queen of France (2); Renée, Duchess of Ferrara (2); Michael Bucy, Archbishop of Bourges (Illegitimate). Died: 1 January 1515, Hôtel des Tournelles. Buried: Basilica of St Denis.

Louise of Savoy – Born: 11 September 1476, Pont-d'Ain. Parents: Margaret of Bourbon and Philip II, Duke of Savoy. Married: Charles, Count of Angoulême in 1488 (he died 1496). Children: Marguerite, Queen of Navarre; Francis I of France. Died: 22 September 1531, Grez-sur-Loing. Buried: Basilica of St Denis.

Margaret Beaufort – Born: 31 May 1443, Bletsoe Castle. Parents: Margaret Beauchamp of Bletsoe and John Beaufort, Duke of Somerset. Married: Edmund Tudor, Earl of Richmond in 1455 (died 1456) (1); Sir Henry Stafford in 1458 (died 1471) (2); Thomas Stanley in 1472 (died 1504) (3). Children: Henry VII (1). Died: 29 June 1509, Westminster. Buried: Westminster Abbey.

Margaret Tudor, Queen of Scots – Born: 28 November 1489, Palace of Westminster. Parents: Elizabeth of York and Henry VII. Coronation: 8 August 1503. Married: James IV of Scotland in 1503 (died 1513) (1); Archibald Douglas, 6th Earl of Angus in 1514 (died 1527) (2); Henry Stewart in 1528 (3). Children: James V of Scotland (1); Margaret Douglas, Countess of Lennox (2). Died: 18 October 1541, Methven Castle, Scotland. Buried: Perth Charterhouse.

Mary I – Born: 18 February 1516, Palace of Placentia (Greenwich). Parents: Katharine of Aragon and Henry VIII. Coronation: 1 October 1553. Married: Philip II of Spain in 1554. Died: 17 November 1558, St James's Palace. Buried: Westminster Abbey.

Mary Boleyn – Born: *c.*1499, Blickling Hall. Parents: Elizabeth Howard and Thomas Boleyn, 1st Earl of Wiltshire. Married: William Carey in 1503 (died 1528) (1); William Stafford in 1534 (2). Children: Catherine Carey, Lady Knollys; Henry Carey, 1st Baron Hunsdon. Both of Mary's children were with William Carey though there is debate whether one or both could be the result of her time spent as mistress to Henry VIII. Died: 19 July 1543, place unknown. Unfortunately, it is unknown where Mary is buried.

Mary Brandon – Born: 2 June 1510. Parents: Anne Browne and Charles Brandon, Duke of Suffolk. Married: Thomas Stanley, 2nd Baron Monteagle. Children: William Stanley, 3rd Baron Monteagle; Francis Stanley; Charles Stanley; Elizabeth Stanley; Anne Stanley; Margaret Stanley. Died: *c.*1540.

Mary Grey – Born: 20 April 1545. Parents: Frances Brandon, Duchess of Suffolk and Henry Grey, 1st Duke of Suffolk. Married: Thomas Keyes in July 1565. Died: 20 April 1578. Buried: it is believed Mary is buried in the tomb of her mother in Westminster Abbey.

Mary Tudor, Queen of France – Born: 18 March 1496, Sheen Palace. Parents: Elizabeth of York and Henry VII. Coronation: 5 November 1514. Married: Louis XII of France in 1514 (died 1515) (1); Charles Brandon, Duke of Suffolk in 1515 (2). Children, all by Charles Brandon: Henry Brandon; Frances Grey, Duchess of Suffolk; Eleanor Clifford, Countess of Cumberland; Henry Brandon, 1st Earl of Lincoln. Died: 25 June 1533, Westhorpe Hall. Buried: 22 July 1533 at Abbey of St Edmund before being moved to St Mary's Church, Bury St Edmunds during the dissolution of the monasteries in 1538.

Introduction

The Tudors are one of the most popular and well-known dynasties, but in comparison to others, such as the Plantagenets for instance, the Tudor dynasty was short, lasting only 118 years and five monarchs (six if you count Lady Jane Grey). When the name Mary Tudor is mentioned, people may initially think of Mary I, daughter of Henry VIII and Katharine of Aragon, and the first queen regnant of England in her own right. Her aunt and possible namesake, Mary Tudor, is most certainly overshadowed by her larger-than-life family members and the events that occurred during her lifetime. But she also has an interesting tale of her own.

The Tudor reign began in 1485 when Mary's father made his bid for the throne. It occurred during one of the most tumultuous periods in English history: the Wars of the Roses. Two cadet branches of the Plantagenet family fought for power and the throne, resulting in differing monarchs. Years later they would be represented by the symbols we know so well: the red rose of Lancaster and the white rose of York. The events of the Wars of the Roses are too complex to cover here but they cannot be skipped entirely. During this period, in January 1457, a young 14-year-old girl was in labour. Within the safety of the walls of the imposing Pembroke Castle, Wales, the teenager gave birth to a boy she named Henry. Henry was named after the Lancastrian king, Henry VI, who was the stepbrother of Edmund Tudor, the father of the newborn baby. Edmund Tudor, 1st Earl of Richmond, was the oldest son of the Welshman, Owen Tudor. Owen had entered the service of Henry V, and fought alongside him in the epic battle of Agincourt. When Henry V died on 31 August 1422, he left behind his dowager queen, Catherine of Valois, and their only child, who succeeded him as King Henry VI. With the loss of his master, Owen remained in service to the dowager queen as clerk of the wardrobe. A relationship blossomed and the unlikely couple allegedly secretly married, and went on to conceive four children: three sons, Edmund, Jasper and Owen, and a daughter.[1] The relationship put both Owen and Catherine in danger. Catherine was forbidden by statute to marry without the consent of the monarch. As her son, Henry VI, was an infant, she would have years to wait before he could consent. Therefore, the only people who could give permission were the council of the young king, of which the brothers of the late King Henry V, Regent-Protector, John of Lancaster, 1st Duke of Bedford, and Humphrey of Lancaster, Duke of Gloucester, were prominent members. The couple did not request consent; statute had already declared that if Catherine married without consent her spouse would be subject to penalties and forfeit his land and goods.[2] Owen was viewed by many as beneath Catherine in station, though he claimed descent from the Welsh royal house of Cadwallader. Catherine and Owen managed to keep their marriage and children secret for a few years until it was discovered upon Catherine's death in 1437. The children were placed under the care of the abbess of Barking Abbey and Owen Tudor was summoned to court to answer to the Privy Council. He refused to attend unless he was granted safe conduct, a request which was denied. Understandably, Owen did not trust that his life would be secure if he travelled to court without safe conduct, so did not attend. Receiving a second summons he sought sanctuary in Westminster Abbey where he remained for several days. Eventually, after facing the Privy Council, Owen and his priest were both imprisoned in Newgate Jail. The pair managed to escape twice, the first time being recaptured. The second attempt was more successful and they managed to flee to the safety of Wales. Owen hoped that when his stepson, Henry VI, reached his majority he would approve the retrospective marriage and acknowledge his sons as his half-brothers.

Owen's hopes were realised. Henry VI awarded Owen with a pension and not only acknowledged his stepbrothers but took on responsibility for ensuring they received an education appropriate for their status as half-brothers to the king of England. The titles given to Edmund (1st Earl of Richmond) and Jasper (1st Earl of Pembroke) were also courtesy of Henry VI. The youngest son, Owen, had chosen a life of piety and entered monastic life until his death in 1502. Edmund and Jasper, along with their father, played prominent roles in the battles which ultimately ended with the Yorkist Edward IV being proclaimed king of England. Edmund Tudor died in 1456, just two months before the birth of his son, leaving behind his very young widow. His brother, Jasper Tudor, 1st Earl of Pembroke, took over responsibility for the young widow and her newborn son, Henry Tudor.

The teenage mother, Margaret Beaufort, was the only child and heiress of John Beaufort, 1st Duke of Somerset. The prominent John of Gaunt, 1st Duke of Lancaster, third son of King Edward III, was Margaret's great-grandfather. Even at such a young age she was intelligent and well aware of her need to protect herself, her fortune, and her son. In order to do this, she would need to remarry. Despite her further marriages, Margaret would not have any more children. Due to his mother's family lineage, Henry Tudor had a distant claim to the throne. Whilst he wasn't in the immediate line of succession, he did have royal blood, so much so that when the Yorkists were in power, he came to be seen as a possible threat. Other than a period when he was a ward of William Herbert, 1st Earl of Pembroke, the young Henry Tudor spent his childhood in the care of his uncle, Jasper Tudor. Following the battle at Tewkesbury in 1471, when the Lancastrians were defeated, Jasper fled from Tenby in Wales, taking his nephew with him. The aim was to shelter in France, but storms led them to the shores of Brittany, which was then separate to France and was governed by Francis II, Duke of Brittany. Henry was only 14 years old when he left Wales and his mother behind. He remained there, under the protection of Francis II.

Edward IV made attempts to have Henry returned to England, including one under the guise of marrying him to one of his daughters. Whether this was his true intent we do not know, but at one point Edward did agree to restore Henry to his inheritance. Henry remained in Brittany, under closer security, until the death of Edward IV in April 1483. Following the coronation of Richard III in July 1483, further attempts were made to convince Duke Francis to send Henry back to England. Francis remained steadfast in his refusal. By this time Henry had already planned to return to England's shores, but with the aim of taking the throne himself. His first attempt failed when the rebellion of Henry Stafford, 2nd Duke of Buckingham, to remove Richard III from the throne failed. Noting a trap on the shores at Poole, Henry sailed back to safety in Brittany.

In the meantime, Margaret Beaufort and Elizabeth Woodville had reached an agreement for Henry and Elizabeth of York to marry. Elizabeth of York was the eldest daughter of Edward IV and Elizabeth Woodville, and following the disappearance of her brothers was now their Yorkist heir. Therefore, on Christmas Day in 1483, Henry took a vow in Rennes Cathedral that when he became king of England he would marry the York princess, uniting the warring factors. Lancastrians and those disaffected by Richard's rule began to join Henry in Brittany. By this time, Duke Francis had maintained Henry for over a decade; he was now aging and continually being pressured to hand Henry over to Richard. Whilst his master was unwell, Pierre Landois, Treasurer to the duke, agreed to hand over Henry. The plan was discovered and Henry managed to escape to France. Duke Francis recovered and was angry at Landois, assisting Henry's remaining followers to join him in France. With assistance from King Charles VIII, Henry left Harfleur on 1 August 1485. He sailed to Milford Haven, landing on 8 August. At the end of a long march, gathering recruits along the way, the army arrived in Bosworth to face the forces of Richard III. Henry came close to failure; Richard had charged at him, killing his standard bearer, Sir William Brandon, in the effort to reach Henry himself. Despite being outnumbered on arrival, the army of Henry Tudor succeeded, Richard III was killed in the battle and Henry was declared king of England.

The Battle of Bosworth had brought about the beginning of one of the most famous dynasties in history.

With the throne won, Henry VII now had to secure it through marriage and children. He kept his vow and married Elizabeth of York on 18 January 1486 at Westminster. The Yorkists and Lancastrian families were now joined but this did not mean all was peaceful and Henry VII would have to continue to fight for his throne. The royal couple now needed children.

Chapter One

A Tudor Rose

Mary Tudor was the fifth child born to the first Tudor king, Henry VII, and his queen consort, Elizabeth of York. Mary was born at Sheen Palace on 18 March 1496.[1] At the time of her birth, Mary had two elder brothers – Arthur, Prince of Wales, born September 1486, and Prince Henry, born June 1491. Her elder sister, Princess Margaret, had been born in between their two male siblings in November 1489. Another sibling, Elizabeth, was born in 1492 but sadly died in September 1495, a few months prior to Mary's birth.

As a baby, Mary was sent to the royal nursey to reside with Henry and Margaret. The royal nursery was mostly based at Eltham but moved on occasion to allow the palace to be cleaned thoroughly. Mary's parents would have employed wetnurses, rockers, maids and nurses to care for their children. Alice Bywimble and Joan Skidmore were two of those employed to care for all three siblings whilst Anne Skeron was the first recorded person employed specifically as a servant to Mary, and was employed as a nurse.[2] Elizabeth of York would certainly not have nursed her children herself. It was customary for women of means to use a wetnurse to feed their children as it was believed at the time that breastfeeding affected fertility and women of royal and aristocratic families were required to return to their duty of conceiving as soon as possible. The records of staff specifically in Mary's service are regrettably scarce, however, there is a payment in October 1496 to Hugh Denes for 10s 10d, though there is no description of what this payment was for other than 'for my lady Mary'.[3]

In December 1497, when Mary was only 18 months old, the royal palace of Sheen had burned to the ground. The royal family were safe but had lost a beautiful home. Whilst Mary is highly unlikely to have any recollection of the event it was no doubt an upsetting event for the family. Henry VII would replace Sheen with the Palace of Richmond, the name taken from his earldom, inherited from his father and held before he was king. The Palace of Richmond as Mary would know it was described in a contemporary record, likely written by Peter Carmelianus, Latin Secretary to Henry VII. He stated:

> If I were to describe in writing the beauty and ornamentation of the royal house of Richemont, as well as the chapel and the great

> hall as well as the most precious equipment of the rooms, it would certainly be long and very wonderful and difficult. Especially in reciting their pompous and proud structure and their splendid equipment, together with the pleasantness and salubrity of the place and the air, together with the most artistic and rich carpets with which at that time the house itself shone and the whole was sparkling. From these facts it could easily be judged that such and such a magnificent house could not be found in so many countries; since it represented an earthly paradise rather than a house or a palace.[4]

By 3 years old, Mary had already been noticed on the marriage market. In 1498, Ludovico Sforza, the Duke of Milan, made the first recorded approach for Mary's hand in marriage for his eldest son. Raimondo de' Raimondi of Soncino, Milanese ambassador to England, was despatched to London with three requests on behalf of his master: firstly, for Henry VII to support Sforza against France in the claim over the Duchy of Milan; secondly, for Mary's hand in marriage; lastly, for Henry VII to bestow the Order of the Garter upon Sforza. The Duke of Milan would be sorely disappointed as Henry VII responded that he could not support Sforza in his dispute with Louis XII of France. According to the Venetians, Henry VII declined as he was friends with France. Henry also declared that he could not bestow the garter as 'the Garter is the badge and first order of King Arthur, and that the knights of old who bore this badge swore to be the friends of friends and foes of foes, and the King of France being a member of the order, the Duke cannot enter it'.[5] With regards to the marriage, Raimondo writes to his master that Henry VII 'thanks your Excellency, but as his daughter is three years old, and cannot be betrothed before seven, he cannot give a definite answer before she attains that age. But when that time arrives, if your lordship cares to treat of the matter, or send an ambassador to ask him, his Majesty sending over to you, he will show every readiness and see that the matter takes effect in every honourable way'.[6] The response is a little different to that recorded by the Venetians who claim Henry VII refused the match on two accounts – Mary's young age and that effectively she is too good for the son of a duke or, in the words of the writer, Marino Sanuto, 'not of the Duke's condition'.[7]

Around the same time, Mary was allocated her own staff but not a separate household and would remain with her siblings, Margaret and Henry. Her servants consisted of a governess, maids and ladies. Her governess, Lady Joan Guildford, was to become an integral part of Mary's life and would affectionately become known as 'Mother Guildford'. At this age she also matured into what we may perceive as an adult wardrobe. Her clothes included gowns of luxurious fabrics; velvet, silk and damask, trimmed with ermine in a variety of colours.[8] Henry VII authorised payments in 1499 for Mary's clothing which included a black velvet gown with crimson edging; another of green velvet edged with purple and lined with black buckram; two kirtles, one of black satin and the other tawny damask; and two pairs of knitted hosen. This sounds very adult-like for a 3-year-old but was standard for the time period.[9]

It is thought Margaret, Henry and Mary were taught to read and write by their mother, or at least received their initial instructions from her. This theory is based on the similarity in signatures and lack of the fashionable italic handwriting style becoming popular at the time. Mary could certainly read and write by the time she was 5 years old, but who taught her is unfortunately lost to history. It is possible she practised with multiple people – her mother, siblings and Lady Guildford.

The royal children would start their day by waking, possibly washing their faces and hands, being dressed, and attending Mass before they broke their fast. During this period people woke early to make the most of the daylight, though the nobility and royals were not required to wake as early as the working classes. After breakfast the children would begin their lessons with their tutors or governess. The main meal of the day was dinner and was served around 11:00 a.m., which seems very early to us nowadays although it did vary within a couple of hours between the classes. During dinner the children would be served a variety of dishes and may have listened to someone read aloud in an effort to keep them entertained whilst eating. More lessons would follow after dinner before once more attending the chapel for Evensong. The next meal would be around 4:00 p.m. when Mary and her siblings would enjoy a supper before having time to play and entertain themselves.

At around 4 or 5 years old, a household was established within the royal nursery for Mary and she received further exquisite clothing: three gowns in the colours of black, blue and crimson, all velvet and all lined with ermine; a fur worn by royalty. It is possible this growing wardrobe was a factor behind the appointment of her own wardrobe keeper around the same time. As well as a wardrobe keeper, a tutor and a number of ladies-in-waiting and gentlewomen were appointed to serve Mary. Lastly, a doctor was appointed with a daily wage, though he was unlikely to reside at the palace and would travel when required.[10]

The first record we have of Mary accepting visitors was in 1500. Though Mary was only 4 years old at the time, she was present at Eltham Palace with her elder siblings, Margaret and Henry, and younger brother, Edmund, who had been born on 21 February 1499. William Blount, 4th Baron Mountjoy, had brought Sir Thomas More and Desiderius Erasmus to the royal nursey to meet the children. Being so young, Mary did not really participate in the visit and continued to play on the floor whilst her elder siblings greeted the visitors but her presence did not go unnoticed and years later Sir Thomas More, when writing a poem of Elizabeth of York's death, recalled her being 'bright as hue'. However, it was her brother Henry who stood out at this visit and the esteemed scholar Erasmus dedicated a ten-page Latin ode named *Prosopopeia Britanniae* to Henry and his father.[11] It was only a year later that Mary would face the first death within her family when the young Prince Edmund died. More would follow but there would also be happier times for the princess to enjoy.

The Catholic tradition of a Jubilee occurs every twenty-five years and fell in 1501. The tradition is a dedicated year for people to ask for forgiveness of sins. Elizabeth of York paid 12d on 13 May for a letter of pardon for Mary from the Jubilee.[12] At such a young age she was unlikely to have sinned but the piety at the time saw people doing all they could to honour God. Elizabeth of York made these payments on behalf of her children, including a further payment of 2s 6d in March 1505 for Mary's offering at Easter.[13]

The Tudor court was a place of chivalry and tradition. Mary would have learned from a young age how to behave, the politics of the royal court and how, being female, she could use the code of chivalry to her advantage. Although Margaret was the eldest sibling in the royal nursey, both Margaret and Mary would have been expected to defer to Henry as the male sibling, and of course their parents. Their father, Henry VII, is thought to have been a miser when it came to spending but he was more than happy to spend on his family and portray his wealth to visiting ambassadors and guests when required. He spared no expense for his family or when it came to royal celebrations.

One such celebration took place in 1501 which saw 5-year-old Mary attending the spectacular event of a royal wedding. This was possibly the first large royal event the young princess attended. Her eldest brother, Arthur, Prince of Wales, was marrying Katharine of Aragon. The ceremony took place at St Paul's Cathedral on 14 November and was followed by large celebrations of pageants, jousts and entertainments. In keeping with the legend that surrounded the bridegroom's name, the jousting at Westminster took on an Arthurian theme. Many courtiers participated in the celebrations and jousts, wearing themed costumes, including Mary's future husband, Charles Brandon. Mary would watch the events along with her mother, sister, grandmother and the ladies of the court and on 21 December would bid her eldest brother farewell as he set off to Ludlow with his new bride.

The guests at the wedding of Arthur and Katharine also included ambassadors of James IV of Scotland who had been sent to progress the marriage negotiations between himself and Princess Margaret. It is perhaps the experiences of her grandmother, Lady Margaret Beaufort, which gave the Tudor family concerns regarding sending Margaret to Scotland at such a young age; she was a couple of weeks away from her 12th birthday at the time of her brother's marriage. The negotiations were concluded early the following year with the marriage treaty being signed on 24 January 1502. James IV would receive 30,000 golden nobles from Henry VII as Margaret's dowry. The amount was to be paid in three instalments of 10,000: the first within seven days of the marriage; the second at the end of the first year; and the final instalment at the end of the second year of marriage. In return Margaret would receive dower lands equivalent to any previous Scottish queen and James would provide any additional funds if there were a shortfall from the income of the lands, up to the value of 2000l per annum. The agreement was a bit strange in that the lands would be in the possession of Margaret's procurators from July 1503 but James would retain the income from them for the term of his life. This meant Margaret would have very little control over her dower lands but was instead promised all of her expenses would be met including 'apparatus of her body, the ornamenting of her residences, her vehicles, stud, furniture, utensils, food, dress, private and domestic affairs, and all other things whatsoever, necessary and becoming the honour, state, rank, and dignity of the said Lady Margaret'. In addition, Margaret would receive a sum of 500 marks per annum which she was free to use as she wished, on the proviso she avoided interfering in her dower lands whilst James was alive.[14] The negotiations resulted in a stipulation that Margaret would remain in England until at least the beginning of September 1503, giving her time to mature before travelling to Scotland to take her place as queen of Scotland.[15]

The betrothal took place the following day, 25 January 1502, at Richmond Palace. Mary, along with Henry, Margaret, Henry VII, Elizabeth of York, the Scottish delegation and courtiers heard High Mass delivered by the Bishop of Rochester, before proceeding to the queen's chamber for the ceremony. After the initial formalities of the reading of the dispensation by Thomas Ruthall, the king's secretary, the ceremony began with Robert Blacader, Archbishop of Glasgow, requesting Henry VII, Elizabeth of York, and Margaret herself to confirm they knew of no impediment to the marriage. Henry VII then requested confirmation by the Scottish delegation of their intent towards his daughter, which was given by Andrew Forman, prelate of Moray. Upon confirmation Margaret was addressed once again by the archbishop and asked to confirm she consented to the betrothal, upon which she replied 'If it please my lord father the king, and my lady mother the queen'.[16] The betrothal vows were then read by the archbishop, firstly to the Earl of Bothwell, who stood as proxy for James IV, and then Margaret, each repeating the words in reply.

> I, Margaret, the first begotten daughter of the right excellent, right high and mighty prince and princess, Henry, by the grace of God King of England, and Elizabeth, queen of the same, wittingly and of deliberate mind, having twelve years complete in age, in the month of November last past, contract matrimony with the right excellent, right high and mighty prince, James, King of Scotland, and the person of whom, Patrick, earl of Bothwell, procurator of the said prince, James, King of Scotland, [represents] and take the said James, King of Scotland, into and for my husband and spouse, and all other for him forsake, during his and mine lives natural, and thereto I plight and give to him, in your person as procurator foresaid, my faith and truth.[17]

Following the vows the court began to celebrate. Margaret had the honour of sitting at the table of her mother, Elizabeth of York. Although no report of where Mary sat for the feast is noted she may have been allowed to sit with her sister, or remained in the care of Lady Guildford. The day progressed with jousting, feasting and dancing. The citizens of London also celebrated with bonfires and wine provided by Henry VII. As Mary had attended the celebrations of the marriage of Arthur and Katharine the year before, it is likely she was allowed to remain for the celebrations, or at least part of them. There are no records of Mary's thoughts of the ceremony but it may have been her sister's wedding where she first started to understand what would be expected of her and, also, what she could expect as a royal princess when she married. Observing the honours bestowed upon her older sister must have been an intriguing experience for such a young lady.

Unfortunately the joy of the celebrations would not last and three months later Mary and her family would suffer another tragic loss. Following their marriage, the newlyweds Prince Arthur and Katharine of Aragon, had travelled to their own court at Ludlow Castle, in the Welsh Marches. Both Arthur and Katharine had fallen ill, possibly contracting the sweating sickness. Arthur would not survive and died on 2 April 1502 at the young age of 15. Mary's reaction to the death of her eldest brother is unknown. She had spent very little time with him as Arthur had not resided in the royal nursery with his siblings, but instead had his own household, first at Faversham then Ludlow where, as Prince of Wales, he was being trained as the heir to the throne. Katharine of Aragon recovered from her illness and returned to London to reside at Durham

House in the Strand. Katharine would become a welcome addition to Mary's life, the pair becoming very close.

Elizabeth of York ensured Mary and her sister, now styled Queen of Scots, were provided clothing respective of their royal status. Robert Ragdale was paid 20d on 7 June 1502 to make a black satin gown, and a further 3d for the hemming of a kirtle for Mary. Ragdale was also tasked with working on a black velvet gown, making sleeves and hemming another gown for Margaret.[18] It is likely these were mourning clothes for the girls as black or dark colours would have been expected at the royal court following Arthur's death.

The year of 1503 brought more loss; this time Mary was to lose her mother, Elizabeth of York, along with the newborn baby, Catherine. Elizabeth of York died on 11 February 1503 at the Tower of London, Catherine passing away a few days later. Elizabeth of York lay in state at the Tower of London for ten days before being conveyed in a procession led by 200 poor persons to Westminster Abbey where she again lay in state overnight, her funeral taking place the following day, 23 February. Mary would not have attended her mother's funeral; the chief mourner was Catherine of York, a sister to the late queen.

Later that year came an event that would likely have been met with both joy and sadness: Margaret was departing for Scotland. The preparations were surely a period of excitement for the two sisters, but also tinged with a sadness that they would be separated and it was unknown if and when they would see each other again. Mary had no doubt spent a lot of time with her sister in the royal nursery and would have learned from her older sister, amongst others, the behaviour expected of her as a royal princess. Now she would be the only Tudor princess left at her father's court. Margaret departed on 24 June 1503 to begin the long journey north. Her father accompanied her to Collyweston, one of the properties belonging to her grandmother, Lady Margaret Beaufort. Here, she would say goodbye to them both and would not see either of them again. The records do not indicate if Mary was present but it is doubtful that she and Prince Henry made the journey without being mentioned. Margaret's retinue on her journey grew to almost 2000 people and did not reach Scotland until the end of July and Margaret spent her first night in her new kingdom on 1 August 1503. The procession had stopped at various towns along the way with Margaret being honoured and celebrated at each place. Back in London, it is possible some of the emptiness created through the departure of Margaret was healed by the presence of Katharine of Aragon, who along with Lady Joan Guildford would provide a stable female presence for Mary.

Chapter Two

'A blossome named Mary'

With her sister gone, it was Mary's time to shine, though that is not to say she did not miss her sister. She remained close to her brother Henry, now Prince of Wales, and spent time with him and Katharine of Aragon. In August 1504 Mary accompanied her father on a trip whilst her brother remained behind, possibly to continue his studies now he was the heir to the throne. From Richmond the party, which included Katharine of Aragon and the ladies of the court, travelled to Westminster. They spent a few days at Westminster before travelling to Greenwich where Katharine fell ill. During a prior hunting trip with Henry VII Katharine had also fallen ill but had recovered enough to proceed with the excursion from Richmond. From Greenwich, Katharine travelled to her home in the Strand to recover whilst Henry VII left for Kent. There is no mention whether Mary accompanied her father or sister-in-law from this point.[1]

At this time negotiations were ongoing for Henry, Prince of Wales to marry Katharine of Aragon. In November 1504, Katharine was invited to Westminster to spend twenty days with Henry VII. The Spanish ambassador, Rodrigo de Puebla, reported to her parents that she was being attended well and Henry VII had ordered Mary to be attended in the same manner.[2]

When not spending time enjoying herself, Mary was busy learning how to be a great lady of the realm. By this time she had a French companion known as Jane Popincourt. Jane had been in the household since at least 1502 as Elizabeth of York paid Robert Ragdale to repair two of her gowns during the same period he was paid to make mourning clothes for Mary.[3] Mary's education would have started from a young age. All Tudor children were expected to learn their prayers. Mary being privileged would have been able to learn from texts and educated individuals unlike the poorer members of society who learnt prayers by memory, not really understanding the Latin they were speaking. Due to her status Mary and her siblings likely had their own prayer books in the form of psalters and possibly used commonplace books for their learning. A commonplace book was the Tudor equivalent of a notebook for modern society; it was somewhere people could make notes of words, passages or quotes they wished to remember. Being male, Henry required a much more academic education than his sisters but that is not to say they did not share some of his lessons. They were all required to learn Latin, though the level required was not the same for the princesses. The girls required a more practical education – they would need to know how to manage a household of their own when they matured so their education was based on practical subjects: housewifery, needlework, languages, perhaps a little arithmetic to assist with household accounts. Other subjects were common and expected amongst the higher ranks of Tudor society such as music and dance.

Mary had an excellent role model in her grandmother. Lady Margaret Beaufort was adept with herbal remedies, religion and the French language. Mary spent time at the home of her grandmother who is known to have read in French and employed a French attendant named Perrot Doryn who could have acted as another practise companion for Mary.[4] It is not known who had the idea to appoint a young French girl to Mary's household but when Mary was 5 years old, Jane Popincourt was placed in her household as a companion but also to assist with Mary's French education. The companionship would help Mary with the spoken language and was a friendship that would last well beyond her youth, and her learning of the French language would also be of benefit later when she spent considerable time with Katharine of Aragon, the latter initially finding English difficult.[5] By spending time with her grandmother, Mary would have access to her library. As a patron of education and printing presses, Lady Margaret would have had an excellent range of texts suitable for a princess. She commissioned a copy of the romance *Blanchardyn and Eglantine* from printer William Caxton. This text is particularly of note as Caxton notes the book is appropriate for:

> … all vertuouse yong noble gentylmen & wymmen for to rede therein, as for their passe tym … And in lykewyse for gentyl Yonge ladyes and domoysellys, for to lerne to be stedfaste & constaunt in their parte to theym that they ones have promysed and agreed to suche as have putte their lyves ofte in Jeopardye for to playse theym to stande in grace, As it is to occupye theym and studye over moche in bokes of contemplacion.[6]

Not all scholars were supportive of ladies reading romances such as *Blanchardyn and Eglantine*. Juan Luis Vives was later commissioned by Katharine of Aragon to write a curriculum of study for her daughter, Mary's niece, and he certainly did not approve of romantic literature. Luckily for Mary, Vives was not around at the time of her own education and if someone as pious as Lady Margaret read romances then Mary certainly could without reproach.

Mary also had the guiding presence of Lady Guildford to supervise her behaviour, ensuring she learnt and behaved with the decorum expected. Her governess was not the only method of teaching Mary the behaviour expected of her as a princess. There was plenty of literature available including Christine de Pizan's *The Three Virtues*. Henry and Mary were both excellent students in music and dance. Mary was accomplished on the lute (one of which had been gifted to her by Henry VII) the clavichord and virginals, having received instruction from Giles Duwes, the same tutor who had taught her siblings in music and sometimes French. Though sharing the royal nursery gave ample time to practise dancing, Mary could not spend all her days studying music and so she would also benefit from Henry's tutors. When Henry's formal education ended in 1509, his tutor William Hone was retained and appointed to tutor Mary. Hone was a member of the growing humanist circle, therefore Mary's education can be expected to have been the new fashionable curriculum of studying the ancient Latin writers, though as noted, her education was nowhere near as in depth as Henry's or even that of her granddaughter, Lady Jane Grey, in later years. Mary likely read classics such as Malory's *Morte d'Arthur* and Froissart's *Meliador* amongst others. These books would instil in Mary the understanding of chivalry.

Growing up was not all splendour and enjoyment. The years of 1504 and 1509 appear to have been years of ill health for Mary and several payments were made to Richard Brabant, the royal apothecary. There is no record of what Brabant was treating, or if she was cured or whether another in her household learned how to concoct the treatment themselves.[7]

Amongst royalty and the aristocracy marriages were often negotiated from an early age to secure alliances, wealth and power, but were not fulfilled until the minimum age of consent, which was 12 for girls and 14 for boys. Mary was no different in this respect and when Henry VII met with Archduke Philip of Austria in the year 1500 when both were in France, they discussed many topics. One of those was the possibility of a future marriage between Mary, then only 4 years old and Charles, Prince of Castile who would later become the Holy Roman Emperor.[8] Nothing came of this discussion and a few years later marriages to France and Portugal were considered as a match for the young princess.

In October 1505, Thomas Lopez, the Portuguese ambassador wrote to his master, Emmanuel, King of Portugal, that Henry VII was seeking a marriage to Marguerite de Navarre (Marguerite d'Angoulême), daughter of Louise of Savoy and sister of the future Francis I of France. At this point Marguerite was only around 13 years old and according to the ambassador Henry VII was also considering Louise of Savoy herself. The report also states that Henry VII was hoping to marry his daughter to the 'dauphin' (Francis). Henry VII had told the ambassador that he would decide 'where best he may' whether his daughter would marry into France or Portugal. The daughter in question has to be Mary as by this point Margaret had already left for Scotland.[9]

Henry VII ultimately decided on neither the Portuguese prince nor the French dauphin. Instead he settled on Prince Charles of Castile, the son of Philip of Burgundy and Juana, Queen of Castile. Juana was sister to Mary's beloved sister-in-law, Katharine of Aragon and became queen of Castile following the death of their mother, Queen Isabella of Castile in 1504. Having Ferdinand of Aragon and Maximilian, Holy Roman Emperor as his grandfathers, Charles would bring England a much greater alliance than that of Portugal. The negotiations began when Mary was still only 10 years old, Charles was even younger, only 6 years old. Unsurprisingly, Mary's thoughts on these early suitors are unknown.

In 1506, Philip and Juana were unexpected guests of the royal court. They had found themselves shipwrecked off the coast of England and had sought shelter from Henry VII. The future Henry VIII was sent by his father to greet Philip at Winchester and escort him to Windsor. On arrival at Windsor on 1 February, Philip was greeted by Henry VII and escorted through a gallery full of the nobility and musicians to a chamber:

> ... where was my lady princess, and my Lady Mary, the king's daughter, and divers other ladies. And after the King of Castile had kissed them, and communed with them, and communed awhile with the king and the ladies all, they came into the king's dining-chamber, where danced my lady princess, and a Spanish lady with her in Spanish array; and after she had danced two or three dances she left; and then danced my Lady Mary and an English lady with her; and ever anon the lady princess desired the king of Castile to dance, which, after that he had excused him once or twice, answered that he was a mariner, "and you", said he, "you would cause me to dance?"; and so he danced not, but communed still with the king. And after that my Lady Mary had danced two or three dances, she went and sat by my lady princess on the end of the carpet which was under the cloth of estate, and near where the king and the King of Castile stood. And then danced one of the strange lords and a lady of England. That done, my Lady Mary played on the lute, and after upon the claregalls [clavicals], who played very well, and she was of all folks there greatly praised, that in her youth, in everything, she behaved herself so well.[10]

The next few days were spent in negotiation and on 9 February Henry VII and Philip signed a treaty. The treaty recognised Philip's rights in Castile and agreed a mutual defence pact between the kingdoms. The Anglo-Burgundian alliance treaty became known by the Burgundians as *Malus Intercursus* due to the favourable nature of the trade aspect towards England. Juana, Queen of Castile, did not arrive at court until Tuesday 10 February as she had remained at the coast to recoup from the journey. On her arrival she was welcomed by her sister, Katharine of Aragon, and Princess Mary. Mary and Katharine left Windsor the next day and travelled to Richmond. Here, they were joined by Henry VII the following day, and lastly by Philip on Monday, 16 February. At Richmond Philip was entertained for a week with tournaments, banquets and jousts.

The visit lasted weeks, possibly as a result of Henry VII attempting to detain the royal couple from leaving until he had his wishes adhered to. By the end of the visit Henry VII had managed to secure not one, but three alliances with Philip. The first was his own marriage to Margaret of Austria, Duchess of Savoy. Secondly, Prince Henry was to marry the daughter of Philip – Eleanora – and lastly Mary was to marry Charles, brother to the aforementioned Eleanora. If Mary's marriage could be negotiated successfully it would be one of the greatest accomplishments of Henry VII's reign. He had already negotiated peace with Scotland and Spain through the marriages of Margaret and Prince Arthur. In June of that year, the Venetian ambassador, Vincenzo Quirini, wrote from Benavente that Dr Nicholas West, ambassador of Henry VII, had arrived to discuss the marriages of Henry VII to Margaret and Mary to Charles. It appears Henry VII had wasted no time in progressing the negotiations.[11] The ambassador goes on to report that a couple of weeks later, on 11 July 1506, a marriage contract pertaining to Henry VII and Margaret was published in the chapel at Valladolid.[12]

Although it would solidify an alliance between the parties, Henry VII may have had other aims in realising both his own marriage and that of Mary. Following the death of Philip in September 1506 and the alleged mental incapacity of Juana, Queen of Castile, the realms of Prince Charles were left to his grandfathers and his aunt, Margaret of Austria, Duchess of Savoy, to govern on his behalf. Ferdinand took on the regency of Castile and Maximilian appointed his daughter, Margaret of Austria, to govern the Netherlands on behalf of her nephew. If Henry VII could gain the support of Maximilian, there was a possibility that he could wrest control of Castile from Ferdinand. Henry VII could then govern Castile himself on behalf of his young son-in-law until the latter came of age. This would be the ultimate power play for England, and Ferdinand was well aware of it.[13]

Henry VII also considered marrying Philip's widow, Juana of Castile, himself. The rumours that had spread of Juana's alleged insanity and that she could not govern her lands, did not discourage Henry VII. Ferdinand, acting on her behalf, was well aware that in marrying his daughter Henry VII would gain control of her lands and gain a very generous dowry to supplement his treasury, therefore this was not a deal he willing to make. In marrying Juana, Henry VII would have become a significant power in Europe, another factor Ferdinand would have been well aware of. Neither of the marriages Henry VII suggested for himself were to progress; Juana would never remarry and died in 1555 after spending many years in and out of isolation whilst Margaret of Austria also remained unmarried.

Regardless of what would come to pass, the visit of Philip and Juana had launched Mary into the spotlight. It was to be the beginning of her public appearances as a beautiful English rose. Mary was asked to preside over a tournament in May 1506 when she received a letter from 'Lady May'. The letter, which had been delivered on the orders of her father, made reference to the jousting Mary had attended when Philip was visiting and noted the success of the event.[14] The tournament, held at Greenwich, was in celebration of the May Day festivities, welcoming the arrival of spring. May Day celebrations were popular in Tudor England; the majority of the population would celebrate in some manner and the royal court was no different, though the celebrations were on a much grander scale. By presiding over the tournament Mary would be expected to award prizes to the winners who competed in her honour. Although Mary had attended court events previously, she would have been in the shadow of her mother and sister; now she was centre of attention and presiding over a tournament for the first time. It was bound to be a time of excitement and joy for a 10-year-old princess.

Henry VII is not often given credit as a family man but his action in playing along with the pageantry of the May Day celebrations by having a letter sent to his young daughter seems to be the modern-day equivalent of a parent arranging a letter from Santa or a 'visit' from the tooth-fairy. He was clearly a family man and proud of his children. Henry VII introduced Vincenzo Capello, Captain of the Flanders galleys, to Mary in August 1506. The Venetian captain had dined with the king at Richmond before being led to another room where Mary and Katharine of Aragon were busy practising music.[15] Capello makes no further comment about Mary but the fact he mentions that Henry VII presented him to Mary can be inferred as an event he is proud to report.

In the meantime, Mary's marriage to Prince Charles was still being discussed. Despite Philip agreeing to the match, following his death the marriage would require the consent of Maximilian, Holy Roman Emperor, Ferdinand of Aragon and Margaret of Austria. However, not all were as enthusiastic as Philip had been. Maximilian had been considering marrying Prince Charles to Claude, daughter of Louis XII of France. In September 1506, Maximilian wrote to Henry VII to inform him that Louis had decided to marry Claude to Francis, d'Angoulême, and warned Henry to 'beware the French Foxes'. Maximilian goes on to confirm he had taken advice on the matter and written to Ferdinand to request he approves the marriage between Mary and Charles.[16] By December 1506, according to Maximilian, Ferdinand was working against his own grandson. He had taken on the regency of Castile following Philip's death and the alleged incapacity of Juana. Ferdinand was purportedly working with the French to remove Charles from the succession. Maximilian sought assistance from Henry VII in the form of 100,000 gold crowns to fund an army, with the promise to repay it within a year. This would obviously be a concern to Henry as the kingdoms of Charles were a major factor in his intention to marry Mary to the young prince.[17]

Mary was likely unaware of the serious negotiations happening and continued to spend time with her brother and Katharine of Aragon. The month of May 1507 brought another opportunity for Mary to take the spotlight. Mary was appointed 'Queen of May' to preside over the May Day jousts held by her brother at Kennington. Mary and her ladies arrived all dressed in green and stood on a stage covered in flowers. Mary would have issued the challenge before receiving flowers and tokens from contenders and in return would gift the winner with a ring, no doubt provided by her father. The events are preserved in history through the following poem:

A lady fayre moost beautyuous of face
With seruauntes foure brought was into a place
Staged about wheron stode lordes and ladyes a grete route
And many a knyght, and squyer also stoute
That the place was full as it be mought
On euery syde that to beholde the Justes dyde abyde
Tyll that the pryse by the Judges was tried
And by the herodes that trouthe wel espied
Therefore puruayde thus these foure seruauntes of this lady foresaid
Entred the felde/ therefor to be assayed
Gorgyously apparayled and arrayed
And for pleasaunce and in a maner for a cognysaunce
Of Mayes month they bare a souenaunce
Of a verte cocle was the reseblaunce
Tatched ryght fast about theyr neckes as longe as May dyde laste

But about theyre neckes it was not caste
For challenge/ but they weere it tyll May was past
Redy to Just theyr armure clere relucent without ruste
Theyr horses barded trottynge on the duste
Procured gentyll hertes vnto luste
And to solace specyally suche as Venus dyde embrace
Or as of Cupyde folowed the trace
Or suche as of Mars desyred the grace
For to attayne and as touchynge this lady souerayne
Had suche beaute/ it wolde an herte constrayne
To serue her/ though he knewe to lese his payne
She was so shene she and her seruantes clad were all in grene
Her fetures fresshe none can dyscryue I wene
For beaute she might well haue ben a quene
She Yonge if aege was set moste goodly hye vpon a stage
Under a hauthorne made by the ourage
Of Flora that is of heuenly parage
In her hande was of halfe an houre with sande rennynge a glas
So contryned it kepte truely the space
Of the halfe houre and dyde it neuer passe
But for to tell how this lady that so ferre dyde excell
Was named yf I aduyse me well
Lady of May she hyght/ after Aprell
Began her reygne.[18]

The next month, Mary was once again presiding over jousts; this time she was not a fictional 'queen' but instead issued the challenge in her own name. The men on this occasion would be competing directly for the honour of Princess Mary Tudor, 'This confortable blossome named Mary, Spronge is to all Englondes glory'.[19] Unfortunately, we have no record of how Mary felt about these events, but considering her love of pageantry, dance and her position at the court, it can be assumed she revelled in her role presiding over such events as these. They would certainly assist her in facing the forthcoming events of her life on the public stage.

Whilst Mary was busy enjoying herself with courtly entertainments, her father had been busy negotiating with the European powers. In the latter half of 1507, Henry VII and Maximilian appointed ambassadors to meet in Calais with the authority to discuss the betrothal and contract between Mary and Charles 'per verba de futoro' (by words about the future), which ultimately means a promise to marry in the future. Maximilian was still doubtful and wrote to his daughter in early December 1507 requesting a clause be added to the draft contract proposed for the marriage between Charles and Mary. The clause would nullify the whole treaty, including fines for causing the marriage to fail, and would take effect if Louis XII was willing to marry his daughter, Princess Claude, to Prince Charles within twelve months.[20] It is surprising therefore that the delegations representing the parties agreed a treaty on 21 December. There was no mention of the additional clause. Perhaps this news did not reach the ambassadors in time or Margaret of Austria neglected to have the clause added, possibly knowing this was likely to be rejected by Henry VII as an insult. It was agreed that a delegation representing Charles, Prince of Castile, would be dispatched to England by Easter the following year to conduct a proxy betrothal between the young couple. Further to making arrangements for the proxy betrothal, the treaty settled a number of points including the financial aspects of the marriage. Mary was to receive a jointure equal to that previously received by Margaret, Duchess of Burgundy (a sister of Mary's grandfather, Edward IV). In addition to those already specified, Charles was to ensure Mary's jointure reflected his position once he was in full possession of all of his dominions, meaning her dower would likely be enlarged, making Mary the recipient of great wealth and land.

In return, Henry VII's representatives also agreed that 250,000 golden crowns would be paid as Mary's marriage portion and was to be entrusted to the merchants in Bruges for safekeeping. Henry VII was to swear on his oath this would be paid, making a pledge that the Mayor of Calais and merchants were bound to discharge the payment if Henry failed to pay. Henry VII was not the only party having to make oaths and pledges. For their part, Emperor Maximilian, Margaret of Austria, Charles de Croy, Henry Count of Nassau and the towns of Flanders were bound to pay 250,000 crowns if Prince Charles refused to consent to the marriage. Each party would be fined if they were at fault and the marriage did not go ahead, for any other reason other than the death of one of the couple.

The delegation further agreed that within forty days of Charles reaching his fourteenth birthday the marriage would be completed 'per verba de presenti' (through words of the present). Neither Mary nor her father were present in Calais so her consent to the proxy ceremony could not be given in person and was therefore given by the representatives of Henry VII. Within the first three months following the marriage, Mary was expected to travel to Hellevoetsluis in the Netherlands, with the expense being met by Henry VII. On arrival, the young couple would have eight days to solemnise the marriage. A further offer was made to Henry VII that Prince Charles would undertake a separate betrothal ceremony himself in the presence of English ambassadors.[21] With all negotiations complete people began to celebrate what the future held.

A French ballad, believed previously to have been written in celebration of Mary's marriage to Louis XII of France, has been connected to the treaty signing. Mary Ann Everett Green explains that the ballad could not have been written in relation to the later marriage as Henry VII was dead when Mary married Louis but is referred to in the ballad as alive. The verses also make reference to the Golden Fleece, aspects of the insignia of Castile (the eagles and castles) and specifically mentions Flemish and Burgundians, both of whom were not subjects of Louis XII but Prince Charles of Castile. It may seem strange that the ballad is in French, inferring the French celebrated the treaty when it would have no benefit to them, but at the time, Calais was still in the possession of the English and thus under the governance of Henry VII. French would have been spoken there and French was also a common language amongst the aristocracy in England at the time.

> Arouse yourselves, ye sleepy spirits –
> Whoever are friends of the English,
> Let us sing AVE MARIA!
> Dame Mary shall join the fleece of gold,
> And the enclosure of the castles, eagles, and lilies,
> Arouse yourselves, ye sleepy spirits –
> Mary, daughter of the true lily,
> Henry the Seventh, that king of worth,
> Prince over all princes,
> Arouse yourselves, ye sleepy spirits –
> Shall deliver all Flanders
> From the great annoyances of its enemies,
> Reinstating the churches –
> Arouse yourselves, ye sleepy spirits –
> Rejoice again I say –
> Sing Burgundians, all unitedly,
> At this lofty marriage –
> Arouse yourselves, ye sleepy spirits –
> For during ten thousand years from this
> There will not be, nor has been in the country,
> Such a peace, such an alliance –
> Arouse yourselves, ye sleepy spirits –
> We all pray, great and small.
> That the kings may be all good friends,

And peace through all the world –
Arouse yourselves, ye sleepy spirits –
And that at last in Paradise
All may sing
With voice and heart purified –
Arouse yourselves, ye sleepy spirits.[22]

It was not just across the Channel where celebrations took place. Henry VII was clearly pleased with his success, issuing letters to the aldermen of towns and cities across the country and the Mayor of London to confirm the negotiations had been concluded and a contract had been drafted, as a result of his 'great labour, study, and policy'. Bonfires were lit across London and fountains flowed with wine, as inhabitants celebrated making it 'evidently known what gladness and rejoicing is generally taken'.[23]

With the Imperial delegation having travelled home from Calais, the culmination of years of negotiations, consultations and setbacks came to a conclusion when the marriage treaty was ratified by Maximilian, Holy Roman Emperor, on 22 February 1508.[24] Despite the initial agreement stating the proxy marriage would take place by Easter, events intervened; one such delay was apparently due to the illness of Henry VII.[25] Notwithstanding delays, the arrangements continued but not all were celebrating. In July 1508, Ferdinand of Aragon, writing to Gutierre Gómez de Fuensalida, Knight Commander of Membrilla, did not want his written ratification to be given so freely, stating he wished Henry VII had discussed it with him prior to the treaty being made. Ferdinand expressed his wishes that 'until the marriage of the Prince and Princess of Wales has taken place, does not wish that any writing of his should appear, confirming the marriage of the Prince of Castile with the Lady Mary. If, however, Henry will not allow the nuptials of the Prince and Princess of Wales to be celebrated unless the said marriage be confirmed, then Membrilla must promise that he will confirm it. But if the said confirmation should not be required, he must confine himself to speaking fair words, saying that his master thinks well of the marriage'.[26] Ferdinand was clearly keeping his options open and using the marriage of Charles and Mary as leverage to influence Henry VII to agree to the marriage of Prince Henry and Katharine of Aragon. As Ferdinand remained evasive, Maximilian wrote to his daughter that 'she knows that the principal reason which has induced him to betroth Prince Charles to the Princess Mary is to get a good sum of money from the King of England. The King of England has promised 100,000 crowns'.[27]

In October, the treaty was ratified by Margaret of Austria followed by Maximilian instructing John de Berghes 'to go over to England, and perform the ceremony according to the rites of the Church, in the name of the Archduke'.[28] A couple of months later, in December 1508, the deputation was despatched to travel to England to make the final negotiations and arrangements for, and complete the proxy betrothal, of the young couple. The details of the visit by the embassy and the betrothal ceremony have thankfully survived.[29] The delegation sent by the Emperor consisted of eight men: John de Berghes, Chamberlain to the Emperor; Laurence de Gorrevod, Governor of Bresse; Sigismund Flucke, Doctor of Law; Jean le Sauvaige, President of Flanders; Master Andrea de Burgo, a knight of the Emperor's council; George de Theimseke, Provost of Cassel; Philip Haneton, First Secretary to the Emperor, and Toyson Dore, Man-at-Arms.[30] The embassy was accompanied by a number of other men of high standing. On their journey to England they travelled to Calais where they were greeted and entertained by Sir Gilbert Talbot before crossing the Channel to Dover. On arriving on English shores they were met by Sir Edward Poynings and Thomas Goldstone, prior of Christ Church at Canterbury, and accompanied to Canterbury where the mayor and aldermen of the city greeted them with gifts. Goldstone and Poynings led the party along the route to London, stopping at various towns enabling others to greet the embassy. Reaching Dartford, they were met by Sir Thomas Brandon, Knight of the Order of the Garter and uncle to Charles Brandon; Dr Nicholas West; George Talbot, 4th Earl of Shrewsbury; John de Giglis, Bishop of Worcester; and Sir Thomas Docwra, prior of the Knights of St John at Clerkenwell. This group of men were to escort the party to the City of London where they arrived on 5 December 1508; they were greeted by the mayor, Sir Stephen Jennings and aldermen of the city. After a long journey, the men were in need of respite before meeting Henry VII, and were escorted to accommodation which had been prepared for their arrival. The group spent the first night being entertained and the next morning were greeted by William Warham, Archbishop of Canterbury and the city sheriffs who welcomed the men with more gifts.

After two days' rest, the embassy was escorted by river, using the royal barges, to Greenwich Palace where the king was residing. A record of the visit states: 'If I were to describe the magnificent and rich equipment of such a king and his royal household, and at the same time the most honorable arrangement established for receiving the Orators themselves again, it would be very difficult and too long for me'.[31] The embassy was guided through the lower court, through a gallery and into the great chamber where the Royal Guard stood awaiting their arrival – 'each one was adorned with a shawl woven of gold and silver, and cloth of gold, velvet, and silk of every colour'. Passing through the Guard who were aligned either side of the room, the group entered the antechamber to find more courtiers present. It must have been an incredible sight to see so many lords, both spiritual and temporal, and members of the royal household present, ready to witness this monumental occasion. When they finally came upon Henry VII he was sitting under a cloth of estate, Henry, Prince of Wales sat below to the left of the king along with the nobility, whilst Rodrigo de Puebla, ambassador to King Ferdinand of Aragon and the churchmen sat to his right. Henry VII, 'The noblest king, and the most distinguished of all kings, bearing divine rather than human majesty and the true excellence of royal dignity, received them with the most humane and gracious words, saying that they had arrived well and happily to himself and his kingdom'.[32]

Following the initial greetings, Jean le Sauvaige, President of Flanders, began to address the court to confirm they were present to conclude the negotiations of the betrothal between Princess Mary and Prince Charles. William Warham responded on behalf of the king, greeting the company and accepting their request to discuss the marriage. The discussions would of course not take place in the presence of the large crowd gathered to witness the encounter and soon after the embassy were escorted into the inner chamber to continue the discourse.

The following day the embassy was met by William Warham, Archbishop of Canterbury; Richard Fox, Bishop of Windsor; and Thomas FitzAlan, 16th Earl of Arundel, amongst others of the king's council, to further the discussions. The contract was reviewed to ensure it matched the agreements previously agreed and the records note:

> By the premysses it is manyfests and openne that this aliaunce and affinitie is by so great afore sight and deliberacion suerly establisshed and knytte on both parties that it can not be dissolved or broken oonles it be by dethe of any of the bothe parties contrahent. Whiche God defende. Howe be it thamitie neuertheles shal stande in full strength and vigour.

Both sides faced large financial implications if they were held responsible for the failure of the contract to be fulfilled. The record continues:

> And it is of trouth and undoubted that there was never amytie or aliaunce heretofore made and concluded betwixt any Prynces with better wyll and mynde, without coloure or dissymulacion, then this that nowe is taken betwixt the sayde Emperour and the kynges hyghnes, whiche at this daye is the most noble aliaunce and gretest Mariage of all Christendome, considering the sundry and manyfolde Regions and Countrayes that the sayde Yonge

> Prynce by right nyghe possibilite, if God sende hym lyf, shal enherite.[33]

This was not just a marriage; it was an alliance between powerful kingdoms which was intended to bring peace and benefits to both sides of the alliance. The final negotiations were confirmed and it was recorded that Emperor Maximilian had signed and affixed his seal of approval. He had also signed and sealed again jointly with Prince Charles as 'tutor and manborne of the said yonge Prynce'.[34] By signing they were 'joynetely as a parte and severally, byndyng thrmself, theyr heyres, lands and subgiettes, under right great sommes of money for penalties whiche they shall forfayte in caas this marriage betwixt ye yonge prynce and the kynges doughter take not effect'.[35] Margaret of Austria, along with the towns, cities and lands under the governance of Charles, were also bound by the contract.

Negotiations concluded, the king, Mary, and the court moved to Richmond Palace on 16 December to celebrate the successful negotiations that, if the marriage took place, offered the possibility of Mary becoming a future Empress but would at the least, make her Duchess of Austria and queen consort of Spain. The embassy was invited to join the celebrations and remained for almost a week. During that time they were treated to beautiful and sumptuous accommodation and plentiful entertainment: 'at that time the house itself shone and the whole was sparkling. From these facts it could easily be judged that such a magnificent house could not be found in so many countries; since it represented an earthly paradise rather than a house or a palace. Indeed, the hall shone on every side with rich curtains of gold and silver and woven silk. Wherein was a great and lofty abacus, laden with vessels of silver and gilt, raised almost from the ground to the very high ceiling, of wonderful value indeed, and not easily estimated in value or price; where different cloths of state of precious gold were set up very high'.[36] Since Elizabeth of York had passed, Mary was able to use the rooms that had previously belonged to her mother. In chambers 'furnished with the most exquisite and precious curtains woven with gold and silk' Mary would have prepared herself, with the assistance of her ladies for the most important public appearance of her life so far.[37]

Chapter Three

Princess of Castile

The betrothal was performed on the morning of Sunday, 17 December 1508 at Richmond Palace. The chapel 'had walls covered with cloths of rich gold. And the royal altar was covered with so many great images of the saints, partly made of gold and partly of silver, and inlaid with an immense number of precious stones and pearls'.[1] Amongst those present were Henry VII, Henry, Prince of Wales, Katharine of Aragon, numerous courtiers and, of course, the ambassadors. Henry VII sat on a dais whilst Mary stood below him, alone under a cloth of estate, 'let them not overlook the fact that to the form and beauty of any other prince or queen she was established at such a tender age (for she was about the eleventh year of her age), there could be no or very rare comparison'.[2] The Archbishop of Canterbury, William Warham, delivered a speech celebrating the union, the benefits of friendship, and the lineage of the couple. In response, Jean le Sauvaige, President of Flanders also expressed joy at the union and the alliance this would create.

Following these ornate and likely long speeches, the young Mary was addressed by Lord de Berghes, acting as proxy for Prince Charles. In the presence of two notaries, acting as official witnesses to avoid any possible disputes about the legitimacy of the betrothal, de Berghes took Mary by the hand and stated his authority to act on behalf of Prince Charles. He went on to repeat the words the President of Flanders read to him, making his vows in the present tense. Releasing Mary's hand, it was now her turn to make her vows. This must have been an anxious moment for the young princess. Taking the right hand of her proxy prince, Mary spoke her long vows in French. The vows translated as:

> I, Mary, by you John, Lord of Berg, commissary and procurator of the most high and puissant Prince Charles, by the grace of God Prince of Spain, Archduke of Austria, and Duke of Burgundy, etc. hereto by his commission and special procuration constituted and ordained, by your means and signifying this to me – take the said Lord Charles to my husband and spouse, and consent to him as to my husband and spouse.

> And to him and to you for him, I promise that henceforward, during my natural life, I will have, hold, and repute him as my husband and spouse; and for this I plight my troth to him and to you for him.[3]

Mary's skill in the language and ability to speak the vows without distraction 'caused many different nobles and others standing and hearing them not only to be amazed and astonished, but also to burst into tears with the greatest joy and sweetness of heart'.[4] With their vows complete, de Berghes kissed Mary and placed a gold ring on her finger. With that final act Mary was betrothed, 'the combination of manners and gestures and good manners was such that I can freely affirm that such excellent and royal virtues could never have been found in any other prince or lady who had been trained or educated for a longer time in these great mysteries'.[5] Before the celebrations could begin, the ceremony had to be ratified: firstly by the contracting parties; secondly it was then certified by a number of men including four bishops, one archbishop, eleven barons, nine earls, one duke and the foreign embassy.[6] It may appear to be a very long-winded process but neither party wanted anything to be denied or rebutted at a later date.

Trumpets blasted in celebration as the court rejoiced. Henry VII, taking de Berghes by the arm, made his way to his chapel, along with the courtiers, to hear Mass given by Richard FitzJames, Bishop of London. Mass was followed by the singing of Te Deums to celebrate the union. Afterwards, Henry VII requested the company of de Berghes and Laurence de Gorrevod, Governor of Bresse, to join him at his table for dinner whilst the rest of the court retired to an adjacent chamber and dined sumptuously from gilt plate and cups, using salt cellars of gold, adorned with gems and pearls.[7]

With all the solemn aspects of the event concluded the court prepared to celebrate with jousting and feasting. Mary, now styled as Princess of Castile, attended as the guest of honour, watching from a gallery with Katharine of Aragon and her ladies. The men would be competing for the honour of the princess, whilst the musicians played from a stage opposite; overall a spectacle Mary likely thoroughly delighted in. For the next three days the royal court enjoyed jousting, hunting, hawking and bear-baiting. Whilst the royal court celebrated, so did the inhabitants of London. Wine flowed and sweet treats ensured nobody went hungry. Bonfires were lit and people of all classes and ages danced and sang, enjoying the festivities at the expense of the court.

On the final day a tournament acted as the grand finale to the celebrations. The day ended with a more intimate dinner. Mary was of course present, as was her sister-in-law, Katharine of Aragon. Henry VII invited the embassy to attend the dinner, at which they presented gifts from Mary's new in-law relations to their new Princess of Castile. The bridegroom, Prince Charles, sent her an item which had a golden letter 'K' for Karolus (Charles) set with diamonds and pearls. The words 'Maria optimam partem elegit, quæ non auferetur ab eâ' (Mary chose the best part, which shall not be taken away from her) were engraved. What the item specifically was we sadly do not know. Emperor Maximilian had sent a ruby and large diamond embellished with pearls. Margaret of Austria had also sent a gift – a balas ruby surrounded by pearls. Although Prince Charles was not present, he would be honoured by Henry VII who agreed to bestow him with the honour of electing him into the Order of the Garter.[8]

The account of the betrothal, written by Peter Carmelianus, concludes with a beautiful poem, praising not only the couple but also both royal families:

> The festive day will shine, for all the mortals of Eve: And the Titan shines brighter than usual in the world.
> Let a good and prudent man, and every lover of peace, rejoice, and above all give a pious prayer to God.
> The illustrious houses of the English and of Burgundy remains clearly linked to the eternal bloodline.
> Behold, there is given to Charles, Mary, a beautiful girl, notable for her virtue, her manners, and her brilliance.
> Henry the Seventh, the famous King, is her father, who is the jewel of kings, and the most honorable.
> As long as Queen Elizabeth, her mother lived, the world flourished among queens without equal.
> Brother Henry, the prince, to whom no one is second, pours out his command throughout the whole world.
> Margaret, daughter of the King, married to the powerful Scots, wise, beautiful, charming, decent.
> I am silent about the deceased brothers and sisters, who hold happy kingdoms in heaven.
> But King Philip had been the father of Charles
> Whom in a short (ah too!) hour he lifted up for himself.
> The only hope of Caesar Augustus, his only son, Magnanimous, willing, energetic and powerful.
> But his queen is the illustrious Joanna, the unquestioned heir of three kingdoms.
> He himself, however, was such a great parent
> Again you have a father, favored by the new lot, Here is Henry, who will support you and your rights, imposing your strong reins on your enemies.

He is the one who will stir up peace with his standard, and can control nations and kingdoms.
Let us, therefore, give praise to the Most High, and to the Lord of power, who has given us so many good things.
And that this Marriage may be salutary for us all, let us offer prayers night and day.
Praise God.[9]

With the celebrations concluded, the embassy had one last task – convince Henry VII to pay 50,000 crowns for a jewel known as 'le riche fleur de lys'.[10] Unfortunately, we have no record of what this jewel looked like but Emperor Maximilian had asked the embassy to pawn it to Henry VII as he was in need of funds. With Henry VII obliging, the embassy declined his invite to remain for the upcoming Christmas festivities and finally departed for home, laden with gifts of horses, hawks and dogs, from the king and court. Mary had made her vows and accepted that she would one day become the wife of a young man who would, in the future, become one of the most powerful men in the world. Despite her training and education in her early years, the next few years would be vital for Mary. It was now time for her to train for her future. There were discussions to send Mary to the court of Margaret of Austria, Duchess of Savoy, who at the time was the regent of the Netherlands on behalf of her nephew. The purpose was to enable Margaret to train Mary and ensure she was taught the necessary customs and fashions of the kingdom, as well as how to rule.

Henry VII was very much involved in the planning of sending Mary abroad. Records of the requirements for her travel have survived and include Henry's own additions. Mary was to have a bedchamber and two additional chambers. Permission was given for items to be taken from Henry's wardrobe for the provision of ensuring Mary was comfortable, and other items were to be ordered in London or Flanders. Her bedchamber was to be hung with cloth of gold, containing a large trussing bed with a counterpoint of cloth of gold and curtains of damask. A featherbed was also included with plenty of pillows made of Holland cloth. Lastly, a pallet bed was to be provided for whichever of her gentlewomen were to stay with her. The floor was to be covered with large carpets and a chair of cloth of gold to be provided. Small carpets of crimson velvet were to cover the windows if required or lay on top of cupboards.

The next chamber included another featherbed as well as 'a riche story of Aras golde and silke'. A large sparver (canopy for a bed) of cloth of gold, was to be placed in the second room with Henry himself adding '*and cramosyn vellet perpale, the vellete embrodred with her bages and other devise*', [the italic indicates Henry's additions] and also added comments regarding the curtains for the sparver that he wished them to be '*dowble sarcenet, perpaled with the colours that the clothe of golde and vellet shalbe*'. This room would also have carpets for the floor and windows as well as a traverse. The third and final room was to contain a bed of estate with a 'counterpoint of *clothe of golde of her colours purpale*'. A large tapestry was to furnish the room along with a chair of cloth of gold and an additional featherbed. Chariots and palfreys were also ordered for Mary and her ladies. The record ends with the numbers of servants who would accompany Mary, including five chamberers and two gentlewomen and ends with a long list of items of jewellery, plate, cups and candlesticks. Henry VII was clearly intending to travel with Mary himself as he is included in the requirements for furnishings and listed as intending to stay at the Castle of Calais on arrival.[11]

Following the proxy wedding, letters were exchanged the same month the embassy departed, with Charles referring to Henry VII as 'father' and Henry, Prince of Wales as 'brother'.[12] To Mary, he wrote:

> My good mate,
>
> With good grace and as cordially as I can, I recommend myself to you. I have charged the Lord of Bergues, and my other ambassadors ordered to your country, to inform you of the good condition of my person and affairs, begging you to believe the same and to let me know by them of your health and good tidings, which is the thing I most desire, as knows the blessed Son of God, whom I pray, my good mate, to give you by his grace your heart's desires. At Malines, the 18th day of December.
>
> Your good husband, CHARLES
> To the Lady Mary, my good mate.[13]

Although the proxy wedding had now taken place, Ferdinand was still obstructing the arrangement by refusing to ratify the agreement. In April 1509 he was still using the marriage of his daughter Katharine of Aragon to Prince Henry in attempts to manipulate proceedings and 'to resolve to make all possible sacrifices of money, but not to consent to the marriage of Prince Charles with the Princess Mary; for the marriage would have been fraught with serious danger to him, to the Queen his daughter, and to Prince Charles himself, while it would also have disturbed the peace of all their kingdoms'.[14]

The same month, another event would impact the political stage of Europe. Despite his intention to accompany his daughter at least as far as Calais,

Henry VII died at Richmond Palace on 21 April 1509. His son, Henry ascended the throne as Henry VIII. The death of Henry VII provided opportunities for new negotiations but Mary had now lost her loving father. There are no records of Mary's reaction to her father's death and although she was close to her brother Henry, it can only have been painful to have no parents at the age of 13. With the court in mourning, Henry VIII ordered new clothing and horse trappings for Mary including two mantles, six kerchiefs and a black velvet-covered saddle and pillion.[15]

Henry VII had made his will on 31 March 1509 at Richmond. He had ensured Mary's future was secure by making reference to the marriage between her and Charles and including a provision in case the marriage did not take place. The provision states 'we wol, our said doughter Mary have for her mariage, fifty thousand poundes paiable of our goods, yf so muche remaigne after the performance of such thinges and charges as in this our Wille'. If there were no funds remaining Henry VII instructs his executors to ensure the funds are provided through rents and income. He then goes on to say that 'in her said mariage she is to be ruled and ordred by th'advise and consent of our said Sone the Prince, his Counsaile, and our said Executors; and soo that she be maried to some noble Prince out of this our Reame'.[16]

Despite the loss of Henry VII and the impact on his children, Ferdinand took the opportunity to encourage Henry VIII to marry Katharine of Aragon without delay. He also finally agreed, in May, to ratify the marriage of Mary and Charles, again on the premise that Henry VIII would marry his daughter.[17] Henry VIII married Katharine of Aragon on 11 June 1509 at the friar's church of Greenwich. We cannot be sure if Mary was present but knowing her close relationship with both her brother and Katharine of Aragon it is easy to assume she would have attended with great joy. The joint coronation of the newly married couple took place on 23 June 1509 at Westminster Abbey. Mary attended the coronation and was present for the following feast at Westminster Palace, where numerous dishes were served. Mary would have witnessed the custom of the king's champion issuing a challenge when Sir Robert Dimmock entered the hall on a large courser 'trapped in tissue, and embroidered with tharmes of England, and of Fraunce'. The knight instructed his herald to declare 'if there any persone, of what estate or degree souer he be, that wil saie or proue that king Henry the eight, is not the rightfoll enheritor, and kyng of this realme, I sir Robert Dimmoke here his Champion, offre my gloue, to fight in his querell, with any persone to thutterance'.[18] Receiving a gift from Henry VIII of a gold cup and cover, the champion left the hall and the feast continued.

The feast was followed by days of celebrations in the form of jousts, dancing, masques and tournaments. For the royal couple to watch the entertainments 'was framed a faire house, couered with Tapisstrie, and hanged with riche clothes of Arras, and in the saied Palaice, was made a curious Fountain, and ouer it a Castle on the toppe thereof, a greate Croune Emperiall, all the imbattelyng with Roses, and Pomegranetes, gilded with fine Golde, the walles of the same Castle coloured, White and Grene losengis. And if euery losenge, either a Rose or Pomegranet, or a Sheffe of Arrowes, or els, H. and K. gilded with fine Golde, with certain Arches or Turrettes gilded, to support the same Castle'.[19] The jousting centred around a competition between two sets of men: 'Schollers' and 'Knightes'. The men also took part in the pageant which signalled the end of the celebrations.

Unfortunately, the joyous occasions of the wedding and coronation would be followed by more tragedy. Lady Margaret Beaufort died less than a week after the coronation on 29 June 1509 at Westminster Abbey, another loss that would have been a blow to Mary. Lady Margaret was an influential figure on her granddaughter, instilling piety, decorum and encouraging Mary's education, the latter continuing after the death of her grandmother.

For the next few years Mary would spend considerable time with her brother and sister-in-law. Henry VIII ensured Mary's expenses were paid including the wages of her household and travel to various residences to join Henry wherever he was. There are numerous payments for carriages sent to transport Mary such as those in July 1509 bringing Mary from Sunninghill to Greenwich and the following July to return Mary to Eltham from Windsor where she had spent time with Henry. Mary appears to have been suffering with some kind of illness in 1509 as in November Henry VIII paid 40s 2½d to Thomas Pereson, an apothecary, for sixty days work in service to Mary.[20] There are no records of what Mary was suffering from but a further payment was made in June the following year of 100l in gold to her physician, Master Lewis.[21] This is approximately an astonishing £66,276 in modern money.[22] Despite illness Mary would have to continue to prepare herself for leaving the safety of her brother and England but until then she could continue to have fun in the many entertainments her brother provided.

With a new king on the throne of England, the royal court changed into a place of enjoyment and frivolity. Henry VIII was a very enthusiastic sportsman, musician and showman. He revelled in court pageants, tournaments and masques and Mary was a constant feature in the entertainments over the next few years. The first disguising recorded featuring Henry VIII took place at Westminster in January 1510. Henry VIII and his companions dressed in 'green coats and hose of Kentish Kenal like [Robin] Hood men' and burst into the chambers of Katharine of Aragon, surprising (or at least attempting to) the queen and her ladies.[23] Unfortunately the record does not state if Mary was present but she certainly was at the next event for Shrove Tuesday the following month. Mary was one of six ladies who were dressed in various disguises:

> ... twoo were appareyled in Crymosyn satyne and purpull, embrowdered with golde and by vynyettes, ran floure delices of golde, with marueylous ryche & strauge tiers on their heades. Other two ladyes in Crymosyne & purpull, made like long slops enbroudered and fret with gold after antike fashion and ouer that garment was ashort garment of clothe of golde scant to the knee facioned like a tabard all ouer, with small double rolles, all of flatte golde of Damaske golde with flatte pypes y straunge it was to beholde. The other two ladies were in kyrtels of Crymosyne and purpul satyn, enbroudered with a vynet of Pomegraneltes of golde, all the garmetes cut compasse wyse, hauyng but demy sleues, and naked doune from the elbowes, and ouer their garments were vochettes of pleasauntes, rouled with Crymsyne veluet, and set w letters of golde lyke Carectes, their heades rouled in pleasauntes and typpers lyke the Egipcians, enbroudered with gold.[24]

The men, including Henry VIII, were also in disguise and danced with the ladies before finally revealing themselves to their audience. Mary did not often spend time away from her brother but in July she was at Eltham without him. Clearly Henry VIII did not forget about his sister when she wasn't around as he sent her a hart, likely one he had caught hunting himself, as a gift.[25] It would not be long before she was in his company again as the records show regular payments for offerings at Mass for both Henry VIII and Mary together.

The next specific mention of Mary attending a courtly entertainment is November 1510 when Henry VIII was entertaining the ambassadors of Maximilian and Ferdinand. After dinner Henry VIII had invited the men into the queen's chamber where they were met with a performance from mummers. After a time the men left but six returned masked. The six men were accompanied by a group of minstrels and followed by six ladies. The ladies were dressed in the Spanish fashion 'in garmentes of Crymosyn Satyn embroudered and trauessed with cloth of gold, cut in Pomegranettes and yokes'.[26] After dancing, the ladies removed the masks of the men to reveal Henry VIII; Henry Bourchier, 2nd Earl of Essex; Charles Brandon; Sir Edward Howard; Sir Thomas Knyvett; and Sir Henry Guildford.

At this point in time Katharine of Aragon was recorded as 'great with childe' so likely did not take part but the Spanish style dress and embroidered pomegranates were likely in her honour. It is therefore possible Mary partnered her brother in the dance and although the men were masked it is very unlikely that she was not aware of who her partner was. Or perhaps her partner was Charles Brandon and this was the beginning of their affection for one another. Mary was still only 14 years old at this point but during this period that was old enough to marry. Although Mary is not noted specifically in *Hall's Chronicle* at this event, we know she was present as she appears in the *Revel Accounts* kept by the diligent Master of Revels. Various materials were ordered for the costumes including satin in various colours, sarcenet in various colours, velvet, ribbons and Venice gold. The only mention specifically for 'the Princess of Castile' was blue satin to line her bonnet, but based on the other items we can surmise she may have worn a gown of satin, possibly blue to match her bonnet or crimson. Mary appears to be the only one whose bonnet was lined with blue satin; four of the other five ladies' bonnets were lined with green satin, though frustratingly the record is unclear on the final piece. Mary was allowed to keep her garments at the end of the revel as a gift from her brother.

It was not long after this that Katharine entered her confinement in preparation for the birth of her child, though sadly this was not her first pregnancy. On Wednesday, 1 January 1511 a Tudor prince was born. The prince, named Henry, was christened four days later on 5 January, his godparents being Louis XII of France, William Warham, Archbishop of Canterbury and Margaret of Austria, Duchess of Savoy.[27] As was custom, Katharine would not have been present at the christening as she would have remained in her chambers for a period of lying-in before attending a churching ceremony to welcome her back to society. Women were usually accompanied to their chambers by their closest women but it was unusual for young, single women to attend childbirth and therefore it is very unlikely Mary was present at the birth, although she possibly attended the christening.

The birth of a male heir was cause for widespread celebration. Henry VIII knew only too well how important it was to have a male heir, he was after all, never intended for the throne. Henry VIII and his court were not alone in celebrating. Throughout London, bonfires were lit, wine was provided by the court for the public and processions took place throughout the city to celebrate and thank God for providing England with an heir. A tournament challenge was issued on the day of the christening by 'Ceure Noble, Vaillant Desyre, Bon Volur and Joyecup [*sic*] Pensere, knights of the Queen Lady Renome'.[28] Although *Letters and Papers Foreign and Domestic* reference a man named 'Ceure Noble' the name is given as 'Cure loial' (Sir Loyal Heart) in *Hall's Chronicle*, a name we are more familiar with. This was of course Henry VIII. Hall goes on to state that Valiant Desire was Sir Edward Neville, Bon Volour (good will) was

Lord William, Earl of Devonshire and Bon Espoir (good hope) was Sir Thomas Knyvett.[29] The *1511 Westminster Tournament Roll* has Henry VIII named as Couer Loyal but two of the men in different roles: Sir Thomas Knyvett as Valiant Desire and Sir Edward Neville as Joyeulx Penser (Bon Espoir).[30]

The tournament was to begin on Candlemas so preparations had to begin swiftly as it was an enormous task to prepare for such an event. Henry ordered crimson velvet to be delivered to John Ketylby, Sergeant of the Chaundery, for the garnishing of tapers for Mary and his newborn son.[31] This was most certainly not the last time Henry VIII would order clothing or materials for his favourite sister. This record also indicates that Mary was present at the entertainments to celebrate the birth of her nephew.

Whilst preparations for the tournament were ongoing the court celebrated Epiphany at Richmond. A banquet was followed by a pageant taking the form of a mountain or a hill 'out of which hill issued a Morryke danced by the King's young gentlemen, as hynsmen, and thereto a lady'.[32] The records are quiet on the identity of the 'lady' but with the christening taking place the previous day, it is not unreasonable to assume Mary was present at the pageant regardless of whether she took part in the performance or not. The entertainment ended with the customary wassailing to signal the end of Christmas.

A few days later, on 12 and 13 of February, at Westminster, the jousts in honour of Henry VIII and Katharine of Aragon and to celebrate the birth of Prince Henry took place. Katharine had left her chambers and had been churched so was able to attend the entertainments. The Master of Revels, once again provides us with an excellent description:

> A forest was constructed within the house of Black Friars, Ludgate, 26 ft. long, 16 ft. broad, 9 ft. high, garnished with artificial hawthorns, oaks, maples, hazels, birches, fern, broom and furze, with beasts and birds embossed of sundry fashion, with foresters sitting and going on the top of the same, and a castle on the said forest, with a maiden sitting thereby with a garland, and a lion of great stature and bigness, with an antelope of like proportion after his kind drawing the said pageant or forest, conducted with men in wodwoos' apparel, and two maidens sitting on the said two beasts; in the which forest were four men of arms, riding, that issued out at times appointed; and on every of the 4 quarters of the forest were the arms of the four knights challengers. And for the second day were provided and made 4 rich pavilions, one crowned, the other three with balls of bornd gold.[33]

Henry and his three companions were to take on all challengers and ran at the lists all day, Henry VIII, unsurprisingly emerging the victor with the most points scored. The second day, the jousts continued after dinner. Henry and his three companions, 'euery one of them vnder a Pauilion of Crymosyn damaske & purple poudred with H. and K. of fine golde, valenced and frynged with golde of damaske', entered the field amidst a procession of musicians and twelve children of honour. Next to enter the field was Charles Brandon, seemingly alone. Brandon was 'fyrst on horsebacke in a long robe of Russet satyn, like a recluse or a religious person and his horse trapped in the same sewte'.[34] Approaching Katharine of Aragon, Brandon petitioned her to allow him to compete in her presence. Permission granted he discarded his robe, revealing rich armour and rode to the end of the lists to await his companions. One by one men would petition the queen for permission to run, then join Brandon at the end of the tiltyard. The men answering the challenge included: Henry Guildford (son of Mother Guildford); Thomas Grey, 2nd Marquess of Dorset; Thomas Boleyn; Henry Stafford, at that time 1st Earl of Wiltshire; Sir Giles Capell; a man named by Hall as Sir Ronlande; and many other knights. The men, all armed, were all granted permission to join the joust and rode to join Brandon awaiting the beginning of the action. With the challengers and answerers ready, the jousting began. Once again Henry won the most points of the day.

With the joust over, the final event of the celebrations was a banquet in the White Hall at Westminster the same day. Dinner was followed by dancing when suddenly Henry disappeared. Possibly to nobody's astonishment, as Henry was known for surprise entertainments, the trumpets blasted and the set of a pageant named 'the Golldyn Arber in the Archeyerd of Plesyr' was brought into the hall.[35] A number of men were hidden inside the setting and emerged to ask the queen if she wished them to perform, which of course, she agreed to. Six ladies participated in the pageant, all dressed in gowns of green and white satin, covered in golden embroidered letters, H and K, though unfortunately we do not know the identity of the ladies. Henry and his initial jousting companions were joined by another two men 'Bon foy' (good faith) and 'Amoure loyall' (Love loyal); all were dressed 'in garmetes of purple satyn, all of cuttes w H. & K. euery edge garnished with frysed gold'.[36] The ladies joined the men to form couples and began to dance.

The pageants held at Henry's court appear to have been a sight to behold but, on this occasion, not only did the floor break with the weight of the set but when the set was moved aside to make room for dancing, the attendees destroyed the set by taking it apart to take pieces with them. Events escalated further when Henry invited guests to take a golden letter from the clothing of the participants. Henry himself ended up almost stripped as people took everything and Sir Thomas Knyvett, despite his best attempts to defend himself, lost almost all of his clothing. The guards were called when the ladies became victims and people began to tear at their clothing, likely in attempt to remove a golden letter but this kind of behaviour could result in embarrassment for a lady at the Tudor court. Henry, Katharine and their companions left the hall and retired to the king's chambers to feast and ended their day amused about the recent events. Mary is not mentioned specifically though this does not mean she wasn't present. The *Book of Payments* does usually note when something is specifically made for Mary with regards to pageants and on occasion, she is made something slightly different to the other ladies, making her stand out, such as the blue bonnet lining previously mentioned. Therefore, on this occasion it may have been that she was present but did not participate, and perhaps instead stayed with the queen to watch.

The Tudor court was once more driven into mourning when Prince Henry died less than two weeks after the celebratory jousts, on 22 February 1511. The records are again silent on Mary's reaction to the loss of her nephew. Henry VIII spent Easter that year at Greenwich. He paid offerings of 20s (£662) for himself and 5s (£165) on behalf of Mary on Good Friday, indicating she was with him. The following month has a record of 100s (£3,313) paid to Anne Jerningham for half a year's wage.[37] The record doesn't state what her role was but as she travelled to France with Mary later on, it is plausible she was a lady of her chambers. Mary's expenses feature quite often in the *Book of Payments*, having been paid by Henry VIII. He not only paid her offerings on Holy days and the wages of her servants but also gave her funds directly. She was provided with payment of 20l (£13,225) in new gold and groats in November 1511.[38] This may appear to be a lot of money but compared to the amounts Henry was spending on entertainments, clothing and jewels it was a drop in the ocean. We do not know what Mary spent these funds on but we do know the Tudors were partial to gambling, including Henry, so maybe this was money intended for Mary to enjoy the holiday season playing games. Mary may have used some of the funds to purchase gifts for her friends, family and servants ahead of Christmas and New Year, the latter being the traditional gift giving day during the Tudor era. The court spent the end of 1511 at Eltham before moving to Greenwich in January where once again there were celebratory entertainments and the Lord of Misrule would take over the social aspects of the court.

For New Years in 1512 Henry once again paid for Mary's offering and spent an enormous 775l (£513,642) on gifts from the goldsmiths.[39] He also included Mary in the wardrobe requests when he authorised an order of 'purple velvet for garnishing the tapers of the King and Queen and crimson velvet for that of the Princess of Castile on Candlemas Day next coming'.[40] Candlemas of 1512 appears to have been spent at Westminster as Henry approved various expenses from there including Mary's offering of 3s 4d (£110).[41]

The year of 1512 in *Hall's Chronicle* is largely taken up by accounts of preparations for war, and the sending of armies to assist Ferdinand against the Mores and Margaret of Austria against the Duke of Guelders. Therefore, unfortunately we do not hear much of Mary until May when she made an offering of 6s 8d (£220) at the marriage of Henry Guildford to Margaret Bryan, daughter of Sir Thomas Bryan.[42] Henry Guildford was the son of Lady Joan Guildford (Mother Guildford) so Mary would have likely wished to attend the wedding or at least make a gift to the couple. Henry Guildford was also a frequent participant in court entertainments so Mary likely knew him well.

It is not until Christmas and Epiphany that we hear more of Mary. The court spent Christmas of 1512 at Greenwich where Henry VIII ordered the preparation of a pageant for New Year. The pageant named 'Dangerous Fortress' comprised of a castle being built within the hall. The set included walls, towers, a dungeon and even artillery. From the records we know that Mary was one of six ladies who participated in the pageant and wore a crimson velvet bonnet, russet sarcenet sleeves lined with yellow sarcenet, a 'partelet of white satin, garnished with damask gold, and a caul of pipes of gold', and a garment, possibly her gown or kirtle, made of cloth of gold. In comparison, the remaining five ladies had gowns of russet satin, crimson satin bonnets and white sarcenet sleeves, so once again Mary would stand out from the others. Henry and Charles Brandon are also noted to have worn garments made of cloth of gold, so they too would have stood out from the other participants.[43] Henry and his five companions acted as the chivalrous knights laying siege to the castle that the ladies were within. The ladies yielded and left the castle to dance with the men before all retired within the castle and it was removed from the hall. Katharine of Aragon did not participate in the pageant but was present to watch the entertainments. As a gift, Mary was once more granted permission to keep her gown afterwards.[44]

Epiphany brought another pageant, this time named 'the Ryche Mount'. The setting is described as 'a rock or mountain of gold and precious stones, set with herbs of divers kinds, and planted with broom to signify Plantaganet [*sic*] and also with red and white roses; on the top, a burning beacon; on the sides, fleurs de lis; at the foot, 6 lords, apparelled in crimson velvet and goldsmith's work, "of korryas kast and ingyen"; above them, 6 minstrels in blue and [yel] low damask; at the entrance, two armed men in green satin. It was drawn by two "myghty woordwossys or wyld men"'. When the mountain was opened it revealed six ladies dressed in 'gold and rich clothes'. The ladies danced with six men, dressed in crimson velvet, before leaving the hall. The *Book of Revels* confirms Mary was one of the six ladies. Mary was the recipient of headwear featuring gold bullion embroidery and along with Lady Courtenay was issued with garments made of cloth of gold and afterwards was able to keep, 'as the King's gift, her head apparel, i.e. the "schaperoun" and "orrelet", set with fine gold, her "cleer", inner sleeves, "sypers", girdle and stomacher.' On this occasion the other five ladies were also allowed to keep their garments.[45] According to Hall the pageant took the form of an Italian disguising known as a masque, not seen before in England and he states some of the ladies did not wish to dance with those masked.[46]

The new year appears to have brought about a push in preparations to prepare Mary for life away from the English court. In January 1513 the first payment to John Palsgrave in his role as a tutor to Mary was made. Palsgrave had previously taught Henry and was appointed to supplement Mary's skill in French on a more formal basis. His annual salary of 6s 13s 4d (£4,418) was paid by Henry, indicating his desire to see his sister receive the best education and care.[47] Although Mary had been studying French since a young age and had benefitted from the presence of her companion, Jane Popincourt, she would not only be required to learn the language formally ahead of her intended move to reside with her husband Prince Charles as Princess of Castile but also to understand her obligations.

Palsgrave was a humanist tutor and published his own French textbook *L'eclaircissement de la langue francaise* in 1530. He began writing the text whilst in service to Mary which gives us an insight into the curriculum Palsgrave set for the princess. Historian, Erin A. Sadlack points out that Palsgrave made use of both English and French texts including Chaucer's *Canterbury Tales*, Alain Chartier's *Quadrilogue invective*, *Le Traité de l'Esperance* and *Lai de paix*.[48] Palsgrave also makes reference to a translation of Ovid's *Heroides* which would most certainly have also been read by her brother who undertook a humanist education. Whether Mary read the literature referenced by Palsgrave we do not know, but as he was writing his text whilst tutoring Mary it could be assumed he recorded what had been used in her lessons. One book that Mary most likely did read is Christine de Pizan's *Book of Three Virtues*. The text acted as almost a conduct book for women during the era. Mary also possibly read *Livre de la cite des dames* (City of Ladies) also by de Pizan. These texts would have given Mary a sound understanding of politics, chivalry and her role as an ambassador between her brother and spouse but would also have provided entertainment in the form of poetry and romance. A further payment was made to Palsgrave in March 1513, just two months after the first payment. This time he was paid 66s 8d (£2,209) and is amongst payments to other men listed as an advance on their wages, so it is possible this payment was also an advance of his salary.

Easter of 1513 was spent at Greenwich, Mary in the company of her brother. The siblings attended Mass on Palm Sunday. Henry paid for Mary's offerings on the holy days including Palm Sunday, and two payments on Easter Sunday – one of 3s 4d (£110) and another of the same amount at High Mass.[49] If by employing John Palsgrave, Henry was making the final preparations to ready Mary for her departure, he was apparently not the only one now taking action. The following month, in April, Margaret of Austria sent a footman to Mary to join her household, indicating she was still keen for Mary and Charles to marry despite any doubts her father and Ferdinand may have been having. Margaret did expect Henry to foot the bill of 20l (£13,255) for the footman which does make it an almost bold action to take on Margaret's part.

For the first time, Mary would experience life without her brother for a lengthy period of time. In his absence Mary spent her time in the company of Katharine of Aragon who had been appointed as regent in Henry's absence. Henry left England at the end of June 1513; he was travelling to join Maximilian as part of the Holy League or League of Cambrai to defend the Papacy against its enemies and France. Henry already had men at Thérouanne and travelled to join them. The English army began a siege of the city of Thérouanne and Maximilian joined them with a small number of men in August. Maximilian, with the utmost display of chivalry, offered to serve as an officer in Henry's army. This would of course appeal to Henry as he didn't like competition, so to have the Emperor under his command was the perfect situation, even it was just a chivalric gesture. The Battle of Guinegate has become known as the Battle of Spurs due to the retreat of the French, and took place on 16 August. The city of Thérouanne fell a few days later on 22 August and the keys to the city were handed to Henry. Hostages of the French nobility were taken including one who would become an important influence in Mary's life later on, Louis d'Orléans, Duc de Longueville.

After this success Henry travelled with Maximilian to Lille where Margaret of Austria was holding court. Henry spent the evening enjoying himself dancing and feasting whilst his army moved to lay siege to Tournai. Henry and Maximilian visited the siege site together on 13 September. Meanwhile back across the Channel, attempting to take advantage of Henry's absence, James IV of Scotland had invaded England at the head of an army. The result was disastrous for the Scots. James was killed on the battlefield at Flodden after Katharine of Aragon, in her capacity as regent, despatched an army to engage him. Katharine wrote to Henry informing him of the victory and stated she had wished to send him the body of the Scottish king but had been dissuaded by the English nobility. Tournai fell on 23 September and Henry attended Mass within the city on 2 October. Maximilian and Margaret of Austria were both present, having been invited by Henry to return the hospitality he had received at Lille. The people of the town presented Margaret with a set of tapestries depicting scenes from the *Book of the City of Ladies*, the very same book Mary is believed to have read.[50]

Another treaty was ratified in Lille on 15 October 1513, the agreement being that the solemnisation of the marriage between Mary and Charles would take place before May 1514, the year Prince Charles turned 14. This date was delayed to July at the Emperor's request as he wished to attend personally.[51] Henry VIII, Mary and his court were to travel to Calais to deliver Mary into the company of Charles, Emperor Maximilian and Margaret of Austria. When Henry finally returned to England, after holding a joust of course, Mary must have been pleased to have her brother home and be happy to discover that the two sons of her favourite Mother Guildford had both been knighted following their actions in France. Mary may have also finally received an accurate description of her future spouse as Henry had met and hosted him whilst in France.

On his return to England, Henry continued to make preparations for Mary's marriage. He instructed Sir Rauf Verney 'to be employed about the necessary charges of the Princess' at a cost of 40l (£26,510).[52] It may have been Verney that was despatched to the court of Margaret to discuss the apparel of the princess. Margaret received a message declaring 'Forasmuch as the king's pleasure is that my lady the princess's apparel for her person shall be according to the fashion and manner of these parts, the king's grace hath provided all cloth of every sort for her, praying her to devise for the making thereof, after such manner as shall best please her'.[53] Whether all the cloth mentioned for Mary's clothing was sent with the messenger or awaiting a response from Margaret is not known but the list compiled originally for her transportations and altered by her father, Henry VII, was used once more; this time it was shared with Margaret to request her input into whether anything was incorrect or missing.[54]

Amidst preparations the Council of Flanders raised an issue with Henry that they 'would gladly receyue to be espowsed to their Prynce, for she was then one of the fairest Ladyes of the worlde but as concernynge the articles of her dowar, they coulde not fulfyll without thassente of the kynge of Arragon and the realme of Castell'.[55] Henry was not going to allow his favourite sister, a princess of England, to leave the safety of his protection without a dower so the marriage was delayed further.

Illness appeared to strike Mary once more around this time. Physician Robert Yaxley was paid 13l 6s 8d (£8,836) in December for attending on Mary for a period of ten weeks.[56] Again frustratingly, there is no further description of what was ailing Mary. Perhaps she was genuinely unwell, or perhaps Mary realised how close she was to her departure resulting in illness.

By this point Ferdinand, who had been avoiding the subject of the marriage between Mary and Charles, was running out of time to find a way to stop the wedding. However, he was not alone in his objections and by early 1514 those surrounding Charles also began to voice concerns. On 3 April 1514, the English ambassador Knight wrote to Wolsey that:

> Those about the Prince of Castile would gladly hinder his marriage with the Lady Mary, saying, he is a child, and she a woman full grown. Unless the King, when the marriage is solemnised, have these officers discharged, my Lady Mary will be in great hazard.[57]

This was the first time an objection relating to her age had been raised. The age gap was not irregular for the time period. Wolsey and Henry VIII were not unwise, they were conscious this was a ruse to call off the wedding so that Maximilian could seek an alternative alliance, using Charles as a pawn. In May Henry once again sent ambassadors to Flanders but the council did not answer favourably and stated they could not receive Mary that year.[58] Ferdinand meanwhile was busy trying to manipulate everyone, attempting to use their armies for his own gain to avoid using his own and wishing his own grandson dead. Ambassadors reported to Henry VIII that: 'He disregards all obligations of Christian princes, and evidently intends mischief. He would be glad if the Prince of Castile were to die, for so he might continue governor of Castile, and do as he liked'.[59] It was also reported that Ferdinand had threatened to disinherit Charles in favour of his younger grandson, Ferdinand, if the marriage to Mary was to proceed.[60]

Maximilian appeared content to ignore the situation, leaving his daughter Margaret to deal with the English ambassadors. In March 1514 she wrote to her father requesting a response to earlier communication regarding the marriage and relays her concerns as to the penalties for calling off the wedding:

> By the treaty made at Tournay the marriage should be solemnised at Calais before 15 May next and yet no preparations for it are seen here and the Emperor is far away. The King of England's suspicions are further aroused by the Emperor's practices with Aragon and France. The English ambassadors have asked her intervention that the marriage may be solemnised at Calais, where the Queen of England will also be and where the King has made costly preparation. To the first treaty for its solemnisation before the end of May most towns here have sealed and their burgesses will suffer great loss in case of failure. The King is bound to pay

> 100,000 cr. at Bruges within four days after the marriage, but she does not know whether he will rebate the loans which he has made to the Emperor.[61]

Maximilian did eventually react and in May 1514 he sent a letter to Mary, addressing her as 'Serenissime principi Mariæ archiduci Austriæ, principi Hispaniæ et duci Burgundiæ, filie nostræ charissimæ', (Most Serenely, to Princess Mary, Archduchess of Austria, Princess of Spain and Duchess of Burgundy, our dearest daughter), and advised her that he had despatched John Colla, Gerard de Pleine and Lord de la Roche to visit Henry VIII and had ordered them to visit her in person whilst they were at court.[62] Maximilian sent a similar letter to Katharine of Aragon. In the meantime Henry VIII was busy ensuring Mary would have everything required to show off the wealth of England. In February 1514 he purchased 'pieces of cloth of gold for the Princess of Castile', amounting to an incredible 793l 0s 9d. (£525,597) and a few months later in June paid 389l 5s 5d (£257,995) for 'plate for the Princess of Castile'. This would be the last reference to Mary as the Princess of Castile in the *Book of Payments*.[63] Henry VIII was going to make sure that when Mary did finally leave England, she would look every inch the royal princess. Not long after the warrant was issued to the wardrobe for the cloth of gold, Henry decided he was not going to be made a fool of, and certainly not by his own father-in-law who was using Henry to support his own war at a detrimental cost to England. Reports indicate that as early as April 1514, Ferdinand and Maximilian were making peace with Louis XII and securing an alternative to Mary as a bride for Prince Charles.

Henry's ambassadors kept him and his council updated and in May Sir Richard Wingfield wrote to Charles Brandon that the council of Charles were attempting to delay the marriage. He reported that only 'poor Hormistorffe' was supportive of the marriage. Hormistorffe told Wingfield that Charles had been asked about a lady at court to which he replied 'on his faith that it was not so, nor never would be of her or any other, only my Lady Mary reserved'.[64] At the end of June, Gerard de Pleine wrote to Margaret of Austria after observing Mary at court on a few occasions. He wrote that he:

> Has never seen so beautiful a lady. Her deportment is exquisite both in conversation and in dancing, and she is very lively. If Margaret had seen her she would not rest till she had her over; she is very well brought up, and appears to love the Prince wonderfully. She has a very bad picture of him, and is said to wish to see it ten times a day, and to take pleasure in hearing of him. She is not tall, but is

> a better match in age and person for the Prince than he had heard say. She seems quite young and does not show that in two years she will be as far advanced as Likerke or Fontaine.[65]

Based on this account it is apparent that Mary was well aware of the expectation placed on her to flatter her betrothed. It also gives us insight into Mary's beauty. Likerke and Fontaine were maids of honour to Margaret and from de Pleine's writing we can assume they looked older than their years, unlike Mary who was youthful in appearance.

Despite the ongoing discussions of war and marriage, July must have been a happy and hopeful time at the court. Katharine of Aragon was again pregnant. Mary must have been ecstatic for her brother and sister-in-law, and hopeful the pregnancy would produce an heir for England. Henry was only too happy to share the news himself. Writing from Eltham on 13 July 1514, he wrote to Margaret of Austria 'Il annonce à Marguerite que la reine sa femme est enceinte' (He announces to Marguerite that the queen, his wife, is pregnant).[66]

In late July, Ferdinand was still conspiring to replace Mary with Renée, the younger daughter of Louis XII, as a bride for Prince Charles. He wrote to Bernard de Mesa, Bishop of Trinopolis on 24 July confirming that 'the treaty of peace between France on the one part and Spain and the Emperor on the other will soon be concluded together with the marriage of Madame Renée and the Archduke'.[67] Less than a week later, on 30 July, no doubt frustrated by Ferdinand and Maximilian making a peace treaty with France behind his back as well as the constant delays and disruptions Henry had the final say:

> Public instrument, notifying that on 30th July 1514, in the royal manor of Wanstead, and in the presence of Thomas duke of Norfolk, Charles duke of Suffolk, Thomas bp. of Lincoln postulate of York, Richard bp. of Winchester, Thomas bp. of Durham, Charles earl of Worcester, and Sir Ralph Vernay, the Princess Mary solemnly renounced her compact of marriage with Charles prince of Spain, and requested the above to intimate the same to the King her brother, Attested by Rob. Toneys and William Edwards, clk. of the diocese of Hereford.[68]

Although it was Mary that repudiated the marriage to Charles, we must remember that Mary lived in a patriarchal society and Henry VIII most certainly made the decision to call off the marriage. Mary's time as Princess of Castile had come to an end but a new arrangement was not too far in the future and would be one that nobody, least of all Mary, would have expected.

Chapter Four

'Nymph from Heaven'

With Prince Charles out of the picture, Henry VIII was able to begin negotiations for another match for Mary, negotiations that likely began far before Mary publicly called off the marriage. In May 1514, Henry VIII had confirmed to Cardinal Wolsey that he was willing to discuss terms with Louis XII and notes 'the alliance of marriage will not be refused'.[1]

Though the note does not confirm who the possible bride would be, Louis XII is rumoured to have been considering marrying Margaret Tudor, then the Dowager Queen of Scots.[2] In May 1514, the Venetian ambassador wrote that Henry VIII was demanding 1.5 million crowns and the towns of Boulogne, Thérouanne, and St Quentin to be delivered to him in order to make peace with France. In response, Thomas Bohier, General of Normandy advised this was not going to be agreed and Louis XII would agree peace with the usual tributes paid. Henry VIII, dissatisfied with this response stated: 'Well, if he chooses to marry my sister, the widow of the King of Scotland, the agreement shall be made'.[3] The following month records note that, 'Others said that a marriage was being; negotiated between the sister of the King of England, widow of the King of Scotland, and the King of France. For certain it was known that the General of Normandy, one of the chief noblemen of France, had crossed over to England to conclude this agreement'.[4] It is conceivable that when hearing that Thomas Bohier, General of Normandy had been despatched to England to negotiate a marriage to Henry VIII's sister they assumed it must be Margaret as Mary was still due to marry Charles at that time and had not yet refuted the marriage. It should also be noted that Margaret did not require the permission of Henry to remarry, she was the widow of James IV of Scotland and mother to James V. Mary however, as an unmarried young lady, did require her brother's permission, not only because she was royalty and therefore under the prerogative of the monarch but also Henry was her last remaining male relative and in a patriarchal society, she was his responsibility.

Louis XII sent ambassadors to England in June 1514, the month before Mary repudiated the marriage with Charles. According to Hall, the French knew the marriage between Charles and Mary was already broken.[5] The same month, Andrea Badoer, the Venetian ambassador, wrote that Louis had confessed to his son-in-law, Francis d'Angoulême, now the dauphin and heir to the throne of France, that he was considering four ladies to marry in the hopes of a male heir: 'The four ladies are (1) Madame Margaret, who was Duchess of Savoy and is the Emperor's daughter, (2) one of the sisters of the Prince of Castile the Emperor's grandson, (3) the Scotch Queen who lately has borne a male child, and (4) the sister of this King who was promised to the Prince of Castile but is still here unmarried'.[6] It is not known what the ladies in question thought about this, but one can only imagine that Margaret of Austria would certainly not be willing to marry the old king.

Maximilian was still relying on Henry to subsidise his military activities and Margaret was still attempting to get funds from Henry for this purpose as per a letter in June where she advises her father that she had asked Henry for a further 30,000 crowns which had apparently been offered to Maximilian previously but at the time he had not accepted the loan.[7] At this time, Margaret of Austria was also still hopeful of a marriage between her nephew and Mary and continued to make arrangements for Mary's travel to Calais. In response to a letter Margaret had written on 23 May 1514 where she pressed her eagerness for the arrival of Mary but wished to amend the locations and delay, Henry replied on 4 June, stating that he 'Regrets that the ceremony cannot take place in the manner which was agreed upon, and refers her to his ambassadors'.[8] Henry was at Eltham when he wrote this so may possibly have been with Mary as Eltham appears to have been her primary residence.

Later that month Henry also responded regarding the 30,000 crowns, saying that 'the Emperor told the English ambassador that a "golden coffer offered as a present, if not accepted in time, might be revoked by the donor". Henry is therefore as free with regard to his offer as the Emperor to his coffer'.[9] Ferdinand and Maximilian had gambled on a treaty with Louis XII, part of which was to marry Charles to one of his daughters. They had tried giving various excuses to delay the marriage including Mary's age and stating they were concerned about the 'feeble constitution' of Charles.[10] His aunt, Margaret of Austria did in fact report that Charles was sick in June. Writing to her father she stated that 'The moon, say the doctors, is prolonging Charles' illness; but he is improving'.[11] Charles himself seems to have still thought he would be marrying Mary. He requested martial assistance in June 1514 to defend Hainault from the French and his request included the use of 2000 of his own men that were in the pay of Henry and also wished to arrange for his marriage to Mary.[12] Neither Ferdinand or Maximilian could foresee that Henry VIII would make terms with Louis XII and reach an agreement resulting in peace for both kingdoms and France receiving the most beautiful princess as their queen.

Whilst Margaret of Austria was still negotiating a wedding and the arrival of Mary, on 29 June 1514 Louis XII commissioned Louis d'Orleans, Duc de Longueville, John de Selva, president of Normandy and Thomas Bohier to form the peace treaty with Henry as well as negotiate the marriage between himself and Mary. Despite de Longueville technically still being a hostage of Henry, he was authorised by Louis to conclude the treaty and promise the payment of 100,000 crowns per year as had previously been agreed during the lifetime of Henry VII.[13] By the end of June rumours were spreading of the possible marriage between Mary and Louis.[14] This must have come as a surprise to Charles, Margaret, Maximilian and Ferdinand when they eventually received the news. News certainly took time to travel across Europe. On 1 August Thomas Spinelly, ambassador to Henry VIII, wrote from Brussels stating the Emperor had written to his ambassadors making statements that if he had received the 30,000 crowns all affairs would have been settled by now. Maximilian also requested that 'Donna Kateryna de Castir, who lately came out of England, may be retained for the service of the Princess, at her coming over. Meanwhile she shall wait upon the Prince's sisters'.[15]

The terms of the treaty dictated that the kingdoms of England and France would remain at peace and Louis would pay 500,000 crowns in addition to the 500,000 consisting of the sums previously agreed by the treaties of Estaples and London and the security bond for de Longueville. The total of one million crowns was to be paid in instalments of 40,000 per year. In return Henry was to return Tournai. The treaty was to remain in situ for a year following the death of either king. With regards to uniting the realms through the marriage of Louis and Mary, it appears Henry initially tried to avoid paying a dowry portion for Mary. Louis expressed surprise 'that the King of England should wish to marry her without a dowry, she being his sister, which might turn hereafter to her reproach'.[16] As Henry VII had bequeathed Mary 50,000 crowns towards her marriage in his will, this ought to have been the minimum stipulated towards her dowry. Henry VIII did capitulate and agreed that he would give Mary a 400,000 crown dowry. Louis should 'receive jewellery and furniture to the value of 200,000 crowns, as the dowry of the Princess Mary, reserving certain conditions as to their restoration'.[17] Henry was also responsible for all of the costs relating to preparing Mary to be presented as queen and her travelling costs. The additional 200,000 was to be offset from the sum of money owed by Louis against Mary's dowry. This meant that in total, Henry was responsible for 200,000 crowns of goods, jewels, travels costs and anything else related to transporting Mary to France.[18]

The new peace treaty was concluded on 7 August 1514 and the previous treaty once more recognised:

> ii. Oath of Lewis XII. to observe a treaty of peace, union and amity concluded 7 Aug. [1514], with deputies of the King of England.
>
> iii. Similar oath to observe a treaty of peace, union and amity concluded 23 March [1510], with deputies of the King of England.[19]

The following day, Louis issued a further grant to Louis d'Orleans, Duc de Longueville to act as his proxy in the marriage between himself and Mary.[20] In light of the treaty, Henry VIII wrote directly to Pope Leo X to explain the new alliance and the reasons Mary's betrothal to Prince Charles had been rebutted:

> To render the peace more binding, he has promised the Lady Mary in marriage to the King of the French, who has most earnestly asked for her. Heretofore, when she had scarcely attained her thirteenth year, his [King Henry's] father affianced her to the Prince of Castile, with a stipulation that on his attaining the age of 13 years, he was to send his ambassadors and procurators to England formally to ratify the espousals, 'per verba de proesenti'. This condition not having been complied with by the guardians of the Prince of Castile, when the King was at Lisle last year, he referred to it by his ambassador on the 15th May 1514, but the Prince's guardians, although frequently reminded, again neglected the matter; so the Lady Mary, after holding prudent counsel, protested before a notary-public and witnesses, that she cancelled whatever had been done by the King's father in her name with the guardians of the Prince of Castile. Being thus freed, she is affianced to the King of the French, whose procurator had already contracted the marriage, by which bond the peace between himself and King Lewis would be more sincere and durable.[21]

Mary would have less than a week from the conclusion of the treaty until the proxy wedding ceremony. The ceremony took place at Greenwich Palace on the morning of 13 August 1514. In attendance were Henry VIII, Katharine of Aragon, William Warham, Archbishop of Canterbury, Thomas Wolsey and the dukes of Norfolk, Suffolk, and Buckingham. Thomas Grey, 2nd Marquess of Dorset was also present along with various bishops and other members of the nobility. Ambassadors were also in attendance including Andrea Badoer, ambassador to Venice but notably the ambassadors of Ferdinand and Maximilian were not invited. This was certainly a shun on the part of Henry.[22] Mary is reported to have worn 'a petticoat of ash-coloured satin, and a gown of purple satin and cloth of gold in chequers; she wore a cap of cloth of gold, and chains and jewels like the Queen'.[23] The ceremony began with speeches made in Latin by the Archbishop of Canterbury and John de Selva. They were followed by the reading of the letters patent of Louis XII by Thomas Ruthall, Bishop of Durham.

Just as in the previous ceremony with the proxy of Charles, the proxy bridegroom (Duc de Longueville) took Mary's right hand in his and spoke, in French, the vows per verba de prœaesenti (by words of the present tense), on behalf of Louis XII. Mary then took his right hand in hers and did the same. After she had finished speaking 'the Duke of Longueville signed the schedule and delivered it for signature to the Princess Mary, who signed Marye; after which the Duke delivered the Princess a gold ring, which the Princess placed on the fourth finger of her right hand'.[24] Although the record held in *Letters and Papers, Foreign and Domestic in the Reign of Henry VIII* does not refer to it, the Venetian account also references that the Duc de Longueville kissed Mary.[25] After the ceremony, the party attended High Mass before enjoying a banquet. After feasting the dancing began, 'the musical instruments being a flute (piva), a harp, a "violetta" and a certain small fife (un certo xifarettó), which produced a very harmonious effect (si accordavano molto bene)'. Henry was apparently in such a celebratory mood he threw off his gown and danced in his doublet. The guests partook in the entertainments for over two hours, after which further refreshments were served before Mary, Katharine of Aragon and their ladies left the chamber.[26]

Unlike her proxy wedding to Charles where both parties were still minors, her proxy to Louis XII was to be consummated. The Duc de Longueville once again had to act as proxy for his master. Mary headed to a chamber to undress and lay in bed. Though the records are silent on Mary's extent of undress, she would have at least kept her shift on for propriety and integrity as she was in view of witnesses. The Duc de Longueville was escorted into the chamber, remaining in his doublet and red hose. He had left one leg bare from the mid-thigh and touched the bare part of his leg to Mary's. This act consummated the marriage of Mary and Louis.[27] Once the consummation was declared the celebrations could begin. The men would have left the chamber to allow Mary to rearrange her attire in the company of her ladies.

From this point on, Mary is referred to as the 'French Queen' in the accounts of Henry VIII, including when he paid her offering for Our Lady Day.[28] Louis XII soon wrote to his new wife, to which she responded, 'Received the letters written with his own hand and heard with great pleasure what the Duke of Longueville said on his behalf. Will love him as cordially as she can'. Mary signed off her letter 'de la main de votre humble compagne, MARIE' (from the hand of your humble companion, MARIE), confirming she had not used a scribe and had taken the time to write herself.[29] Mary was clearly showing that she respected the fact Louis had written in his own hand when it was common for members of the royal family to use scribes to write on their behalf. Louis also wrote to the magistrates of Paris on 24 August to advise them that they should begin making preparations for Mary's arrival, 'desiring with all our heart that she will be received, honored, and admitted the most honorably and grandly that it will be possible to do'.[30] In response the city of Paris commissioned Pierre Gringore to create a series of elaborate pageants to welcome their new queen.

With the formalities concluded, news began to spread about the occasion and celebrations. The Venetian ambassador, Andrea Badoer, reported that 'The Queen [Princess Mary] did not care for the French King's being an old man of -, and gouty'.[31] Henry was clearly pleased with the outcome and the resulting alliance with France. Although previously a prisoner, the Duc de Longueville had been treated according to his status and he was now treated even more honourably and rewarded extensively. Following the ceremony, Henry rewarded him with 2,000l (£1,325,529) and even gave him the gown he had worn himself for the ceremony.[32] Henry wrote to Louis on 23 August to confirm he was despatching his ambassadors: Charles Somerset, Earl of Worcester; Thomas Docwra, Prior of St John's; and Dr Nicholas West, Dean of Windsor.[33] Though the English ceremony had taken place the formalities were not over and Louis was to conduct his own proxy ceremony. Mary appointed Charles Somerset, Earl of Worcester to act on her behalf at the ceremony. This was the Tudor form of a modern Power of Attorney.[34] She too wrote to Louis on the same day as her brother to advise Louis that she had given Worcester a message 'touchant les fyansailles d'entre vous et moy en parolle de present' (hearing the wedding between you and me in word of the present). She went on to say that her 'greatest desire is to hear of his prosperity'. Mary signed off her letter once more with 'De la main de votre humble compagne Marie' (From the hand of your humble companion Marie).[35]

It was not only England and France that celebrated the union. News of the marriage arrived at the Venetian court on 25 August with the arrival of gentleman, Zuan Francesco de la Croce, who had previously been at the French court.[36] On 27 August 1514, the Venetians were to 'go to St. Mark's Church; a prelate "in pontificalibus" to sing high mass; and, as solemn thanksgiving, "Te Deun Laudamus" be chaunted. Also that the bells throughout the whole city be rung, and torches and lights displayed in the evening from the steeples. Also that letters and orders be sent to the army to make demonstration of gladness, and that the like be done in such other of the towns and places of the Signory'.[37] The Venetian nobility attended High Mass in their finery of velvets, damask and cloth of gold to give thanks and celebrate the peace and marriage between England and France. Bells were rung in various towns, fireworks lit up the sky and the Venetians were provided with wine, courtesy of the Senate.[38] For the people of Venice, the union meant peace. They had often referred to Henry as a friend but were consciously aware of Louis' continued ambition to invade Italy. Through Henry, this treaty gave the Venetians much more security that their domain would remain safe from invasion, at least for the near future. Leonardo Loredan, the Doge of Venice, wrote personally to Henry VIII on 28 August to congratulate him on the treaty with France and thank him for including Venice amongst his allies within the peace treaty.[39]

Others were not in a celebratory mood and did not receive the news with the same joy as others. Writing from Brussels, Sir Richard Wingfield advised Henry VIII that the dominions of Prince Charles were deeply unhappy with the union. He continues:

> The Archduchess alone will not believe it, but 'taketh great thought and displeasure therewith, insomuch that some fear she shall take hurt thereby'. She is going to send to England, the Esquire Bonnett, with whom she is advised to join the Provost of Cassell, to remonstrate. If the report prove true, think 'they shall send incontinently into France to desire the alliance of the second daughter of the French King, and put themselves entirely into his [hands]'.[40]

Prince Charles himself is reportedly to have reacted by going:

> ... immediately into his council chamber and said to his councillors, 'Well! am I to have my wife as you promised me?' with other words to that effect; whereupon his councillors answered him, 'You are young, but the King of France is the first King in Christendom, and, having no wife, it rests with him to take for his queen any woman he pleases'. And thus did they seek to excuse themselves. During this conversation, Duke Charles, looking out

> of a window, saw a man with a hawk on his fist, and calling one of his councillors who was his chief friend, said to him, 'I prithee go buy me that hawk.' The councillor replied 'I know that hawk; he is a young bird, and does not yet know how to quarry (non sa ancora paissar): he is not a bird for your Lordship.' The Prince again said, 'I prithee go buy it'. The councillor still seeking to excuse himself, the Duke at length exclaimed, 'Come with me'; so he bought it himself, and put it on his fist. Then, having returned into the council chamber and seated himself, he commenced plucking the hawk, the councillor meanwhile inquiring, 'Sir what are you doing?'; The Duke still continued plucking the bird, and when he had done so to his heart's content, made answer: 'Thou askest me why I plucked this hawk; he is young, you see, and has not yet been trained, and because he is young he is held in small account, and because he is young he squeaked not when I plucked him. Thus have you done by me: I am young, you have plucked me at your good pleasure; and because I was young I knew not how to complain; but bear in mind that for the future I shall pluck you.' He also used other very strong language.[41]

Clearly, those who had spent time delaying the marriage between Charles and Mary were now in disbelief that Henry VIII would make alternative arrangements regarding his sister. As a result, Mary was now Queen of France and all that awaited was for her to travel to her new home, and her coronation. It was arranged that Mary 'was to cross over to Boulogne, and the King of France would come as far as Abbeville, it was said, to meet her, and there consummate his marriage with this "*nymph from heaven*" her beauty and affability warranting the expression'.[42]

Chapter Five

The French Queen

Arrangements were now underway for Mary to travel to meet Louis XII. The *Sanuto Diaries* report that Henry was intending to travel to Calais with his sister and would also meet Louis there.[1] It was intended that Mary should begin her journey on 15 August, only two days after her proxy wedding. In early September she had not yet left and Marco Dandolo, Venetian ambassador to France, wrote to the Senate to report that Lous XII was expecting Mary to arrive in Paris on 29 September.[2]

In the meantime, Mary was busy adjusting to her new role as both queen and an ambassador between her birth country of England and France. Only a couple of days after her marriage, Mary was already being approached for her intermediary ability. The Duc de Longueville wrote to Mary on 16 August. Addressing his letter to 'the Queen, my Sovereign Lady' he requested her 'mediation in favor of a merchant named John Calvacanty, dwelling at London, who had done the writer some service in a matter of business with the King her brother'.[3] He also advised that he was happy to act as messenger between her and her new husband and counselled that Louis was eager to meet her in person and had suggested Abbeville as their meeting place. Thomas Bohier, who was with the Duc de Longueville at Canterbury, also wrote to his new queen confirming the same message but his letter states that rather than Abbeville being a mere suggestion, Louis would be at Abbeville to await her arrival.[4] By the end of August, Louis had travelled to 'Temps to see his daughters, and will afterwards come to Paris on his way into Picardy to meet his wife coming from England'.[5]

On 28 August Thomas Bohier wrote to Wolsey requesting that Wolsey write to Louis to communicate the expected date of Mary's arrival in Boulogne. Bohier expresses that Louis is eager to meet Mary in person stating 'he is marvellously anxious to see her'. He also advises that the Duc de Longueville would be writing to request details of Mary's suite.[6] On the same day Bohier also wrote to Mary that her husband 'desires news from her every day, but above all things to see her in France'.[7] Mary of course obliges and writes to Louis advising that Henry was making preparations for her departure which she believed would be soon.[8] Louis was evidently eager for the arrival of his bride; writing to Wolsey he thanked him for his service and requested him to ask Henry to send Mary to him as soon as possible.[9]

Meanwhile, Margaret of Austria was still shocked by the turn of events. According to the English ambassadors she 'declares the penance is too great for their offence towards England'. It appears Margaret understood that the alliance between England and France was as a result of the continuous delays and actions taken behind Henry's back.[10] Margaret was not the only person who was feeling anxious. Mary received a further letter from the Duc de Longueville, written 2 September, advising that Louis 'greatly regrets not having heard from her. Begs she will hasten her coming, which will give his Majesty the greatest pleasure in the world'.[11] The message was supported by another sent by Bohier stating that Louis was unhappy not to have heard from her.[12] On the same day Louis also wrote to Wolsey once more urging him to hasten Mary's departure from the English court.[13] Anger was the reaction reported in Flanders by Richard Sampson, whilst Sir Edward Poynings reported from Tournai that 'The marriage is unpopular, and he will find great danger in keeping Tournay, as it cannot be victualled without the good will of the surrounding people'.[14] Maximilian was also unhappy with the union stating that 'he was sorry "such a fair and virtuous princess should com[e to] an impotent, indisposed, and so malicious a prince as is the French King"'.[15]

Regardless of the anger felt by Charles' subjects, in early September both Henry and Louis were busy making preparations for Mary to leave for France. The embassy, consisting of Charles Somerset, Earl of Worcester, Thomas Docwra, Prior of St John's and Dr Nicholas West, Dean of Windsor arrived in Boulogne on 3 September 1514. Louis was not yet there but was on his way to meet the party. Travelling in the opposite direction, leaving France for England, was Charles Brandon, Duke of Suffolk. He met the ambassadors and offered one of them his horse as he was about to board a ship home. Brandon was rewarded handsomely for his service to Louis.[16] The following day, on 4 September, Sir Nicholas Vaux, Lieutenant of Guisnes and his wife, Anne, were amongst those appointed to accompany Mary to Abbeville. Vaux reported that he was to have '40 horses in his train, and all with scarlet cloth. There will be more than 2,000 in all'.[17] The sheer number of horses gives an indication just how sumptuous Mary's entry to France was to be.

The embassy travelled from Boulogne to Montreuil, arriving on 6 September. Here they were accommodated for one night and the French representatives gifted them 'a goodly present of partridges, quails, lapwings, snites, charcells, ducks, chickens, pigeons, muttons, lambs, pigs, veal, fish, and two hogsheads of wine'. More gifts were presented on their arrival at Abbeville the following day. Louis was now in Paris awaiting their arrival but had already sent the royal furriers to begin readying the royal lodgings at Abbeville in preparation for his and Mary's arrival. It appears at this point that Mary's retinue had not yet been finalised, or at least had not yet been communicated with the ambassadors who were keen to obtain the details in order to make preparations.[18]

Correspondence still flowed between Henry and Margaret of Austria regarding the union. Margaret had threatened to publish the promise made by Henry that Charles and Mary would marry. In response Henry replied via Sir Richard Wingfield that he also had written promises from her but they had failed to conclude the agreement. Henry also makes reference to publishing 'various promises made to him by Margaret in secret matters'. Lastly, Margaret expresses concern that Mary would not be received well in France and was worried about the treatment she would receive, indicating it may be similar to her reception when she was proposed as a bride for Charles VIII. It is not known if this was a last-ditch effort to convince Henry to marry Mary to Charles instead; regardless he responded that 'her solicitude is needless, as Henry has taken sufficient precautions in that matter'.[19] Unfortunately, we do not know any details of these precautions taken by Henry though it is likely he ensured her train was full of those he felt he could trust with the safety and happiness of his sister.

Whilst Henry was arranging Mary's retinue, she would have the exciting opportunity to make sure she had an exquisite wardrobe to take with her. She had to appear no longer as a princess, but as the queen of France. Lady Guildford was in Mary's service once more by this point and acted on her behalf to assist in getting her wardrobe ready. On 12 September a clerk, acting on behalf of Lady Guildford, accepted a payment made by Sir John Daunce to the amount of 23l 7s 4d (£15,486) for 'bonnets and other stuff bought for the French Queen'; a second payment of a similar nature, though lacking detail, was also received for 53l 4s 10d (£35,286).[20] Louis was only too happy to assist Mary in creating a new wardrobe, ensuring she was comfortable with the French fashion. Louis informed Wolsey that he had sent one of his gentlemen to meet Mary and with him sent 'certain accoutrements for her head after the French fashion'. Louis wished Wolsey to introduce the man to his wife and deliver the headwear. Wolsey made a further request on behalf of Louis – he wished Lord Berners to discuss with Henry the matter of Louis wishing to 'send a gentlewoman hither to dress her head from time to time after the French fashion'.[21] At this time Mary was staying at the home of the Archbishop of Canterbury in Croydon along with Henry VIII and Katharine of Aragon. The arrival of new headwear to try must have been an exciting time for Mary that she likely shared with her sister-in-law. Henry is known to have been an admirer of expensive clothing so it is easy to assume he also would have been party to the trying on of new things. Henry is also likely to have been pleased that Louis was asking his permission to send people to assist Mary rather than doing as he wished. Mary's presentation, including her wardrobe, was a matter of great importance to both kings.

Lord Berners would later be awarded 100l (£52,002) by Henry for 'attendance and advice in the "setting forward of the French Queen"'.[22] Just as Henry was grateful for the service of Lord Berners, Louis was thankful for Wolsey's assistance, writing to him in September that he 'Thanks him for the trouble taken by him in the apparel of the Queen, his wife, as the Seigneur de Marigny and Jehan de Paris [Jehan Perréal] have written. Is very anxious to see her, and will be glad to have these preparations abridged. Is contented he shall retain for a time Marigny and De Paris to assist in arranging her apparel à la mode de France. Begs Wolsey will convey in reply to the kind expressions of his said wife that the writer is quite as desirous of her presence as she can be of his'.[23] Louis is granting his permission for two of his men to remain in England in order to serve Mary to ensure her wardrobe befitted that of a queen and help her become accustomed to the French fashions.

Mary's trousseau, once complete, with the assistance of Jehan Perréal, consisted of a vast range of garments in the fashions of the English, Milanese and French. Her wardrobe consisted of gowns, petticoats, bonnets, mantles, sleeves, smocks, kerchiefs, and rails, amongst other items. Rails were worn whilst a lady's hair or toilet was being completed. From the inventory it appears Mary had a fondness for purple, black and shades of red – there are many gowns in crimson. Her gowns were made of a variety of materials including damask, velvet and satin and lined with taffeta, ermine and mink amongst other types of fur.[24] Henry paid for a total of '15 "gowns devised for the French Queen, of the French fashion," 6 "gowns after Milan fashion," 7 "gowns after the English fashion," 3 "jackets for her footmen," 3 "jackets for the second sort," 3 "jackets for the third sort," a gown, altar cloths, cushions, &c. for the closet, 7 "kirtles of the French fashion," and 6 "kirtles after the English fashion and Milan"'.[25] It was not only Mary who had to be dressed appropriately, so would those accompanying her. As well as paying for the apparel of her footmen and the liveries of her servants, Henry rewarded Sir Walter Devereux '25l., ... "for a gown of tinsel for Mistress Anne Devereux, sent over with the French Queen"'.[26]

Clothing was not the only necessity for a queen, she also needed jewels and once more Louis was only too happy to oblige. Amongst the gifts sent by Louis were pieces made with emeralds, rubies, diamonds and pearls. Mary had an ornament for her headpieces which bore twenty diamonds and apparently also had the initial 'M' on a pendant with pearl drops.[27] Unfortunately, this pendant which sounds very similar to that well known piece of jewellery worn by Anne

Boleyn, is lost to us, though perhaps Mary was the influence behind Anne's famous pendant. Henry also provided jewels for Mary including bracelets, coronets, rings and imitation flowers, including roses and fleur-de-lis, set in gold with sparkling gems.[28] A goldsmith named Amadas was paid the large sum of 1021 14s 4d (£68,077) to make items for Mary. Unfortunately, we have no specifics of the items made by Amadas; he may have been responsible for the majority of the items referred to previously, but as queen of France Mary would have been expected to look resplendent and therefore required the jewels to do so.[29]

More practically, Mary required new seals, two of which were paid for by Henry. One was her Great Seal, made in silver, engraved with the arms of both England and France and the other her Privy Seal, which was made of gold and bore a crown and four roses.[30] He also gifted parcels of plate, furniture (including beds), litters and chapel furnishings for her to take with her.[31] The chapel furnishings included altar cloths, hangings and images of silver-gilt of Edward the Confessor, St Thomas of Canterbury, St George and the Dragon, St Margaret, St Catherine and Mary Magdalen.[32] Henry also made a gift of tapestries 'of cloth of gold and of silk of very large dimensions, more beautiful than any ever seen, with the arms of France and England united' which Mary took with her and were seen upon her entry to Abbeville.[33] Whilst all the preparations were ongoing, numerous nobles attended court to take their leave of their princess and bid her farewell and celebrations and jousts were held in Mary's honour.[34] Henry was not about to limit the festivities concerning his sister.

On 14 September, Mass was heard at the Church of the Celestines in Paris. Following the service, Louis gave his oath to the treaty in the presence of witnesses including Francis d'Angoulême; Louis of Bourbon; Louis d'Orleans, the Duc de Longueville; John Stuart, Duke of Albany; Louis of Graville, Admiral of France; George d'Amboise, Archbishop of Rouen; and many others of the nobility and church. As well as making his oath to the peace treaty, Louis also performed his own proxy ceremony. Just as Mary had done, Louis spoke his vows and Charles Somerset, Earl of Worcester acted in place of Mary. The events were recorded and notarised and copies issued to Henry. The following day Louis, in the presence of the Bishop of Paris, bound himself to the amount of one million crowns payable to Henry VIII with the penalty of excommunication for default. Excommunication from the Church was an incredibly serious matter, the threat of which would not be taken lightly, indicating how serious Louis was about the treaty and the union with Mary.[35]

In France, whilst awaiting Mary's arrival, great preparations had been made to receive their new queen and celebrate the union. The Venetian ambassador, Marco Dandolo, reported that Francis d'Angoulême had already spent 60,000 crowns on arranging entertainments.[36] Louis had given permission for Francis and nine other men to arrange and participate in a tournament. Francis issued the challenge on the same day Louis observed the proxy ceremony, the events to take place once Mary had arrived. The tournament was proclaimed 'as noble knights ought to meet, to encourage mutual affection, and also to avoid laziness, the mother and nurse of vice'.[37] Whilst they awaited Mary's arrival the men celebrated the proxy ceremony.

Mary left court for Dover on 19 September. Amongst those appointed to accompany Mary on her journey to Abbeville were Thomas Howard, 2nd Duke of Norfolk and his wife, Agnes Tilney; Thomas Grey, 2nd Marquess of Dorset and his wife, Margaret Wotton; Thomas Ruthall, Bishop of Durham; Thomas Howard, Earl of Surrey; Sir Edmund Howard; Charles Somerset, Earl of Worcester; Lord Edward Grey; Thomas Docwra, Prior of St John's; Nicholas West, Dean of Westminster; and Sir Nicholas Vaux and his wife.[38] The ambassador to Margaret of Austria reported that many had declined to attend upon and accompany Mary as they were unhappy with the alliance with their common enemy of France.[39]

Henry gave explicit orders to his councillors regarding Mary's journey to France. As well as confirming to Louis that Henry wishes to strengthen the alliance between them the councillors 'shall also say that he now sends his sister furnished with all things appertaining to so great a princess and they are ready to present her when the French King appoints a time for the solemnisation of the marriage: foreseeing always that they nowise deliver the Princess till the matrimony is celebrated. They take with them a minute approved by the King and Council of the French King's letters patent of the dower or donation propter nuptias, which they shall cause to be engrossed at the French Court; and they shall endeavour to get two copies signed and sealed with the French King's hand and great seal, so as to bring one with them at their return and leave the other with the French Queen'.[40] Henry had already selected some of the retinue to remain with Mary. Henry Courtenay, 2nd Earl of Devon was amongst those selected to remain in Mary's service being paid 50 marks for six months 'to give his daily attendance upon the French Queen [in] the parts of France'.[41]

Although the accounts of the nobility who accompanied Mary to Abbeville are fairly consistent, the records of the numbers appointed to remain with Mary are inconsistent between sources. As well as the large retinue of the nobility to accompany her, Mary also had her household initially recorded to consist of two ladies-in-waiting; five gentlemen-in-waiting; three chamberers; twelve gentlemen; three chaplains; fifteen yeomen; twenty grooms; nine footmen; five pages; and thirty-six servants including Elizabeth Saxby and Elizabeth Langton, the latter as her wardrobe maid.[42] Elizabeth Langton was responsible for ensuring Mary's clothing was stored safely and for selecting gowns, sleeves and bonnets for her mistress. She would also have liaised with the launderess and tailors for cleaning, alterations and mending. The role of Elizabeth Saxby is not explicitly known, but she was awarded an annuity in September 1514 of 20l (£10,400) for services to Mary and previously to her mother, Elizabeth of York.[43] The records of grants for September also include annuities for: Elizabeth Catesby, 40 marks; Mary Redyng, 50l; Elizabeth Chamber, 20l; and Dorothy Verney, 20 marks. Each of these women were granted a sum for services to Mary and in some cases previous service to her mother. Some payments were a one-off whilst others, such as Elizabeth Chamber, received an annuity for life.

Of course, her reliable childhood governess 'Mother Guildford' was included in her retinue. Lady Guildford had been called out of retirement to prepare Mary and then accompany her as her lady of honour, and in July of 1515 'Old Lady Guylforde' was paid her annuity of 10l (£6,627), a sign of gratitude from Henry for her service to his sister.[44] A later account in October 1514 records that as well as Lady Guildford and Mistress Anne Devereux, there were seven other ladies appointed to accompany and remain with Mary: Lady Elizabeth Grey; Elizabeth Ferrers; M. Boleyn; M. Wotton; Alice Denys; and Anne Jerningham. It is believed M. Boleyn refers to Mary as at that point Anne is thought to have been at Mechelen in the household of Margaret of Austria. M. Wotton is probably Margaret Wotton, wife of Thomas Grey, 2nd Marquess of Dorset. Also travelling but with the intention of only remaining for the wedding was Anne Howard, Countess of Oxford (sister of Thomas Howard, Earl of Surrey and daughter of Thomas Howard, 2nd Duke of Norfolk), as well as either Elizabeth Stafford, the second wife of Surrey, or Agnes Tilney, Duchess of Norfolk.[45]

Mary also had a designated treasurer, Sir Edward Bensted; her almoner, Dr James Denton; her master of horse, Richard Blount; her chamberlain Lord Berners; as well as several chaplains. In addition to those allocated to her by Henry, Mary also took her tutor, John Palsgrave with her. Palsgrave was appointed in the capacity of her secretary but it is probable Mary also received some comfort from his presence as he had been her French tutor since 1512 and therefore she could rely on his language skills in her new country.

The councillors accompanying Mary were ordered to find out who in Mary's service would be permitted to remain in France with her and who wished to remain. They were also ordered to return following the marriage and not to travel further than Abbeville, instead returning to England rather than attending the coronation.[46] One person who was not able to remain a part of Mary's household was Jane Popincourt, Mary's childhood friend. On hearing that Mary wished to bring Jane with her, the Earl of Worcester reported to Wolsey that Louis had responded 'he wished she were brente [burned], for Worcester and his fellows had shown him enough of her evil life; "that there should never man nor woman be about his wife, but such as should be at her contentation"; and that he had only spoken for Jane at the suit of Lord Longevile, as he told Worcester and his fellows before; "for he told him that the Queen loved and trusted her above all the gentlewomen about her; but if the King made her to be brent," he should think it a good deed'.[47] Henry also paid for his own trumpeters to accompany Mary, paying eight men 16d each for a period of twenty days.[48]

A record of the procession by Venetian merchant, Lorenzo Pasqualigo, provides the best account of the size of the retinue as well as the sight observers would have the chance to view. He writes on 23 September that Mary 'left for Dover tour [*sic*] days ago, accompanied by four of the chief lords of England, namely, the Treasurer, the Lord Chamberlain, the Chancellor, and Lord Stanley, besides 400 knights and barons, and 200 gentlemen and other squires, with their horses. The lords, knights, and barons were all accompanied by their wives, attended by their damsels (damizelle). There would be about 1,000 palfreys, and 100 women's carriages (carette de clones)'. Carriages were not in existence at this time so it can be assumed he refers to litters. He continues, 'There are so many gowns of wove gold and with gold grounds, housings for the horses and palfreys of the same materials, and chains and jewels, that they are worth a vast amount of treasure; and some of the noblemen in this company, to do themselves honour, had spent as much as 200,000 crowns each. Many of the merchants purposed going to Dover to see this fine sight, and about a week ago all the merchants of every nation went to the Court. The Queen (of France) desired to see them all, and gave her hand to each of them'.[49] This mention of Mary greeting the merchants gives a clear insight into Mary's appreciation of people of all ranks. Mary did not have to greet the merchants but she made a point of greeting them personally; no doubt some of those merchants were responsible for the beautiful trousseau she was taking with her. Not only did Mary greet the merchants but she spoke to them in French, much to their delight.

When describing Mary herself, Pasqualigo states:

> She wore a gown in the French fashion, of wove gold (oro tirado), very costly; she is very beautiful, and has not her match in all England, is a young woman 10 years old, tall, fair, and of a light complexion, with a colour, and most affable and graceful; on her neck was a jewelled diamond, as large and as broad as a full sized finger (un diamante in zoielo grando e grosso un bendedo), with a pear-shaped pearl beneath it, the size of a pigeon's egg, which jewel had been sent her as a present by the King of France, through; and the jewellers of 'the Row,' whom the King desired to value it, estimated its worth at 60,000 crowns. It was marvellous

> that the existence of this diamond and pearl should never have been known; it was believed they had belonged to the late King of France, or to the Duke of Britanny, the father of the late Queen.[50]

The jewel described is likely the 'Mirror of Naples', a jewel that would become the focus of arguments at a later point. The writer clearly has Mary's age incorrect; she was most certainly not 10 years old but aside from the error in age, this is a valuable description of Mary at the time of her departure from court.

As Mary had been travelling towards Dover, William Blount, 4th Baron Mountjoy was returning to England, bringing with him the tournament challenge issued by Francis. The challenge was proclaimed at Canterbury, but Henry was unhappy with the short notice, the opening date being delayed until 13 November to give the Englishmen time to prepare and travel.[51] Initially it was reported that Henry would travel as far as Calais with Mary. This was later changed to Henry accompanying Mary for ten miles out to sea aboard his new ship *Henry Grace à Dieu*.[52] The weather, after causing delays of a few days to Mary's departure, put a stop to Henry's plans, and he decided to remain on firm ground. Mary bid farewell to her pregnant sister-in-law, Katharine of Aragon, at Dover Castle before making the short trip to the shores where she took her leave of her brother – Henry holding her hand and kissing her goodbye. It is at this point that Mary obtained a promise from Henry that he 'wolde never provoke or move me but as myn ounn hert and mynde shulde be best pleased'.[53] This promise was Mary's hope for the future and something she would later rely on.

It was reported nine ships were made ready to make the journey, though the accounts specifically name twelve along with their captains: '*The Great Elizabeth*, Sir Weston Brown; *Great Bark*, Sir William Pyrton; *Great Galley*, William Gonson; *Less Bark*, Sir Stephen Bull; *Swallow*, Sir John Wallope; *Sweepstake*, Sir Henry Sherborn; *Rose Galley*, William Sabyn; *Catteryn Gally*, William Cocke; *Myhell Younge*, William Fyscher; *Pettyr of Lye*, Adrian Doncken; *John Hopton's galleon*, John Hopton; and *Lysard*, Christopher Coo'. The total cost for preparing these ships to transport Mary was an astonishing 10051 9s 9½d (£522,878).[54] *Henry Grace à Dieu* was also prepared but as Henry changed his mind it does not appear this ship actually sailed. In January 1515, an unnamed man was paid 66s 8d (£2,209) to act as the pilot to take Mary across the English Channel to France.[55] With the preparations all complete, and Mary arriving at Dover, it would have been an anxious time for Louis awaiting the arrival of his bride as she now had to cross the unpredictable Channel. With the weather appearing to abate, Mary set sail at 4:00 a.m. on 2 October 1514.

Chapter Six

'She is a Paradise'

Mary finally arrived on the shores of France at around 10:00 a.m. on 3 October. Storms had scattered the ships and only four ships arrived together at Boulogne. *The Great Elizabeth* succumbed to the sea, being wrecked off the coast of Calais where only 100 of the 500 on board survived.[1] Efforts were later made to recover what could be salvaged and Christopher Coo, captain of the *Lysard*, transported the survivors back to England. It must have been terrifying and upsetting for Mary to lose sight of so many ships and later find so many had lost their lives in the attempt to transport her to France. According to Hall the ships came under jeopardy when entering the haven of Boulogne. Boats were despatched to transport those on board to the shore and 'at the landyng Sir Christopher Garnyshe stode in the water and toke her in his armes, and so caryed her to land, where the Duke of Vandosme and a Cardynall with many estates receyued her'.[2]

A letter from an unnamed individual notes the 'Arrival in France on the 3rd at Boulogne of the Queen, the sister of the King of England (a most beautiful young woman), with 80 damsels and English lords. The King was at a distance of 18 miles, with 200 French damsels [having gone] to meet the Queen'.[3] The Earl of Worcester was with Louis on the day Mary and arrived and wrote to Wolsey to state:

> I assure you he hath a marvellous mind to content and please the Queen; and since he heard of her landing, which was this morning, there is nothing can displease him, and is devising new collars and goodly gear for her. There was in his chamber but my lord of Paris, Robertet, and the General, and I; where he showed me the goodliest and the richest sight of jewels that ever I saw. I would never have believed it if I had not seen it; for I assure you all that ever I have seen is not to compare to 56 great pieces that I saw of diamonds and rubies, and 7 of the greatest pearls that I have seen, besides a great number of other goodly diamonds, rubies, balais, and great pearls; and the worst of the second sort of stones be prizes and cost 2,000 ducats. There is 10 or 12 of

> the principal stones that there hath been refused, for one of them, 100,000 ducats. And when he had showed me all, he said that all should be for his wife. And another coffer also was there, that was full of goodly girdles, collars, chains, bracelets, beads of gold, and other divers goodly jewels; but, merrily laughing, he said, 'my wife shall not have all at once, but at divers times;' for he would have many and at divers times kisses and thanks for them. I assure you he thinketh every hour a day, till he seeth her; he is never well, but when he heareth speak of her. I make no doubt but she shall have a good life with him, with the grace of God.[4]

Though Louis was clearly ecstatic at the arrival of his new bride, others were still angry about the union. Peter Martyr, a gentleman of the Spanish court wrote 'King Louis is at Abbeville waiting for his new bride, who will be his death. What an old valetudinarian, suffering from leprosy (elephantia gravatus), can want with a handsome girl of 18 his correspondent may infer, and what the French think of it'.[5] Louis certainly did not have leprosy, with Henry's fear of illness there is absolutely no way he would allow his sister to marry a man with any known infections. The message is clearly one of vitriol intended to provide amusement to a Spanish favouring audience but the remark that Mary would be the death of Louis would later become much more prominent amongst the gossips of Europe.

Although Mary was now on French soil, the lost ships had caused transport issues. There was not enough horse to transport the retinue. Jacques Leest, Abbot of Saint-Vulmer in Boulogne recorded that the town and abbey lent Mary their own mounts. A procession of monks from the abbey and the church of Notre Dame attended Mary, proffering relics for her to kiss. Mary and her retinue were then led to the town, halting at the entrance bridge for the first of what would become a series of pageants and entertainments as Mary made her way to Abbeville. As Mary approached the bridge a ship decorated with fleur-de-lis and roses was lowered and a young lady and two children greeted her; the young lady representing the Virgin Mary and the other two, angels. The three had rehearsed verse composed by Leurens Framery. The young lady quoted lines from the Song of Solomon then asked who is 'the beautiful and triumphant maid/full of honour, beauty, and sense'. One of the angels responded:

> This is the flowering rose of beauty,
> The sovereign and illustrious princess,
> Your goddaughter named Mary,

By whom war and discord have taken cease
As of peace you were the goddess,
Daughter and spouse of the celestial king,
Likewise this flower of nobility
Is the root of peace and of joy
And the dear spouse of the most Christian king.[6]

With the second angel confirming the words of the first, the young lady presented a gift to Mary – a silver swan with a heart of gold. The verse centres Mary in her role as the peacemaker, her marriage forging peace between England (the rose) and France (the fleur-de-lis). This reference as peacemaker would be one of the central themes of the coming celebrations. Mary and those who had travelled on her ship remained here for a few days to rest and await the arrival of the scattered ships carrying the rest of her retinue along with her belongings.

Two days later, on 5 October, Mary reached Montreuil-sur-Mer where she would be greeted by five pageants in her honour, all of which were recorded in an illuminated manuscript. The nobility of France escorted Mary to the city amidst the sounds of crowds cheering, artillery firing, and trumpets blasting. She was greeted by the ecclesiastical and secular men of the town before hearing a speech delivered by the lawyer Guillame de l'Espinoy. Once more, Mary as peacemaker was central to the theme and would continue to be so. The first two pageants were based on mythology whilst the final three took on a biblical theme. The first sees Mary depicted as Perseus slaying a monster which represented war. In the second Mary is presented as Diana and offered a crown by Apollo (representing Louis), once more depicting Mary in her peacemaking role by giving her fealty to Louis in marriage. The Virgin Mary and the Annunciation were the focus of the third pageant, believed to have portrayed the union of Louis and Mary whilst in the fourth, Mary is portrayed as the Queen of Sheba and Louis as Solomon, their marriage once more bringing peace to their dominions. Lastly, the final pageant was the portrayal of Esther, and inferred Mary would play a prominent role in keeping the peace between England and France through her influence on both kings.[7]

The following day Mary met the mayor and received gifts on behalf of the town including a tableau featuring Saint Anne, Saint Margaret and the Virgin Mary. Mary was given the opportunity to enjoy the company of some of the French ladies that day, allowing her time to get to know some of the prominent ladies who would be present at the royal court.

Mary finally reached the outskirts of Abbeville on 8 October, having left Montreuil-sur-Mer the previous day. On hearing of her approach, Louis had despatched Francis d'Angoulême, and others to meet her. Louis himself later rode out, under the guise of a hawking trip where he happened to come across Mary. Louis 'rode a very beautiful Spanish horse, caparisoned with cloth of gold and black satin, in chequers; he himself being clad in a short riding dress of cloth of gold on crimson. He found a great multitude of horsemen and others who had come to witness this interview between the parties, and went up very boldly to the Queen as if they had been on intimate terms, and having first kissed his own hand to her, he then threw his arm round her neck, and kissed her as kindly as if he had been five and twenty'.[8] Mary attempted to dismount to show her respect but Louis would not allow her to do this, instead Mary chose to 'blow' Louis a kiss, an action he did not quite understand but was delighted by her beauty. Having spoken briefly with Mary, Louis departed back to Abbeville via a secret avenue to avoid stealing Mary's spotlight as she entered the town.

According to the Venetian records there was a downpour of rain just before the procession entered Abbeville, soaking the company. The party was met in the suburbs of Abbeville by the mayor, captain of the castle and numerous men including archers, the castle guard and elected officials. The clergy then came to meet Mary, offering a white canopy for her to travel under. They entered the town in the afternoon. Mary was preceded by fifty of her squires 'dressed in silk of several sorts, with gold collars worth from 50 to 60 ducats', the primary noble, the Duke of Norfolk came next followed by pairs of nobles, ambassadors and the aristocracy 'all clad either in cloth of gold or silk of various qualities, in riding gear, and all wearing enormous gold collars, some doubled and some trebled, round their necks, whilst some wore them prisoner fashion; so that never was such pomp witnessed; and the greater part of them had velvet bonnets, some of one colour and some of another'.[9] Just ahead of Mary came 'her two heralds with the coats of arms, in the fashion and with the devices of England; farther on marched eight trumpeters clad in crimson damask; then came the macers with gilt maces surmounted by a royal crown; near them were two grooms dressed in short doublets of cloth of gold with velvet caps, who followed, each leading a palfrey; and there were two other palfreys caparisoned with cloth of gold, ridden by two pages dressed in like manner in cloth of gold with velvet caps'.[10]

Finally came Mary, who according to Hall appeared in 'cloth of silver, her horse was trapped in goldsmythes work very rychly. After her followed xxxvi ladies, al ther palfreys trapped with crymsyn veluet, embraudered after them folowed one charyott of clothe of tyssue, the seconde clothe of golde and the third Crymsyn veluet embrawdered with the kyngs armes and hers, full of roses'.[11] Mary's litter is reported to have had bannerettes 'with the arms of Henry VII, Queen Elizabeth and Edward IV and his consort; an azure canopy of state, wrought with a figure of our Lord, sitting in a rainbow, attended by the four evangelists'. Mary's motto *La volonté de dieu me suffit* was embroidered in cloth of gold on the valence.[12]

The Venetian account goes into more detail stating:

> ... the Switzers entered first with their banner; then the French gentlemen; then the English gentlemen, and the French princes with the English princes and barons, together with the ambassadors from the Pope, the Venetians, and the Florentines. Then followed the Queen, under a white canopy, above and around which were the roses, supported by two porcupines. She was alone beneath it, and Monseigneur [d'Angoulême] on her left hand, but outside. She rode a white palfrey, with rich trappings, and was herself clad in very handsome stiff brocade. Next came her litter, very beautiful, adorned with lilies; then five of the principal English ladies, very well dressed; then a carriage of brocade, on which were four ladies, followed by a second carriage with as many more ladies. Next came six ladies on horseback; and then a third carriage of purple and crimson velvet, with four ladies; after which a crowd of ladies, some twenty in number; then 150 archers in three liveries. In this order they went to the Queen's house, which was near that of the King. It was a sumptuous entry, and these noblemen of England have very large chains, and are otherwise in good array.[13]

Mary carried a white sceptre, the trappings of Mary's palfrey were cloth of gold on white and her own gown was 'cloth of gold on crimson with close English sleeves; her head-tire consisted of certain gold ornaments in their fashion, with two large pearls on the left side. On her head she wore a shaggy hat of crimson silk, cocked over her left eye.[14]

Fortunately there remains descriptions of Mary, 'She is generally considered handsome and well favoured, were not her eyes and eyebrows too light; for the rest it appears to me that nature optime suplevit: she is slight, rather than defective from corpulence, and conducts herself with so much grace, and has such good manners, that for her age of 18 years – and she does not look more – she is a paradise'.[15]

Although Mary had entered the city riding her white palfrey, at the church of Notre Dame de la Chapelle she entered her litter to continue her procession. The residents had come to welcome their new queen and did not disappoint in their welcome. As at Montreuil-sur-Mer, artillery was fired and bells were rung to announce Mary's arrival. Proceeding to the first gate, decorated with two angels holding shields bearing the arms of the two kingdoms, Mary was met by the king's physician. He gave an oration, addressing Mary and stating the 'lilies of France were hers to gather'.[16] Several pageants awaited Mary as she progressed through the town, the most impressive being an entire ship that was built for the sole purpose of the pageant. Elsewhere in the town Mary witnessed a seven-headed serpent spouting wine and another fountain of wine coming from a construction of a lily surrounded by roses. Children also participated and in one pageant dressed as soldiers carrying fleur-de-lis banners and driving porcupines (the symbol of Louis), ahead of a young girl representing Mary. The efforts by the townspeople must have been a delight to Mary; the symbolism of Mary as the rose of England and her role as peacemaker was once more prevalent throughout. It was reported that Mary 'delighted in listening to music, singing, and dancing'.[17] As a princess who enjoyed dancing with her brother, it is easy to understand the enjoyment she would have received through witnessing such spectacles.

The same day, on 8 October, Louis issued letters patent declaring his 'agreement to give as a large dower to his beloved consort Marie, as was held by Ann late Queen of France, he endows her by these presents with the town and castlery of Chinon, the county of Saintonge and town of Rochelle (with great fee, &c., of Saintonge, St. Jean d'Angely and Rochefort), the county of Pezenas (Pedenacii), the lordships of Montigny, Cessenon and Cabrieres, the little seal of Montpellier, the money of St. Andrew and rent of Villeneuve lès Avignon, the rent of the Seneschalcy of Beaucaire, the impositio foranea of Languedoc and the profits of salt of Pezenas, Montpellier, Frontignan and Narbonne to the value of 10,400 livres Tournois; and also, instead of St. Menehould and Moret (which used to be dower of queens of France but are otherwise disposed of by the King's predecessors), Loudun and Roquemaure'.[18] This was a very generous dower which would provide Mary with regular income and wealth. As Louis was busy approving letters patent, Mary ended her procession at the church of St Wulfran where she was met by the dean and chapter. After paying her respects at the high altar, Mary was conducted to the Hôtel de la Gruuthuse where Louis was waiting for her. She was formally presented by the Duke of Norfolk who gave a lengthy speech on behalf of Henry before a small banquet was held in Mary's honour. The English nobles were entertained separately by Francis d'Angoulême but when they returned Mary was present in the hall being entertained by a ball. After hours of dancing and singing, Mary departed for her own lodgings, accessed along a temporary gallery that had been raised across the gardens from Louis' accommodations.[19]

If those in attendance had been impressed by the efforts, ceremony and pomp leading up to the wedding, they would certainly be surprised by what the wedding day held. At around 7:30 a.m. on 9 October 1514, Mary left her own lodgings to process through the gardens towards the king's chambers, once more on her white palfrey. The retinue was preceded by heralds and musicians. Mary was accompanied by the Duke of Norfolk, the Marquess of Dorset and other lords and nobles 'all in pairs well arrayed, some in cloth of gold and some in velvet, damasks, and satins, though the greater part of them were clad in cloth of gold, some of one sort and some of another, the greater part of their gowns being lined with most beautiful sables, and some with other very fine furs, which they did not wear on their entry. They had all most massive gold chains, so that some, I think, must have found it burdensome to carry them; some wore them single round the neck, but very large, some doubled and trebled, and some doubled six times, whilst others had them a hand's breadth and very long, so that never was such magnificence beheld'.[20] On entering Louis' chambers, Mary was preceded by thirteen pairs of knights, macers and two heralds. Mary then entered, the English nobility accompanying her, now with their caps in their hands to show reverence. Mary wore a gown of white cloth of silver in the English fashion, lined with ermine, her loose hair was partly covered by a jewel covered coronet, as according to French custom she could not wear a crown until after her coronation but it was reported that 'she wore jewels of very great price'.[21] Louis also wore white cloth of gold lined with martins, so the couple would complement one another and dazzle observers. He also wore the collar of St Michael, the French equivalent of the Order of the Garter.[22]

Mary and her retinue entered the hall around 9:00 a.m. The hall was hung with cloth of gold, and mosaics and stained-glass windows depicted the deeds of St Wulfran. The chamber was already attended by the French nobility, Mary curtseyed to Louis who doffed his cap in response to her, kissed her and presented her with a necklace featuring two jewels. The pair then both sat on chairs near the altar to hear Mass with a canopy held over them by the Count of Guise and the dukes of Angoulême, Alençon, and Vendôme.[23] Mass was performed by René de Prie, Cardinal of Bayeaux, Louis kissing the *pax* then kissing Mary. Following Mass, the Cardinal offered the consecrated wafer; one half to Louis and one half to Mary who kissed the wafer before swallowing it.[24] With the marriage solemnised Mary curtseyed once more and the royal couple departed, each to their own lodgings to rest before the celebrations later that day. Louis' daughters, Claude and Renee, both attended Mary in her chambers until the court reunited for celebrations. It may have been difficult for the princesses as their mother had only died on 9 January 1514 and Claude had been asked to give an offering to Mary following the ceremony to allow Mary to make an offering at the altar. It was also Claude that was destined to be queen if Mary did not produce a son, making this perhaps a tense situation.

Maybe even more so considering the fact that Mary was closer in age to her stepdaughters than she was to her husband.

At 1:00 p.m. the feasting began, Mary and her entourage once more processing to the chambers of Louis. This time Mary appeared to dress in the French fashion, delighting observers. One Venetian reported 'I promise you that she is very handsome, and of sufficiently tall stature. She appears to me rather pale, though this I believe proceeds from the tossing of the sea and from her fright. She does not seem a whit more than 16 years old, and looks very well in the French costume. She is extremely courteous and well mannered, and has come in very sumptuous array'.[25] This compliment certainly would have pleased Henry, that the trousseau he had provided had been a success; his sister was the star of the French court, just as she had been of his. Louis was also delighted with his queen's wardrobe and thanked Jehan Perréal for 'devysing new collars and goodlie gear'.[26] After feasting, the court partook in dancing. During the banquet Mary was served her drinks by an 'Englishman clad in gold brocade, who knelt the whole time, as did the one who tasted for her, bareheaded'.[27] For Mary, the festivities lasted until 4:00 p.m. when it was time for her to retire to Louis' bedchamber for consummation. Mary was escorted by her stepdaughter Claude. Though it is not recorded, it is likely the remainder of the court continued with the celebrations.

The marriage and the celebrations were well attended by both French and English nobility. Of the French nobility were:

> The Duke of Valois and Bretagne, the Duke of Alençon, the son of the King Don Frederic of Naples, the Earl of Vendôme, the Duke of Longueville, the Prince de la Roche Suryon, the Duke of Albany, the Earl of St. Poll, the Earl of Guise, brother to the Duke of Lorraine, Louis Monsieur, brother to the Earl of Nevers, the Earl of Roussy, the Lord of Lautrec, the Earl of Sancerre, the Lord de Lespar, the Earl Manfroy, the Lord de la Palice, Grand Maistre de France, the Earl Galiace de Saint Severin, Grand Esquire, the Earl of Alexandrie, the Earl of Maleverer, Grand Seneschal of Normandy, le Sr. de Graville, Admiral, le Sr. de Monmorancy, Premier Baron Chamb., le Sr. de Testeville, le Sr. de la Tremoille, le Prince de Talmon, son fils, le Sr. de Piennes, Lieutenant de Picardie, le Sr. de Bouchaige Chambrelan, le Sr. de Dourriers, le Sr. de Chesnes, le Sr. Daubigny, le Vidame D'Amiens, le Sr. de Boysy, Monsieur de Bonyvet, le Vidame de Chartres, Monsieur de Fou, Monsieur de Cursoll, Monsieur de Wansay, Monsieur Louis D'Ars, le Sr. du Pont de Remy, les trois Generaux de France, viz., Normandie, Languedoie, Languedoc, Monsieur de

> Beaudiner, Mons. de Gynry, Mons. de Rouville, Grand Veneur, Mons. Denebatt, Cappne des Toilles, Monsieur de Boucheron.[28]

The English also had a large number of attendees. In addition to those already named were:

> the Lord Lawarre, the Lord Berners, chamberlain to the French Queen, and the Lord Montaigle and my Lady his wife; the Lord Richard Grey, the Lord John Grey, the Lord Leonard Grey, brethren to my Lord Marquis; Sir Nicholas Vaux, Sir David Owen, Sir Andrew Windsor, Sir John Husee, Sir John Peche and Sir Henry Wyot, bannerets; Sir Morice Berkeley, Sir Wm. Sandes, Sir John Hungerford, Sir Robert Drury, Sir Tho. Botrym, Sir Philipp Calthorp, Sir Thomas Clynton, Sir Robert Cotton, Sir John Heydon, Sir John Carre, Sir Edward Greville, Sir Will. Essex, Sir Philip-Tylney, Sir Nicholas Applyard, Sir Edward Bensted, Sir Will. Rows, and Sir John Wallop, knights; John Broughton, Rich. Weston, Giles Strangways, Tho. Cheyney, Ralph Chamberlain, Rich. Blont, Gerard Danet, and Robert Jonys, esquires; Garter Principal King of Arms, and his four servants; Thomas Pawlet, _ Manners, George Cobham, and Anthony Saintliger; Richmond Herald; John Myclow with 50 officers of the King's household servants that were officers with the French Queen; Hen. Webb, gentleman usher; Tho. Rushe and Ambrose [Bradman], serjeant at arms.[29]

The day after the marriage ceremony, Louis appeared jovial reporting that 'thrice last night did he cross the river, and would have done more, had he chosen'.[30] For Mary, it was not such a jovial day as the majority of her attendants were dismissed by Louis. Louis had two main reasons for dismissing the staff: (a) he did not want anyone he didn't know to influence his new wife and; (b) he was accustomed to a very simple life and the large retinue was being paid for by Louis himself, a cost he did not wish to burden. Many of the English lords departed the day after the wedding, Louis having made them a gift of 30,000 francs each, whilst her trumpeters were gifted 150 crowns. Louis appointed Monsieur de Concresault as Lord Steward to Mary's household. Although Louis had initially agreed to Mary's retinue, it was amended and those who were approved to remain with Mary from the English retinue consisted of: Francis Buddies, bailiff of the chamber; Richard Blount, squire; Robert West, master of horse, Dr Denton, Mary's almoner; Master Guille, physician; three pages; master of the pantry; cupbearer; usher; carver; and Henry Calays, groom of the robes. In addition Louis approved four maids of honour and two chambermaids.[31] The fours maids of honour are thought to have been Margaret Wotton, Elizabeth Grey, Elizabeth Ferrys and M. Boleyn. Again we do not know if this refers to Mary or Anne Boleyn but as Eric Ives argues, it is hard to believe that both sisters were present at that time as they would have been named. I am therefore of the opinion this refers to Mary Boleyn and Anne joined the household at a later date after travelling from the court of Margaret of Austria.[32] There is a payment made in October 1516 to 'a servant of the French Queen who "went over with her and tarried there still", 40s' (£1,325) but unfortunately there is no further information as to who this refers to.[33]

Louis replaced Lady Guildford with Madame d'Aumont. The lady was responsible for remaining in Mary's company, just as Lady Guildford had done. She would sleep in Mary's chamber unless Louis was visiting or Mary was summoned to spend the night in Louis' chambers. Louis also placed the most prominent ladies at the French court in Mary's company. Amongst them were his daughter, Claude; Marguerite d'Angoulême, sister of Francis and her mother, Louise of Savoy; and Mary of Luxembourg.[34]

Of those dismissed, Mary was greatly upset about the dismissal of Lady Joan Guildford. Lady Guildford had of course been a part of Mary's life since she was a child and had honoured Mary by agreeing to leave retirement to enter her service in this new part of her life. Louis had complained about the influence of Lady Guildford since the arrival of the wedding party. He was unhappy that she was always present in Mary's company, that other ladies could not attend her, and that he himself could not visit without her presence. Lady Guildford clearly cared for Mary but it is hard to believe she would remain near her mistress if Mary asked her to leave; this would be disobeying an order, an act that goes against all protocol and etiquette. She had looked after Mary for many years and Mary likely felt safe in her company, trusted her advice and it is likely she asked her faithful lady in waiting to remain at her side regardless of who came to visit. It should be remembered that although she was now queen of France, Mary was still a young 18-year-old now residing in a foreign country and uncertain whom she could trust other than those she had brought with her. Even then there were factions in the English court with the Duke of Norfolk on one side and Charles Brandon and Wolsey on the other. Therefore, Mary may have felt Lady Guildford was her only constant companion at that time who really did have her best interests at heart.

Mary did the only thing she thought may help, she wrote to her brother on 12 October voicing her concerns and worry:

> My good Brother as hertly as I can I recomaund me unto youre Grace, mervelynge moch that I never herd from you syns …

> re depertynge, so often as I have sent and written to you. And now am I left post a lone in effect; for on the morn next after … e maryage my chambirlayn with all other men servants wer discharged and in lyke wyse my mother Guldeford with other my women and maydyns, except such as never had experience nor knowlech how to advertise or gyfe me counsel yn any tyme of need, which is to be fered more schortly then your Grace thought at the tyme of my depertynge, as my mother Guldeford can more playnly schew your Grace then I cann wryt; to whom I beseche you to gyve credens. And yf hit may be by eny meane possible, I humbly requyr you to cause my seyd mother Guldeford to repayr hither once agayn. For ells yf any chauns happe other then weale I schall not knowe wher nor of whom to aske any good counsell to your pleasur, nor yet to myn own proffit. I merveill moche that my Lord of Northfolke wold at all tymes so lyghtly graunt every thynge at ther reqwests here. I am weale assured that when ze know the trouth of every thyng as my mother Guldeford can schew you, ze wold full lyttyll have thowght I schold have ben thus intreated: that wold God my Lord of Zorke (Wolsey) had com with me yn the rome of Northfolke: for then I am sure I schuld have bene left moch more at my herti…. Then I am now. And thus I byd your Grace fare weale with …….. as ever had Prince; and more hertis ease then I have now.[35]

Mary ends the letter by asking Henry to give greetings to Lady Guildford and signs 'Be your lowyng syster MARY QUENE OF FRANCE'.[36] The interesting part of this letter is that Mary, for the first time, gives an indication of which factor of Henry's court she favours. Rather than blaming her husband for the dismissal of her household and in particular, Lady Guildford, Mary chose to firmly plant the blame on Thomas Howard, Duke of Norfolk, and confirming she wished Henry had chosen Wolsey to accompany her rather than Norfolk, thereby stating she favours the Wolsey/Brandon faction. It would have been very unwise to blame Louis but that is not to say she didn't, she just did not commit that in writing. What the message was she asked Lady Guildford to convey is unfortunately not recorded but she has clearly given a verbal message to be passed to Henry and requests he gives credence to this message.

Henry was not the only one Mary sought assistance from. Mary also wrote to her 'lovynge frend Th'archebischop of Zorke' (Wolsey) on the same day, pleading for his help:

> But for eny thynge I myght do, yn no wyse myght I have any graunt for her abode here, which I assure you my lord is moch to my discomffort; besyd meny other discomffortis that ze wold full lytyll have thought. I have not zet seen yn Fraunce eny lady or jentill woman so necessary for me as sche ys nor zet so mete to do the kynge my brother service as sche ys. And for my part my lord, as ze love the kynge my broder and me, fynd the meanes that sche may yn all hast com hither agayn, for I had as lefe lose the wynnynge I schall have yn France as to lose her counsell when I schall lacke it, which is not like long to be required, as I am sure the nobill men and jentillmen can schew you more then becometh me to wryte yn this matter.[37]

At this point Norfolk and his son had already left the French court along with those dismissed. Mary was making a plea to have Lady Guildford returned to her. Wolsey did attempt to restore the faithful lady to her mistress. He wrote to the Earl of Worcester who had remained at the court, hoping that since Norfolk had now left, it may be possible to change Louis' mind. Worcester had no success and responded that Louis had stated that he and Mary were 'both of age to rule themselves, and not to have servants that should look to rule him or her. If his wife need of counsel, or to be ruled, he is able to do it; but he was sure it was never the queen's mind nor desire to have her again; for as soon as she came to land, and also when he was married, she began to take upon her, not only to rule the queen, but also that she should not come to him, but she should be with her; nor that no lady nor lord should speak with her but she should hear it'. Worcester also reports that he had spoken to Mary about the dismissal and states 'the French queen told me that she loved my Lady Guildford well, but she is content that she come not, for she is in that case that she may well be without her'.[38]

Wolsey didn't stop there, he wrote to Louis himself, being very careful not to inform Louis that it was Mary who had complained. Wolsey feigned surprise at hearing the news and attempts to garner sympathy with Louis, stating that Mary 'is a young lady, and that when she should be abroad, not understanding the language perfectly, and having no acquaintance with any of the ladies there, to whom she might disclose such feelings as women are given to, and that she had no one of her acquaintance to whom she could familiarly tell and disclose her mind; that she might find herself desolate, as it were, and might entertain regret and displeasure; which peradventure, might cause her to have some sickness, and her bodily health to be impaired, which God forbid and should such accident happen, I believe, Sire, that you would be most grieved'. Having tried to use Mary's health as a reason to reinstate Lady Guildford he goes on to say 'Mistress Guildford is at Boulogne, on her return here, and that she was entirely discharged; doubting lest the king, my master, should he know it, might think it somewhat strange, I have ventured to write to the said lady, to tarry awhile at the said town of Boulogne, until I had written you my poor and simple opinion on this subject, which, Sire, I now do. And by your leave, Sire, it seems to me that you should retain her for some time in the service of the queen, your wife, and not discharge her so suddenly; seeing and considering that the king, your said good brother, has taken her from a solitary place, which she had never intended to quit, to place her in the service of the queen, his said good sister'.[39] Despite the attempts by Wolsey and Worcester, Louis would not be swayed.

In November 1514, Mary requested the treasurer, Nicolas de Carisay, pay 600 crowns of soleil gold to a goldsmith named William Verner usually residing in London but who at that time was in France. The payment was for the purchase of jewelled ornaments intended as gifts 'to some ladies and damsels of the said country of England, nearly related to us, whom we do not wish to be named or otherwise mentioned here'.[40] The ornaments are described as 'a polished ruby and an emerald, enchased in a golden cross, weighing ten ounces and a half, worth two hundred crowns soleil; a fine diamond and two sapphires, enchased in a golden collar, weighing two marks, three ounces, and three quarters, worth 300 crowns soleil; and for another table-diamond, chased in a pendent *agnus Dei* of gold, weighing six ounces and half a quarter, worth 100 crowns soleil'.[41] As she did not wish to name the recipients it is possible the gifts were for her English attendants recently dismissed by Louis XII. Mary may not have wished the treasury to inform her husband of the generous gift, lest it anger him that she had rewarded them so. In November, Henry awarded Lady Guildford with an annual pension of 20l in an effort to reduce the impact of the dismissal but there was little else he could do, though seven months later he awarded her an annuity of 40l.[42]

Mary also made additional efforts to secure a replacement opportunity for her secretary John Palsgrave who had also been dismissed. On 13 November Mary sought assistance once more from Wolsey in an attempt to secure a position for him in Paris so that 'he may continu at scole yff he hadde ben retaynyd in my service I wold have done for hym gladly my sellff but sins he was put owt off my service I wyllyd hym to cum to paris party by cause I trust veryly that you wyll provyde for hym he may be abyll to continu and allso bycause I intend my sellff som what to do for hym howe behytt by cause my estat ys not yett made I wott nott howmyche I shall be gladde to helpe hym that he schall not need to cumm home praying you hertely not to forget hym'.[43] Whilst we do not know if Wolsey managed to secure him an income we do know that Palsgrave did remain in Paris so Mary's influence on this occasion may have been a success.

On the same day that Louis dismissed her servants, he also gifted Mary a 'rubie two unches and a half longe, and as bigge as a mannes fynger, hangyng by two chaynes of gold at every end', possibly with the intention on softening the blow. The following day came with another gift, this time 'a great Diamont a tablet, with a great rounde Pearle hangyng by it', and as the days continued so did the gifts, 'every day he gaf her also Rynges with stones of greate estimation'.[44] The councillors of both Henry and Louis were tasked with completing an inventory of Mary's possession including furniture, tapestries and jewels. The inventory notes that Mary's bed had a blue counterpane, embroidered with roses, continuing the symbol of England and Mary's position as an English princess. Her tapestries, gifted by Henry, and other items of furniture are also recorded.[45] Henry could rest assured his sister had arrived safely with the expensive trousseau he had provided for her. For Louis, the inventory was to ensure the agreed trousseau and expense's related to Mary equalled 200,000 crowns. Louis issued letters patent on 13 October confirming his satisfaction that Henry had 'transmitted our beloved consort to Abbeville, adorned with costly equipments and jewels, &c., most honourably, sumptuously, and splendidly, we acquit the said king and his heirs of the 200,000 crowns which should have been paid in the year 1514, considering the aforesaid jewels as full recompense'.[46] With Mary and Louis now married and her household amended, her coronation now awaited.

Chapter Seven

Crowning a Tudor Rose

A bout of gout delayed the departure of the royal couple who were intending to leave Abbeville for Paris within days of their marriage. Ambassadors reported to Henry on 13 October that 'The Quene is continually with hym, of whom he maketh asmuch, as she reporteth to us herself, as it is possible for any man to make of a Lady'.[1] Whilst Louis rested, Mary took to her role as queen. Through her education and reading of works such as Christine de Pizan, she would have been well aware she was expected to act as an intermediary and assist her people where she could. Mary had already taken efforts to support those dismissed from her service, now she would begin to work on assisting the French.

Mary wrote to her brother on 18 October requesting that a Frenchman, François Descars be released upon receipt of a small ransom. Mary had been petitioned by Louis, Duke de Longueville, and Francis to use her influence with Henry to secure the release of the man who had been taken hostage by Lord Darcy when fighting the Scots. Mary was hoping Henry would pay the ransom and be reimbursed once Descars was released. Two days later, Mary wrote once more, again petitioning Henry for the release of Descars. This time she also admonished her brother, 'since my departing from you, I have sent you divers letters, and as yet I have had no manner of word from your grace, whereof in part I marvel, considering that certain letters be come from your grace hither. I trust, though I be far from you, that your grace will not forget me'. Mary reiterates that she hopes Henry will intervene in the matter of the prisoner, 'I beseech you that his ransom might be as favourable, and driven to as small a small as might be'. To further influence Henry's decision Mary informs him that Francis and the Duc de Longueville had successfully petitioned Louis to release the English prisoners held at Boulogne. She also mentions that '200 marks, or 250 marks, I hear say they would be content to give'. The alternative was for the 'poor gentleman' to remain in prison.[2] By including an amount which Mary states she overheard, she is indicating to Henry the sum the French would be willing to repay, though whether it was information overheard or Mary was encouraged to include that in her correspondence is unknown. Unfortunately, we do not know the outcome of Mary's petitions on this matter.

Louis and Mary eventually departed Abbeville to travel to Beauvais around 24 October. Here they were joined by Thomas Grey, Marquess of Dorset and Charles Brandon who were on their way to Paris to take part in the celebratory jousts to be held in honour of Mary. Brandon was granted an audience with Louis on 26 October and reported:

> … I was brought straight into his chamber, where he lay in his bed, and the queen sitting by his bedside; and so I did my reverence, and kneeled down by his bedside; and so he embraced me in his arms, and held me a good while, and said that I was heartily welcome; and asked me 'how does mine especial good brother, whom I am so much bound to love above all the world?' and, Sire, I showed his grace that your grace recommended you to him, as unto your most entirely beloved brother; and further I showed him that you commanded me to give unto him thanks on your part, for the great honour and love that he had showed unto the queen, your sister. And upon that, his grace said that there should [be nothing] that he will spare, to do your grace's pleasure, or service, with as hearty manner as ever I saw a man; and, Sire, I said unto him that your grace would do unto him in like case, and he said, 'I doubt it not; for I know well the nobleness, and trust as much in your master, that I reckon that I have of him the greatest jewel that ever one prince had of another;' and so I rose up, and made my reverence unto the queen, and made your grace's recommendations unto her, and the queen's also. And, Sire, I assure your grace that there was never queen nor lady that ordered herself more honourably nor wiser, the which I assure your grace rejoiced me not a little; your grace knows why: for I think that there was never queen in France that hath demeaned herself more honourably, nor wiselier; and so says all the noblemen in France that have seen her demeanour, the which letted not speak it; and as for the king, [there was] never man that set his mind more upon [woman] than he does on her, because she demeans herself so winning unto him, the which I am sure, [will be] no little comfort unto your grace.[3]

Brandon was obviously keen to report back to Henry how well Mary was conducting herself in her new role as queen and how his favourite sister was being treated, but it is interesting that he makes a comment that 'rejoiced me not a little; your grace knows why'. It has been suggested that this implies there was already a bond between Brandon and Mary that Henry was well aware of, though whether at this point it was a romantic bond can only be speculated upon.

Henry, in response to the positive reports he had received, wrote to Louis expressing his happiness of how Mary was conducting herself and went on to say 'our will, pleasure, and intention is, that in acting, she should persevere from good to better, if she wish and desire to have our love and fraternal benevolence; and thus we gave her advice and counsel, before her departure from us, and we make no doubt that you will, day by day, find her more and more all that she ought to be to you'.[4] Whilst this may seem to be a threat that Mary would anger Henry if she upset Louis, it should be noted that whilst this was a patriarchal society, and Mary was well aware of the expectations placed on her as a princess and sister to a king, Henry is likely paying lip-service, using the art of chivalry to flatter Louis.

The court took a more leisurely journey from Beauvais to St Denis on the outskirts of Paris, travelling through the towns of Picardy, arriving on 30 October.[5] Mary once more showed her compassion by exercising her prerogative of releasing prisoners in each town. Mary was welcomed by the clergy and residents of St Denis and remained there, as French custom dictated that she could not enter Paris itself until after her coronation. Louis continued on to Paris as he had matters requiring his attention, one of those matters being another audience with Brandon who arrived in Paris on 2 November. Henry had sent Brandon not only to joust, but also to discuss a secret diplomatic matter. Louis was too busy with the preparation of the coronation and celebrations and declined to enter any further negotiations at that point.

On Sunday, 5 November 1514, Mary Tudor was crowned Queen of France. The coronation took place at the abbey of St Denis. Ambassadors and those of the aristocracy who were not part of the procession, flocked to their places whilst the public sought a good viewpoint. Louis chose to attend from a private viewing point so he could watch the ceremony without being seen whilst the English ambassadors were escorted into the abbey early to ensure they reached their prominent seats. Around 10:00 a.m., trumpets signalled the arrival of Mary, preceded by the French nobility. Francis d'Angoulême had the honourable role of escorting Mary by the hand towards the altar. Mary knelt upon a cushion where she remained for several minutes. The Cardinal of Brie anointed Mary before placing the crown sceptre in her right hand. The rod of justice was placed in her left hand, he placed a ring on her finger, and finally the crown matrimonial of France was placed upon her head. With the necessary trappings, Mary was led to chair of estate underneath a canopy, next to the altar. Francis stood behind Mary and gently lifted the crown slightly from her head. He held it there for the remainder of the service to alleviate the weight upon her head. When Mary was seated, Mass was sung before Mary once again approached the altar and presented her offering. Lastly, she received the sacrament before departing from the abbey to her lodgings. Louis joined her whilst the English ambassadors dined with the French nobility. The following day would prove to be the most extravagant event Mary had witnessed since her arrival in France – her entry into Paris as Queen of France.

It appears there was, at one point, a concern regarding Mary's entry to Paris. The Duke of Norfolk wrote to Wolsey advising that he had received a response from Francis regarding a possible delay, to which Francis had protested he was unable to 'command nor alter or defer any time of doing of the said enterprise from the time appointed of her entry into Paris, albeit that the herald had anything done to the contrary and old custom of the realm of France, which concerned the preparations made for the meeting by a great number of answerers and noble persons'. He goes on to say that he 'Thinks this great triumph in her honor should not be delayed by England, and the yit rawnes of the preparation of ours'.[6]

It was determined Mary's entry should follow the precedent set by the previous queen, Anne of Brittany. The officials and representatives of Paris travelled to the Chapelle St Denis to await Mary who had left St Denis at 9:00 a.m. to dine at the chapel. Princess Claude, Louise of Savoy and her daughter Marguerite d'Angoulême were amongst the nobility who came to pay their reverence to Mary. They were followed by a small deputation of the provost, sheriffs and select representatives who went to her lodgings to welcome their new queen. Mary sat in state, in the company of French ladies, to receive the party. Mary relied on the Bishop of Paris to assist her in thanking the men and she promised them she would act on their behalf if she could do anything for the city of Paris. On their departure, the next delegation entered – this time it was men of parliament, led by Anthony du Prat, their president. The Bishop once again helped Mary as she replied through him to the delegations offer of welcome and compliments. Each man filed past Mary and she was presented with gifts of welcome by each group.

After the delegations had left it was time for Mary to make her entry into Paris through the Porte St Denis. With the crowds waiting for a glimpse of their beautiful, young, new queen, Mary was preceded into Paris by a huge entourage. The Swiss guard led the procession, along with the heralds-at-arms, including those of England and France as well as those of the nobility, all wearing their appropriate livery. The French nobility came next with their pages, then the maître d'hôtel of Louis. Mary's palfrey in its beautiful trappings and a royal courser came next, being led into the city. Finally, came Mary, seated in her litter with Francis d'Angoulême riding at her side and followed by Charles Brandon, Thomas Grey, and the dukes of Longueville, Vendôme, and Bourbon. Mary wore a robe of cloth of gold covered in gems, a jewelled carcanet, rings and her crown. Lastly, the ladies of the French court rode behind with Mary's carriages coming last.[7] It really must have been an extraordinary event to witness.

At the city walls, Mary was approached by a delegation of burgesses who gifted a canopy made of cloth of gold, and embroidered with roses and fleur-de-lis, to be held over the queen. At the entrance Mary was met with the first of the pageants arranged by Pierre Gringore – a scaffold covered with a tapestry depicting a vessel which had four winds blowing upon it. The city of Paris was at the helm, Ceres and Bacchus on the deck, Honour at the mast, whilst sailors standing on the scaffold bid their welcome:

> Noble lady – welcome to France!
> Through thee we now shall live in joy and pleasure,
> Frenchmen and Englishmen live at their pleasance;
> Praises to god, who send us such a treasure![8]

Mary was then met by the sheriffs, merchants and select citizens who brought another canopy to be added to the previous one.

As the procession continued, the second pageant was waiting for Mary's arrival. At the Fontaine du Ponceau, three ladies 'named the graces' in costume tended to a rose tree and a fleur-de-lis whilst a beautiful fountain watered them. The graces were named 'Gratia preveniens' (Prosperity), 'Gratia gratis data' (Mirth), and 'Gratia gratum faciens' (Beauty). The graces were meant to symbolise that Mary possessed all of these virtues. An orator then spoke about the union of the red rose and the French lily, a theme that would continue throughout the entertainments. The third pageant took place near Trinity convent and was organised by the Brothers of the Passion. On a scaffold stood two figures, representing a king and queen. The queen presented the king with a white shield with a red cross, symbolising the Queen of Sheba visiting Solomon after hearing of his wisdom. The pageant intended to indicate that Mary had come to visit Louis after learning of his wisdom and with her had brought peace. Continuing to Painters Gate, the fourth pageant featured minstrels playing and a figure representing God. In his right hand he held a heart surrounded by the Order of St Michael, in the left a rose and lily intertwined. Directly under God stood a king and a queen and below them five ladies. Two represented England and France, sitting either side of the scaffold whilst Amity, Confederation, and Peace stood between them.

The fifth appears to have been incredibly elaborate. It was sponsored by a guild and took place at the church of the Holy Innocents. A two-tier scaffold had been erected and at the top was a gold 'throne of honour' with a lily in the 'orchard of France'. The four virtues – truth, pity, mercy and strength – stood around the throne. The lower scaffold had been decorated to look like a wall, featuring towers and a gate with a rosebush in the centre. The rose was identified as 'the rose of Jericho'. A rosebud grew from the bush upwards towards the upper tier, whilst the lily trailed downwards to meet it. Together they then rose to the throne, the rosebud opening to reveal a young maiden who spoke in French:

> Scented flower of honeyed favour,
> Branch of peace where all grace flows,
> Vermilion rose in Jericho planted,
> Humble Mary, of whom everything is so clear and fluent,
> You are welcome in this country
> To which through you good peace has come.
> Divine thanks to your increased faith
> If only to see you France takes delight,
> As if God had fed you
> In his orchard made a pigmented flower
> To decorate the noble fleur-de-lis.[9]

Also on the lower tier were four figures: 'the Great Pastor' representing the Pope; 'the sole wish of the Princes'; 'Peace'; and 'Discord'. Each figure had a motto which referenced the rose and the lily and symbolised the peace the union brought to the two realms. Lastly, the towers of the pageant had a motto again referring to peace.

The sixth was held at the Châtelet of Paris. A blue covered scaffold represented the sky. Members of the nobility and the clergy participated; a figure representing Truth ascended towards the sky, whilst another representing Justice and carrying a sword descended to meet Truth under a crown. On a lower level twelve members of the nobility and clergy stood as still as statues on individual platforms, lower still were 'Phœbus, Diana, Minerva, Stella Maris and Bonaccord. Stella Maris (star of the sea) signifies the Queen. As the moon derives light from the sun, Phœbus was intended for the King and Diana for France'.[10] This pageant symbolised Mary bringing accord to France.

Finally, the last pageant took place at the gates of the Palais Royal. The angel Gabriel was saluting the Virgin Mary, a lily growing in between them. Lower down the arms of Louis and Mary featured prominently. Below the arms were the king and queen, Justice and Truth stood either side whilst on the bottom tier figures representing shepherds and shepherdesses sung in praise of Mary. Each pageant was accompanied by orators, mottos and banners praising the marriage and reinforcing the hope of peace. Gringore recorded his work in a beautifully illuminated manuscript to gift to Mary to commemorate the events.[11]

The pageants over, it was not yet time for Mary to rest. Instead she visited the church of St Genevieve des Ardans where she met with the clergy and a group of scholars from the University of Paris. Before she returned to the Palais Royal, she visited the church of Notre Dame where she made her devotions. *Te Deums* were chanted and the archbishop welcomed Mary to France saying 'Dearest Lady, most welcome are you into this realm.'[2] By the time Mary had enjoyed all seven of Gringore's pageants, visited the churches and met with the scholars it was 6:00 p.m. when she arrived for the banquet at the Palais Royal.[13]

The chamber selected for the banquet held the effigies of the French kings. The walls were hung with tapestries and the sideboards full of gold and silver plate. As minstrels entertained the guests, Mary sat at a marble table in the company of Princess Claude, Louise of Savoy, and Marguerite, surrounded by the nobility of France and of course, Louis, for a magnificent feast that 'no living man had ever seen so sumptuous a supper at the entry of a queen'.[14] It was reported that some of the dishes served to end the feast were extraordinary to see: a phoenix that was consumed by fire, St George, the arms of France held by a porcupine (Louis' emblem), and a joust between a hare and a cockerel.[15] Mary, being very fond of music, rewarded the minstrels with a gift of plate, and a silver and gilt ship, believed to have been valued at 200 crowns.[16] After an extremely long day, Mary finally retired to her chambers but the celebrations were not over; the next day would see Mary riding in state through Paris.

Louis, wishing to ensure his new wife remained in the spotlight, travelled ahead to the Hôtel des Tournelles, a favourite residence of the king, though sadly no longer existing. Mary attended Mass at the chapel of the Palais Royal in the morning and spent time being shown all the relics belonging to the chapel. On reaching her husband they remained there for a few days, Mary likely being grateful for the short rest after all the travelling and entertainments. Whilst Mary was settling in, Louis was busy with his duties as king, one of which was awarding Brandon a pension of 1000 crowns.[17] A few days later, on Saturday, 11 November, a delegation of provosts and merchants attended Mary at the Hôtel des Tournelles to present her with a gift on behalf of the city of Paris. The gift was silver gilt plate, valued at over 6,000 francs – an exceptional offering. The men also requested a favour from their new queen – the honour of her attending a banquet they wished to host in her honour. Mary, of course, graciously accepted the gift and the invite, advising she would speak

Mary Tudor, Queen of France, Duchess of Suffolk

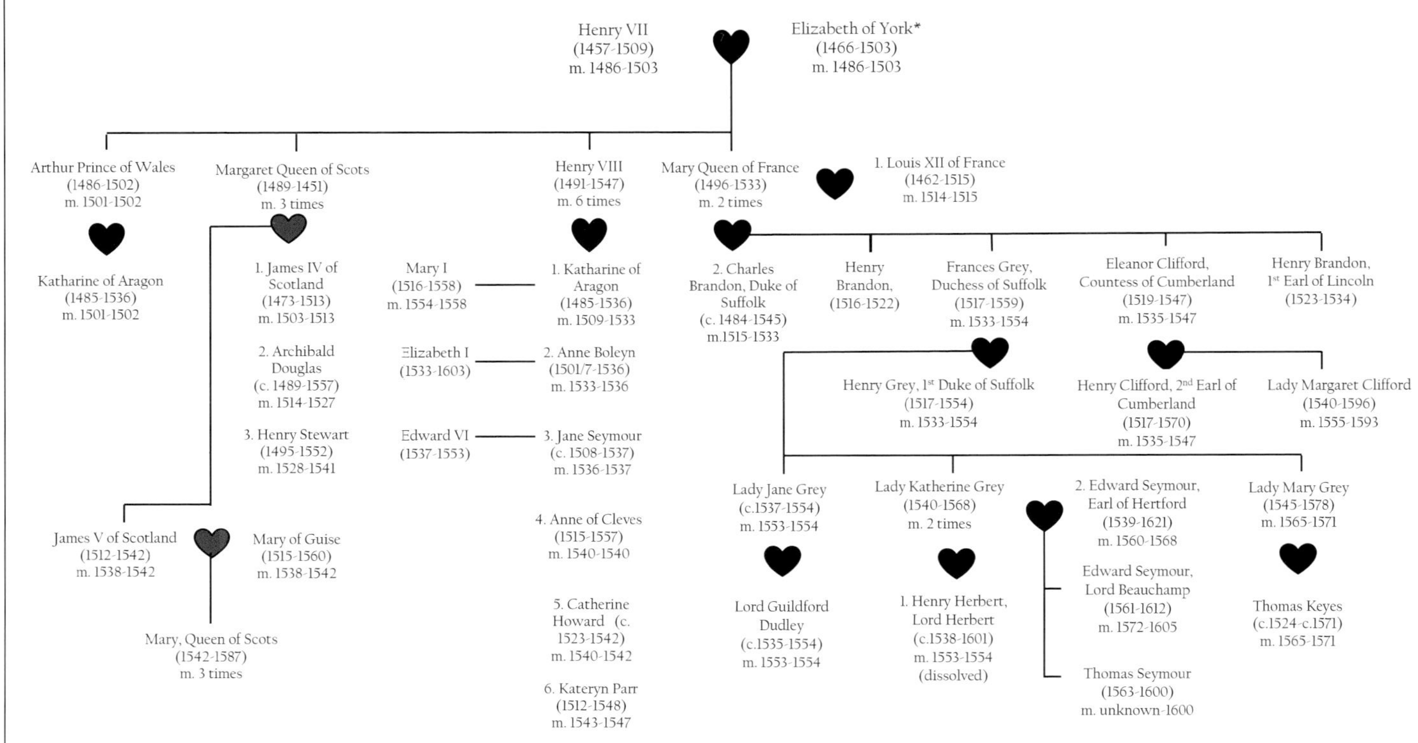

Note:

*Elizabeth of York gave birth to seven children, only those who survived infancy have been included here

m = married

Not all marriages/children are represented

1. Mary Tudor Family Tree.

2. Statue of Henry VII, Pembroke Castle.

3. Lady Margaret Beaufort.

4. Pembroke Castle, birthplace of Henry VII.

5. Henry VII and Elizabeth of York.

Above left: **6.** Arthur, Prince of Wales. Stained Glass window at St Laurence's Church, Ludlow.

Above right: **7.** Margaret Tudor.

Right: **8.** Portrait of Henry VIII.

9. Queen Katharine of Aragon.

10. Charles V, Holy Roman Emperor.

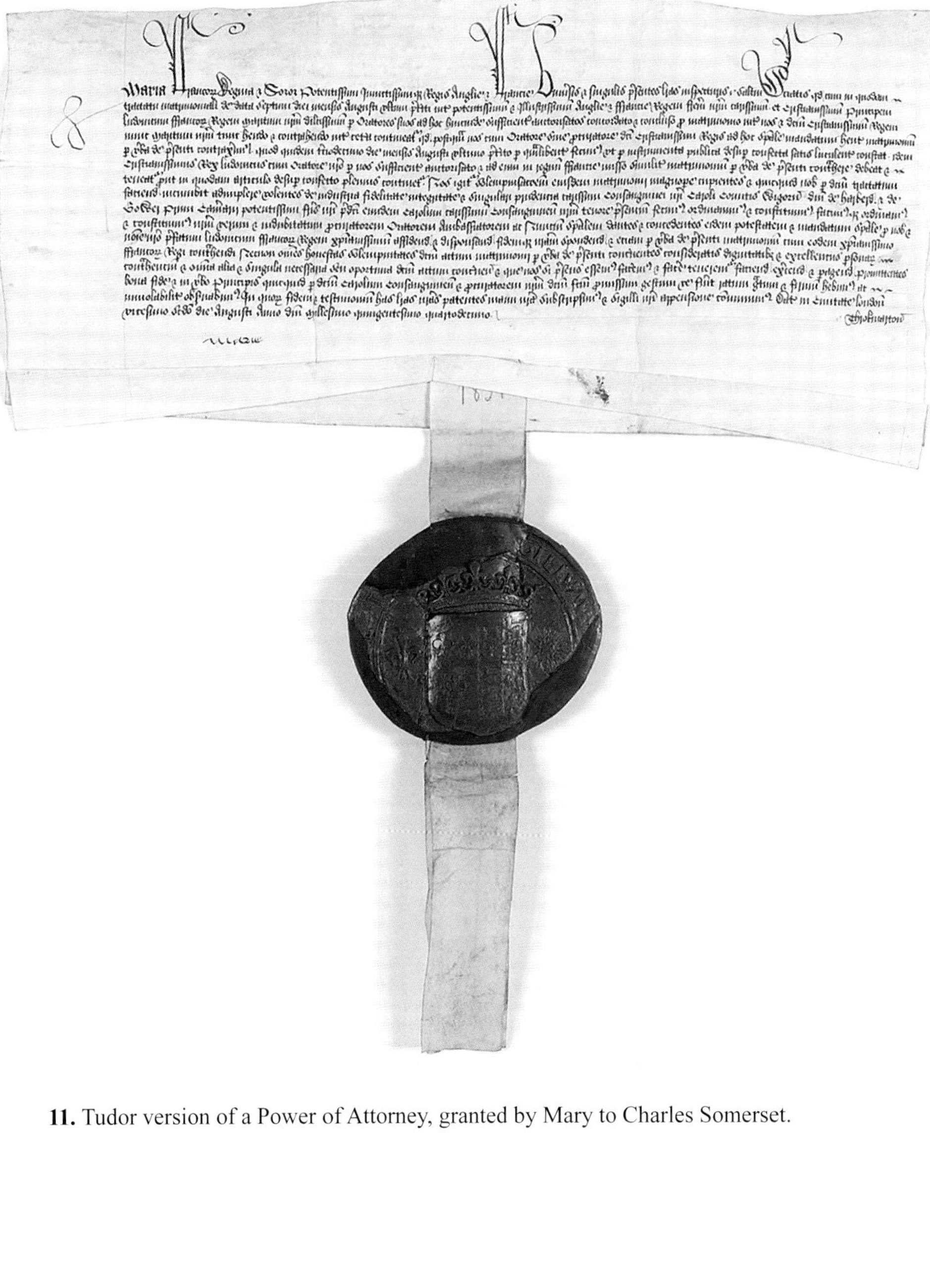

11. Tudor version of a Power of Attorney, granted by Mary to Charles Somerset.

Above: **12.** Anne of Brittany and Mary Tudor.

Left: **13.** Portrait of Mary Tudor.

14. Medallion with portrait of Louis XII of France.

15. Charles Brandon, Duke of Suffolk.

Left: **16.** Cardinal Thomas Wolsey.

Below: **17.** Mary Tudor and Charles Brandon.

Right: **18.** Westhorpe. The hall Mary knew as her home was demolished in the late 1760s.

Below: **19.** St Margaret's Parish Church, Westhorpe. Mary and Charles would have worshipped here.

20. An image believed to be either Katharine of Aragon or Mary Tudor.

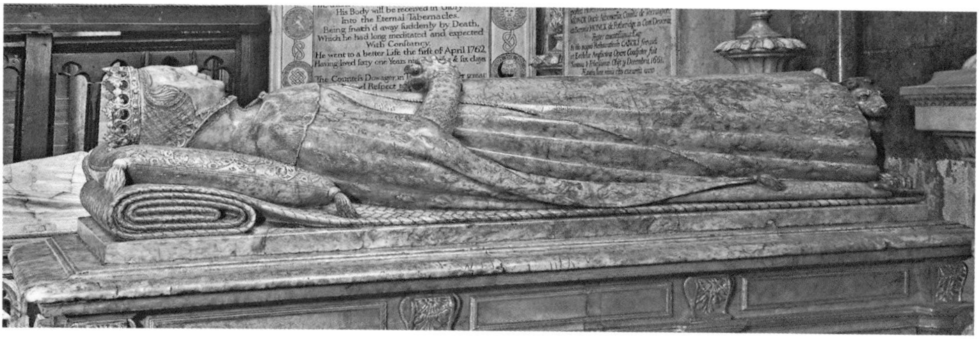

21. Tomb of Frances Brandon, Duchess of Suffolk.

Above: **22.** Lady Jane Grey.

Right: **23.** Plaque within the Barrow Chapel of St Margaret's, Westhorpe.

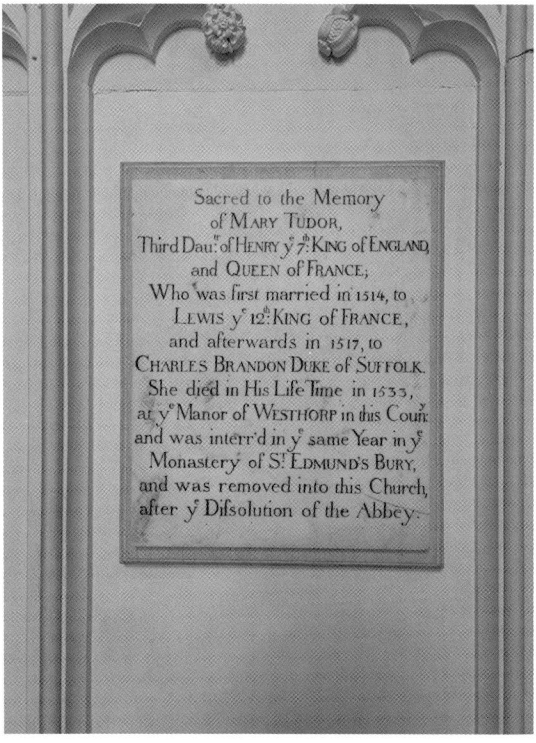

Above: **24.** Mary Tudor's tomb, St Mary's Church, Bury St Edmunds.

Left: **25.** Plaque near Mary's tomb, St Mary's Church, Bury St Edmunds. Note the error in the date of Mary's marriage to Charles Brandon, they were married in 1515.

26. Mary Tudor window, St Mary's Church, Bury St Edmunds.
The window tells Mary's story.

27. Beginning of the story in Mary's window, St Mary's Church, Bury St Edmunds.
The story begins with the foot panels of the upper half:
Left: Erasmus and Sir Thomas More visiting Eltham.
Centre: Betrothal to Prince Charles of Castile at Richmond.
Right: Mary departs Dover for France.

28. Next part of Mary's story
Larger scenes on upper panels:
Left: Marriage at Abbeville.
Centre: Entry into Paris with Francis of Valois.
Right: 'La Reine Blanche', Mary meets Charles Brandon.

29. Final part of Mary's story
Lower Panels:
Left: Marriage to Charles Brandon at Cluny.
Centre: Meeting Henry VIII and receiving forgiveness at Greenwich.
Right: Abbott John Reeve conducting Mary's funeral service at the Abbey of St Edmund.

The small images in the upper tracery depict:
Mary, Henry VIII, Charles of Castile, Louis XII of France, Charles Brandon, Duke of Suffolk.

with Louis and confirm a date she would visit them.[18] She later confirmed she would attend on 26 November.[19]

Two days later, on Monday, 13 November, the anticipated tournament was due to begin at noon. The events were to take place over the course of weeks, beginning with a four-day joust. Prior to attending the events, Mary spent time catching up on correspondence. One of those letters was another letter to Wolsey requesting his assistance to help John Palsgrave. She had requested Wolsey help her faithful servant remain in Paris, so it is possible Palsgrave had managed to see Mary once she was now in the same city.[20] The tournament had been delayed as the English men intending to partake had not yet arrived. Henry had paid for men of the English nobility to travel to France to participate in the jousts, in honour of Mary and England. Amongst them were Charles Brandon, Duke of Suffolk; Thomas Grey, Marquess of Dorset; and Sir Edmund Howard who was paid 100l 'to prepare myself to do feat of arms in the parts of France at jousts and tourneys royal there to be holden'.[21]

In preparation for the tournament Francis, along with his companions, had 'erected in the Rue St. Anthoine near the Tournelles a Triumphant Arch supported by 5 great Pillars, unto which 5 shields were fastened. Whereof – 1st. One was of Silver, which whosoever touched was admitted to run 4 Courses with a lance, and a 5th pour la Dame if he required it. 2nd. Who touched the Golden Shield, was admitted to one Course with the Lance and coups d'espé sans nombres. 3rd. Who touched the Black Shield was admitted to fight on foot with a Lance or Pike, and afterwards with a single sword. 4th. He that touched the Tawny Shield was admitted to fight on foot likewise, casting a Lance with one hand and holding a Target in the other, and after this to fight with a Two-handed sword. 5th. They that touched the Grey Shield which the Defendants should keep against all comers with the Arms above mentioned'.[22]

The first day of jousting began with Louis, Mary and the French nobility all present. The tournament was opened with a proclamation by the heralds announcing the events were 'for the joyous advent of the queen to the said Paris'.[23] Francis and his men were first to arrive on the field dressed in 'cloth of golde cloth of syluer and crymsyn veluet'. They approached the purpose-built stage where the nobility and Mary were waiting, 'the quene stode so that all men might see her and wondered at her beautie'.[24] Louis was unwell and remained lying on a couch to watch the feats of arms. It is reported that 'the English Duke of Suffolk broke many spears, and was one of the challengers, as also the Marquis of Dorset: and on the second day the two English lords, the Duke of Suffolk and the Marquis of Dorset, did remarkably well, and shivered many spears'.[25] Another account reports that Brandon ran fifteen courses on the first day alone, the highest number of all contenders.[26] The next two days the English continued to distinguish themselves and on the fourth, the nobility refrained from entering the lists, instead the lower classes put their skills to the test. Hall reports that over the four days, over three hundred men took part, running five courses.

After a days respite, the fighting with lance and sword on horseback began on Saturday, 18 November. Dorset reported that he and Brandon had only participated on the first of three days of this activity as there was a lack of noble participants. Francis hurt his hand in the fighting so could not continue for the remaining events, instead placing one of his men in his place. It must have been very difficult for Mary to maintain a degree of impartiality watching the close friends of her brother, men she had known for a long time, competing against her new subjects in a dangerous sport where, 'the Duke of Suffolke hurt a gentleman that he was like to die, the Marques strok Mounsire Grew an Albanoys with his spere and perced his hed pece & put hym in jeopardy. The duke of Suffolke in the tournay ouer threwe a man of armes horse and man, and so dyd the lorde Marques another, and yet the Frenchmen woulde in no wyse prayse them'.[27]

Lastly, on Tuesday, 21 November the general melee began. After having spent so much money on the event, and it being in his homeland, Francis was not too happy with the English beating the French in the events so far. He took the underhand decision to bring in 'the tallest and the strongest man; and he was an Almayne, and put him in the place of another person, to have had the Duke of Suffolk rebuked. The same great German came to the bars fiercely, with face hid, because he would not be known; and bare his spear to the Duke of Suffolk, with all his strength; and the duke him received, and for all his strength, put him, by strong strokes, from the barriers, and with the butt end of the spear, strake the German that he staggered; but for all that, the German strake strongly and hardly at the duke, and the judges suffered many more strokes to be foughten then were appointed; but when they saw the German reel & stagger, then they let fall the rail between them'.[28] With the rail down Brandon used the pommel of his sword to hit the man until he was bleeding and left the field, being ushered out by Francis before anyone could question the man's identity and the devious tactics of Francis.

Whether Mary had romantic feelings for Brandon by this time we cannot know, but we can only assume the anxiousness she must have felt at seeing him face such an opponent and knowing how her brother would react if his best friend was hurt, or worse, killed, through Francis' scheming. Mary did not need to worry, the English were victorious and the actions of Francis had been noted, even by Louis. Mary, clearly amused and proud of the English, reportedly told Dorset and Brandon that Louis had merrily stated they had shamed Francis and should receive the prizes for England. When reporting the events to Wolsey,

Dorset also commented on Mary stating that she 'continues her goodness and wisdom, and increases in the favor of her husband and the Privy Council'.[29]

Whilst the tournament was ongoing, Mary did not forget her brother and on 15 November she wrote to Henry thanking him for 'his kind letters and good counsel'.[30] Two days later she wrote once more asking him to intervene for a priest named Vincent Knight. Knight had accompanied their father when he returned to England to fight for the throne and had remained ever since. The Privy Council had commanded Knight to travel to France to fight in the wars on the promise of a benefice upon his return. However, he was instead imprisoned in Tournai for seven weeks and afterwards returned to England and placed in Fleet prison. Mary expressed her concern that 'he has been in your prison of the Fleet, without any veritable cause, for the space of forty-four weeks, and has lost and spent all his property in prison, as we have been duly advertised by some of our especial servants in England'. Mary then continues with a request 'I pray you earnestly, both for my sake, as a reward of the services he has done you, and that he may more eagerly supplicate God for you and me, to do him some good, and, if it please you, to command the bishop of York to have his money restored to him and to be gracious to him'. Just in case Henry requires a further enticement to do the right thing, Mary adds, 'By so doing you will bestow great charity and alms'.[31] This letter gives insight into Mary as a caring person; she clearly did not forget about England once she left, being kept up to date by her staff. She valued the service individuals gave to her family and sought to reward them, or in this case at least ensure their freedom. By referring to charity and alms, Mary is relying on Henry to agree according to the art of chivalry and Christian virtues.

On the same day, Brandon was offering his concern that Mary had found herself without counsel following the dismissal of her household. Brandon wrote to Wolsey that he and the English ambassadors had requested a meeting with the Duc de Longueville, the General of Normandy and two bishops and explained to them that Mary had 'desired us that we send for them, and desire them, on her behalf; and in the name of the king our master, that they would be good and loving to her, and that they would give her counsel from time to time, how she might best order herself to content the king; whereof she was most desirous, and in her should lack no good will. And because she knew well they were the men that the king loved and trusted, and knew best his mind, therefore she was utterly determined to love them and trust them, and to be ordered by their counsel in all causes; for she knew well that those that the king loved must love her best, and she them'.[32] The men of course agreed. This was a master stroke by Mary. Not only did she secure the loyalty of the most important men at Louis' court by playing the damsel but she knew they would tell Louis of the meeting, and Mary declaring herself open to the counsel of his advisors would be sure to please him.

Soon after the end of the tournament and the prizes being awarded, the majority of the Englishmen left for home, their costs being met by Louis as far as Calais. Brandon remained as they still had secret business to attend to. That secret business was the organisation of a meeting between Henry and Louis plus an expedition into Spain. The aim was to expel Ferdinand from Navarre and ensure Castile was passed to the daughters of Isabella, one of those being Katharine of Aragon, and therefore as her husband, would be Henry's to control. Louis in return wished Henry to assist him in his claim to Milan and further requested a loan of 200,000 crowns for a year.[33]

Mary and Louis left Paris on Thursday 23 November and travelled to Saint-Germain-en-Laye to hunt. As promised, Mary was back in Paris by 26 November. Whilst at the Hôtel des Tournelles she received a delegation of scholars from the University of Paris. An oration was delivered by Doctor of Theology, Maître May de Breuil, on behalf of the deputation. The oration was recorded on an illuminated manuscript and an original copy remains in existence today.[34] The oration refers to the university as 'the eldest daughter of the king' and in essence requests Mary, as Louis' wife, take on the role of 'most Christian mother and sovereign lady' to the university, thereby offering her support and patronage. The manuscript shows the delegation offering Mary a crown featuring three red roses, three white roses and three fleurs-de-lis. The red roses were to represent her beauty; her virtue and grace, and her wisdom. The white roses represented the nobility of the royal house of England, the English accomplishments in learned sciences, and the fertility of England. The fleur-de-lis of course represented Louis.[35]

Around midday Mary rode in to the city to dine, Francis rode at her side, Brandon and the nobility rode ahead whilst the ladies followed Mary. There was such excitement at Mary coming to dine that on reaching the Hôtel de Ville, Mary could not get inside the gates due to the large crowds gathered. Rather than allow her guard to force their way through using violence, Mary decided to wait but after a while it was clear the crowd were not dispersing; they all wanted to see her, or possibly receive alms or the leftover food from the feast. Mary had to enter through the concierge and was directed through a narrow staircase and finally to the chamber where the feast was being held in her honour. The number of people inside the chamber was also vast making it difficult to get dishes to all of the tables, though that would not have been something affecting Mary as she was the guest of honour and the dishes for her table had been cooked in chambers appropriated specifically for that purpose. After dining, Mary was invited into the council chamber where she was presented with a gift consisting of coffers of various spices. Mary not only accepted the gift but selected six of them to be sent to her stepdaughter, Princess Renée, who had not been present at the banquet.

Later that day Mary returned to Saint-Germain where Louis was waiting for her. The couple remained there for a few weeks, Mary caring for Louis whose health had deteriorated again. The aging king had been used to a humble life; he preferred to spend time with family and would wake early, eating around 10:00 a.m. before retiring to bed around 6:00 p.m. Having a young bride, Louis attempted to ensure he was present for the welcome entertainments which the nobility and people of France had so thoughtfully prepared for Mary, but the extravagance, constant travelling and entertaining had all taken their toll on Louis. As a young lady, it might have been expected that Mary would continue to spend her time hosting feasts and entertaining the court; instead she chose to remain at her husband's side, rarely leaving unless her presence was requested by the nobility in their attempts to honour and entertain her. Louis was only too happy for Mary to attend these entertainments as it meant the nobility grew affectionate of Mary, but when she was with him, she kept Louis in good spirits, playing her lute and singing to him.

By the middle of December, Brandon had finally returned to England, having left the French court at the end of November. He reported to Henry that Mary was being treated very well following which Henry wrote to Louis personally thanking him for his kind treatment of his sister. Louis and Mary had travelled once more to the Hôtel des Tournelles, but it was now becoming apparent that Louis was seriously ill, though he was still planning on meeting Henry at the end of December.[36] Louis, ever the courteous monarch responded to his brother-in-law – it was to be his last remaining letter:

> I understand the pleasure you have to hear of my welfare, from my cousin the Duke of Suffolk, and the satisfaction that I have with the queen, my wife, your good sister; who has hitherto conducted herself, and still does, every day, towards me, in such a manner that I cannot but be delighted with her, and love and honour her more and more each day; and you may be assured that I do, and ever shall, so treat her, as to give both her and you perfect satisfaction, and as to the reception and good cheer which my cousin Suffolk tells you that I have given him, and for which you thank me, it needs not, my good brother, cousin and compeer, that you should render many thanks; for I beg you to believe that, independent of this place I know he holds with you, and the love you bear him, – his virtues, manners, politeness, and good condition, deserve that he should be received with even greater honour.[37]

Chapter Eight

La Reine Blanche

At around 6:00 a.m. on New Year's Day 1515, aged 53 years old, Louis XII of France died at the Hôtel des Tournelles. He and Mary had been married 82 days and now Mary was a widow and queen dowager at only 18 years old. Unfortunately, no records have yet come to light to inform us if Mary was with Louis when he died, or if not, how she was informed.

French custom dictated that a royal widow should go into mourning closed off from the world for a period of forty days. Before retiring Mary had been visited by Francis who assured her that she would be kept entertained during this time. As per the custom, Mary retired to the Hôtel de Cluny the day after Louis' death. The chambers would be kept dark, lit only by candlelight. Mary was required to dress all in white to signify mourning, giving her the epithet *la reine blanche* (the white queen). She would not be entirely alone; her ladies were to accompany her but it still must have been an overwhelming experience for Mary.

Ambassadors from the Venetian Council of Ten had previously been despatched to France to issue congratulations on the wedding of Louis and Mary and present a gift to Mary worth 1000 ducats.[1] The ambassadors were reported to have been given a 'box of black velvet, with a gilt handle, enclosing a white silk hat and appendages. Would also find a small case containing two rings, in one of which was a large ruby, and in the other diamond, also a pendant balass, (ruby) with a pear-shaped pearl beneath it, which balass was to be fastened to the hat'.[2] By the time they reached the French court, Louis had died. The Venetians ultimately decided they did not wish to gift such a sum to a dowager queen so they did not make the gift to her, the ambassadors were instead ordered to find out who was close to Francis, no doubt so the gifts could be given to them instead.[3] It was widely known that the way to gain a favour from Louis was to approach Mary, or make her happy in some way. With Louis gone the Venetians had no reason to try and win her favour. Francis, now referred to by ambassadors as the new king, visited Mary every evening and is reported to have said that 'with the exception of the late King, whom she desires, she may dispose of the whole kingdom, even more than before'.[4] This led the Venetian ambassadors to believe that Mary would retain an immense amount of power in France. One possible reason for Mary retaining so much power would be as the mother of the next king, if she were pregnant.

The central question surrounding Mary's future was whether she was carrying a child and if so, would the child be male. Francis must have been anxious at this point; if Mary was pregnant, his hopes to become the next king would be destroyed. News was already spreading that she may be pregnant.[5] Sir Robert Wingfield writing from the court of Emperor Maximilian, on 14 January, warned Henry that 'if the Queen of France be with child, she be kept from danger. If she be a maid, "as I think verily she is," to obtain possession of her person'.[6] He was obviously concerned about her future if she was not returned to England. Another report stated that Mary was desperate to remain in power and padded her clothing to fabricate a pregnancy.[7] There is no other evidence to substantiate this statement, in fact Mary's own actions dispute this. Francis did visit Mary regularly, perhaps keen to learn what his future was. After a couple of weeks he allegedly asked Mary if he could name himself king, to which she replied, 'that he might, and that she knew of no other king than he, for she had no idea of having any offspring that could prevent'.[8] Although there were already concerns around Mary's future, with the matter of Mary not being pregnant concluded, her future became even more of a concern to Henry and Francis. Now that she was widowed, she was back on the marriage market. Thomas Spinelly, from the court of Margaret of Austria wrote of his concerns about Francis, 'he in nowise suffre the frenche qwene to departe tul she be maryed at his pleasyr'.[9]

Although Mary was secluded from the court, she was still able to write. Wolsey had written to her on hearing of the failing health of Louis and proffered advice on Mary's actions if he were to die. Wolsey wrote 'Assuring your grace, that the king, your most loving brother, will never forsake, but most fastly stick unto you, in all your needs. Wherefore, Madam, for the old service that I have done unto your grace, I most humbly beseech the same never to do anything but by the advice of his grace; referring to all things to him whatever fair promises, words, or persuasions, shall be made to the contrary; having always a special regard to his common honour, and letting nothing pass your grace's mouth whereby any person in those parts may have you at any advantage. And if any motions of marriage or other thing fortune to be made unto you, in no wise give hearing to the [same]. And, thus doing, you shall not fail to have the king fast and loving unto you, and attain to your [own heart's] desire, [and to return] then again unto England, with as much honour as [ever woman] had'.[10] In Mary's response, dated 10 January 1515, she replied, 'as it please the King my brother and his Council I will be ordered. And so I pray you, my lord, to show his Grace, seeing that the King my husband is departed to God, of whose soul

God pardon. And where as you advise me that I should make no promise, My Lord, I trust the King my brother and you will not reckon in me such childhood. I trust I have so ordered myself so since that I came hither, that I trust it hath been to the honour of the King my brother and me, since I come hither, and so I trust to continue'.[11]

Wolsey would have been well aware that if the French kept Mary in their possession, she would not be able to return to England and therefore her trousseau, dower and her wealth would also not return. Her dower had been agreed so that she should retain it after the death of Louis, regardless of whether she remained living in France or not.[12] Within a week of his death there had already been an inventory completed of Louis' tapestries, jewels and plate, a copy of which was sent to Henry. The inventory estimated the total at over 400,000 crowns.[13] Whilst the clause relating to Mary's dower was beneficial for Mary, it would be disadvantageous for France to pay this sort of revenue if she returned to England or married anywhere other than in France. The new king, Francis I, therefore initially sought to keep Mary in France, ideally through marriage to a French nobleman. It was reported that the Duke of Lorraine and the Duke of Bourbon were amongst the favourites of the suitors.[14] Prince Charles and his grandfather, Emperor Maximilian, were also suggested as potential matches. This must have been a very anxious time for Mary, once more in the hands of others to make decisions about her life.

Louis' death resulted in uncertainty. The treaty between England and France stated the peace would be kept for a year following the death of either monarch. Other kingdoms were unsure what the death of the French king meant for them. Up until his death, Louis had been insistent he would invade Milan, but with his death, Francis had the financial obligations of Mary's dower to fulfil before he could make war on anyone, if that was what he wished to do.

Before he died, Louis had wanted nothing more than to please his beautiful bride and had heaped gifts upon her. He had sent gifts before she left England but once she was in France, Louis showered Mary with even more gifts from the vast selection he had previously shown to the Earl of Worcester. Amongst them were:

> First a cronell for her head of golde and stone in the day of her marriage.
>
> Item a goodlie devise for her neke set with stone and perle.
>
> Item a gooflie gurdill of golde of as goodlie facion as may be devised.

Item ii braseletts of golde set with stone and perle.

Item on the nexte day for her change a Riche Juell of golde with a Cheyne of golde for her nekke.

Item a goodlie gurdill of golde.

Item a goodlie Crosse gilte poisaunt xiijxx unc.

Item a faire coffer of silver to lay in her Juellis.[15]

Some of the gifts of jewels became a point of contention between Francis I and Henry VIII as Francis argued some of them belonged to the crown and could not be kept by Mary. Henry sent a delegation of ambassadors under the guise of paying their respects following the death of Louis and to congratulate Francis on ascending the throne, but Henry also wanted to ensure his sister was returned to him. Heading this delegation was Charles Brandon who had only returned to England a few weeks before.

Whilst Mary was secluded, the French made preparations for the funeral of Louis. In the great hall at the palace his body lay in state, wearing his crown, robes and sceptre. An effigy replaced the body when it was no longer acceptable for it to remain exposed. Through the streets which were hung with black cloth, Louis' body was transported to Notre Dame and then into St Denis where he was interred. Louis' tomb still exists and is one of magnificence, indicating how much he was loved and respected by his people and his successor. Mary would not attend his funeral, it was not customary, especially for the nobility, to attend the funeral of a spouse.

Mary did not dwell in isolation. As well as writing to Wolsey and her brother she also issued charters from her place in seclusion. Three of those still exist, dated 12, 23 and 27 February 1515. All three are orders to her treasurer to pay money to her attendees, one above his normal wage and another was the award of a marriage portion to a female servant.[16] Even when in mourning, Mary was still the caring mistress to those who served her.

Brandon and his companions, Dr Nicholas West and Sir Richard Wingfield, arrived in Senlis on 27 January. Francis had left Paris on 18 January and already travelled to Rheims where his coronation took place on 25 January. Francis agreed to meet the delegation at Noyon on Thursday, 1 February. The delegation was well received and a formal audience granted for the following day. During this audience the ambassadors passed on Henry's gratitude for how Francis had treated Mary whilst she was in mourning. They referenced a letter Francis had written to Henry, 'that he would neither do her wrong, no suffer her to take wrong of any other person, but be to her as a loving son should be to his mother'. Francis responded that he 'could do no less for his honor, seeing that she was Henry's sister, a noble princess married to his predecessor; and he expressed a hope that she would write to England, and report "how lovingly he had behaved to her"'.[17] Brandon had also brought a letter from Henry for Mary, in which Henry advised her not to consider remaining in France. Mary responded directly to Henry; and it is at this point we can begin to wonder if Mary had already made a decision:

> ... there is nothing so great a store [to] me as for to see you, the which I would very fain have the time for to come, as I trust it shall be, or else I would be very sorry, for I think every day a thousand till I may see you.
>
> Sire, whereas your grace sends me word that I will not give no credence [to the] for no suit, nor for no other words that shall be given me; sire, I promise your grace that I never made them no promise, nor no other fo[r the]m, nor never will [until] that I know your [grace's mind] for nobody alive; for [your grace] is all the comfort t[hat I have] in this world.[18]

Mary is conforming to the dutiful sister here by stating she trusts Henry will make the right decision by her. She goes on to say that she will be ready as soon as he sends for her before finally ending her letter by thanking Henry for allowing his surgeon to remain with her. Whilst this does act as a genuine show of appreciation it also hints at the stress she is under and could have been Mary's way of eliciting sympathy from her brother with one final request that she asks Henry to 'give him leave for to tarry here awhile with me, for because I am very ill-diseased with the toothache, and the mother withal, that some times I wot not what for to do; but [an I] might see your grace I were he[aled]'.[19] The 'mother' was apparently another term for *hysteria passio*. It is described as a 'uterine malady' with symptoms 'primarily respiratory distress along with a sensation of strangling or pressure sometimes leading to a complete cessation of visible breathing'.[20] It may be this which led to later unsubstantiated accounts that Mary was hysterical when confined in the Hôtel de Cluny. She relies on flattery to convince Henry to bring her home stating seeing him would make her well again.

By 4 February, Brandon and the ambassadors were in Paris. When Mary met with them the following day she ensured they were aware that she had felt pressured by Francis to marry someone of his choosing. This is exactly what Henry would have feared. The ambassadors wrote to Henry that although Francis had tried pressuring Mary 'she never consented nor never wole do [but rather] suffre thextremitie of death and astouching her here she never was nor is mynded therto for she [counts] every day an hundred till she may see your grace'.[21] Once more this letter both flatters Henry but instils a fear that his favourite sister would rather die than marry against her will or be forced to marry in France. Mary is ensuring her brother is in a position where to deny her anything would go against the code of chivalry he was so eager to enforce and show himself as the true knight in shining armour. Brandon wrote separately to Henry concerning the matter. Whether his letter embellishes the truth or not we do not know but he wrote that during the meeting with Mary on 5 February, he had enquired about the behaviour of Francis to which Mary responded that 'he had been in hand with her of many matters; but on hearing that Suffolk was come, he promised to trouble her no more'.[22] In their letter, the ambassadors also added that Mary trusts that Henry 'knoweth her mynde therin'.[23] Although it would be easy to assume that this reference is a direct hint that she wants to marry Brandon, it could also be Mary just reminding Henry that she wishes to marry someone of her choosing. Before leaving England, Mary had made Henry promise that as she had married Louis out of duty, he 'wolde never provoke or move me but as myn ounn hert and mynde shulde be best pleased'.[24]

For Brandon, the matter was already serious. On the day he had met with Francis for the formal audience, he had later been called into the Francis' chambers for a private meeting. Here he was accused of coming to France with the sole aim of marrying Mary. For Brandon, this was a matter of life and death. It was treason to marry royalty without the monarch's permission and he was now faced with accusations that could see his head cut off. Brandon wrote to Wolsey on 3 February to confide in him the accusation he had faced from Francis. He wrote that he hoped Henry did not believe this and stated that he had told Francis that he 'had none such [t]hyng, nor it was never intended on the King my master's behalf nor on mine'. He told Wolsey that Francis had told him Mary herself had admitted this secret to Francis and in turn he had promised to help the couple achieve their wishes. When all Brandon could do was thank the French king and fearfully state that he would be in much trouble if Henry were to know of this, Francis went on to say that 'I and the Queen shall so instance your master, that I trust he will be content. And because[I] would gladly put your heart at rest, I would, [as] I come to Paris, speak with the Queen; and s[he an]d I both will write letters to the King your master, with our own hands, in the best manner that can be devised'.[25]

Wolsey was quick to respond and this letter gives rise to the suggestion that Henry knew all along what would happen when he despatched Brandon to bring Mary home:

> ... as joyous I am as any creature living to hear, as well of your honourable entertainment with the French king, and of his loving

> mind towards you for your marriage with the French queen, our master's sister, as also of his kind offer made unto you, that both he and the said French queen shall effectually write unto the king's grace, for the obtaining of his good will and favour unto the same. The content of which your letter I have, at good leisure, declared unto the king's highness; and his grace marvellously rejoiced to hear of your good speed in the same, and how substantially and discreetly you ordered and handled yourself, in your words and conversation with the said French king, when he first secretly broke with you of the said marriage. And therefore, my lord, the king and I think it good that you procure and solicit the speedy sending unto his grace of the letters from the said French king and queen, touching this matter: assuring you that the king continueth firmly in his good mind and purpose towards you, for the accomplishment of the said marriage: albeit that there be daily, on every side, practices made to the let of the same, which I have withstood hitherto, and doubt not but so to do, till you shall have achieved your intended purpose.[26]

Wolsey then ends his letter by confirming the lands granted to Brandon, 'The Lady Suffolk is dead. The King has granted her lands to Suffolk, and given him the lordship of Claxton, formerly the Lord Admiral's'.[27] That Wolsey voices no surprise on receipt of Brandon's letter and the comment that Henry is happy with his 'discreet behaviour' indicates both were supportive of the match. The encouragement of both Henry and Wolsey to obtain the letters of Francis and Claude shows that it is likely that Henry was well aware of the reaction the match would cause amongst the rest of the court and was intending for Brandon to have the French support in the face of the criticism he would receive, and was acting alongside Wolsey to avoid the criticism of the nobility. Of course, it could have been Wolsey feigning Henry's support in the matter but as Brandon was supportive of Wolsey against the Norfolk faction this is highly unlikely. Therefore, it seems Henry was party to the secret; a secret that could see Mary imprisoned and Brandon dead.

Chapter Nine

A Secret to Die For

With Mary in isolation she was well aware that her future lay in the hands of two kings: her brother, Henry VIII, and the new king of France, Francis I. Both had their own reasons for having Mary under their control but by becoming a widow with a very generous income, she was a highly attractive match on the European marriage market. For his part, Francis dismissed her English attendants, likely thinking this would isolate Mary even more and therefore bend her to his will in his choice of suitor. Mary had to make the most of her situation, relying on her brother and Francis I to be the chivalrous men they professed to be. But that did not mean she would not use her own skills to get what she wanted, and what she wanted was Charles Brandon, Duke of Suffolk. This decision would cause outrage, but why? Who was Charles Brandon?

Charles Brandon was the son of Sir William Brandon, who had been the standard bearer to Henry Tudor at the Battle of Bosworth. Having lost his father defending Henry, it is thought Charles Brandon was taken in by his uncle, Sir Thomas Brandon. Grateful for his sacrifice, Henry VII maintained an interest in the young Brandon; he was welcome at court with his uncle and was later given a position attending upon Prince Henry. From there a friendship grew that some may not have survived but Charles not only survived but flourished under his friend, eventually being buried in the same place as him. On the accession of Henry VIII, Brandon was appointed an esquire of the body and chamberlain of the principality of Wales. This was the beginning of his glittering court career.

Mary was certainly not the first wife of Brandon. He had been contracted to marry Anne Browne, daughter of Sir Anthony Browne, when he was much younger. For reasons unknown, Brandon did not go through with the marriage and instead, at some time prior to February 1507, he married Margaret Neville, daughter of John Neville, 1st Marquess of Montague, a younger brother of Richard Neville, Earl of Warwick, the 'Kingmaker'. Margaret was widowed from Sir John Mortimer and had wealth; or at least more wealth than Anne Browne. The marriage was declared void sometime later that same year on the grounds of the degree of consanguinity and, in early 1508, Brandon married Anne Browne. Anne was actually related to Margaret – she was the stepdaughter of Margaret's sister, Lucy Neville. Just to complicate matters further, the father of Margaret's deceased spouse was married to Brandon's grandmother. Together, Anne and Brandon had two children: Lady Anne Brandon (1507–1557); and Lady Mary Brandon (1510–1542). Following Anne's death, Brandon was granted the wardship of Elizabeth Grey, 5th Baroness Lisle in 1512. Through this arrangement Brandon had access to Elizabeth's wealth and lands and was awarded the title of Viscount Lisle on 15 May 1513 in consideration of a prospective marriage to the young heiress when she became of age. The title was later surrendered.

1513 would have been a difficult year for Mary – her brother was in France with an army and her sister-in-law, Katharine of Aragon, whilst acting as regent had successfully defended England by defeating the Scottish army, resulting in the death of James IV of Scotland. It should not be forgotten that James was the brother-in-law of Mary and Henry through his marriage to Margaret, so it must have been difficult to manage emotions knowing her sister was now a widow but as a result of invading her homeland.

Brandon was in France with Henry where another possible match was raised, this time a possible marriage between Brandon and Margaret of Austria, Duchess of Savoy. Philippe de Brezilles, ambassador to Margaret, who was situated in the camp of the English at Thérouanne wrote to Margaret that Brandon 'heartily desired to serve you. I think you are well enough aware that he is a second king, and it seems to me that you would do well to write him a courteous letter; for it is he who does and undoes'.[1] High praise indeed to be noted as a 'second king' though probably not something that would be wise to mention in the presence of Henry VIII. Margaret and Brandon did indeed meet in person. Henry VIII, encouraging his friend in the potential of a match with the daughter of an Emperor, allegedly acted as an interpreter for the pair given that Brandon was not fluent in French. Henry went as far as asking if there was any possibility of a match between her and his friend, to which Margaret replied 'it was impossible, and would bring upon her the evil grace of her father (Emperor Maximilian) and all that country; "that it was not here the custom, and that I should be dishonoured, and holden for a fool and light"'.[2] Margaret did give a promise to Henry that she would not marry anyone else until Brandon returned; in response Brandon agreed not to marry without her consent.

Brandon did have a diamond ring belonging to Margaret which was thought by some to be a token of a promise but when Margaret was questioned about Brandon showing off the jewel, she responded that:

> ... one night at Tournay, being at the banquet, after the banquet he put himself upon his knees before me, and in speaking and him playing, he drew from my finger the ring, and put it upon his, and since shewed it me; and I took to laugh, and to him said

> that he was a thief, and that I thought not that the King had with him led thieves out of his country. This word laron he could not understand; wherefore I was constrained to ask how one said in Flemish laron. And afterwards I said to him in Flemish dieffe, and I prayed him many times to give it me again, for that it was too much known. But he understood me not well, and kept it unto the next day that I spake to the King, him requiring to make him to give it me, because it was too much known – I promising him one of my bracelets the which I wore, the which I gave him. And then he gave me the said ring; the which one other tyme at Lylle, being set nigh to my Lady of Hornes, and he before, upon his knees, it took again from my finger. I spake to the King to have it again; but it was not possible, for he said unto me that he would give me others better, and that I should leave him that. I said unto him, that it was not for the value but for that it was too much known. He would not understand it, and departed from me. The morrow after he brought me one fair point of diamond, and one table of ruby, and shew me that it was for the other ring; wherefore I durst no more speak of it, if not to beseech him that it should not be shewed to any person; the which hath not all been to me done.[3]

Whether anything romantic happened between the couple is a matter of opinion, though for Margaret, Brandon would likely not have been of a high enough rank so she may have just given words of encouragement to maintain peace with Henry VIII. There was, of course, still the matter of the marriage of her nephew Charles and Mary for Margaret to be conscious of, so she could not afford to lose the goodwill of the king. On 23 May 1514 Margaret stated that all she required was the goodwill of Henry VIII and desired 'as much as his coming, and the same of my Lady Mary'. It is apparent that the rumours that had spread about the relationship between Margaret and Brandon were a cause of distress to Margaret who confessed that she 'shall not dare speak nor shew good semblant to the said personage; whereas I would make to him much honor and good cheer, I shall not dare behold him with a good eye, what displeasure shall be the same to him and to me', and urged Wingfield to advise Henry and Brandon that her honour could not allow anything further.[4]

Margaret was not just a wealthy woman, she also had a reputation of being a well-educated, intelligent woman. Brandon was well aware of this and took the opportunity to secure a place in her household for his eldest daughter, Anne. Anne would have the opportunity to serve and learn from one of the most influential women in Europe during the sixteenth century. Another young lady was also left in the care of Margaret; a young girl that Brandon had saved during the warfare. The TV show *The Tudors* depicts Brandon as a womaniser and he brings a lady back from France to England and engages in a romantic relationship with her. There is no evidential basis for this, but it is reported that he did save a young lady and left her with the opportunity of a secure future with Margaret. Sadly, we do not know what the future held for the girl but it is possible she was still at Margaret's court later when Anne Boleyn was also placed there.

Brandon was elevated to the Dukedom of Suffolk in February 1514. Some may assume this was to make him of a high enough rank to be acceptable for Mary, but at this point the preparations to marry Mary to Charles were still ongoing. However, there were rumours about Brandon and Margaret of Austria at this time and the latter was not pleased and begged Henry VIII to ensure Brandon had married his ward Elizabeth Grey by the time the group were to meet once more in Calais for the solemnities of Mary and Charles' marriage later that year. By creating Brandon, Duke of Suffolk, Henry VIII was effectively raising him to the highest rank possible and therefore, more than an acceptable match for Margaret. Whether this was Henry's plan or not, we do not know, but it was a significant favour to bestow. Alternatively, Henry may have genuinely wished to reward Brandon for his work, success in France and loyalty; there may even have been no marriage to consider when the honour was bestowed. However, if Brandon were to secure a marriage with Margaret, it would ensure Henry had influence as Brandon would take over all of her lands, wealth and income as her husband. What Mary thought of the gossip surrounding Brandon and Margaret of Austria is not known. We do not know if Mary had any feelings for Brandon at this point; if she did then the possibility of him marrying Margaret must have been upsetting but Mary was also well aware that her future lay in the hands of her brother, not her own will, at least not at that point.

On 1 February 1515, with a few exceptions, Henry granted Brandon 'all the possessions forfeited by Edmund de la Pole Earl of Suffolk and John Earl of Lincoln, with reversion of the possessions now held by Queen Katharine and Margaret Countess of Suffolk for life.'[5] This grant would provide a generous income and though the grant states it is in support of his title, he had been elevated to the dukedom a year before this, so maybe it was Henry's way of ensuring his sister would be comfortable on her return as the Duchess of Suffolk. The grant was ratified by parliament on 5 February.[6]

By this point, Mary had apparently already made Francis a party to her secret desire to marry Brandon when Francis was attempting to encourage her to marry someone in France. In a letter to Wolsey, Brandon reports the conversation between Mary and Francis where she had allegedly stated: '"Sir, I beseech you that you will let me alone and speak no more to me of the matter; and if you will promise me by your faith and truth, and as you are a true prince, that you will keep it counsel and help me, I will tell you all my whole mind. And he gave her his faith in her hand that he would keep it counsel, and that he would help her to the best of his power." Having told him her mind, and said she could not think "but the King her brother w[ould be disp]lysed (?)" with her, she besought him to get the King['s consent]'.[7] Brandon also wrote to Henry and advised that Mary had become afraid that Francis would do something to harm him.[8] Again, we do not know whether this is true but this would likely have infuriated Henry that Francis was causing distress to his sister and putting his best friend at risk of harm.

Mary was allowed to end her official mourning on 11 February and return to society. On 15 February, from a window at the Hôtel de Cluny, she watched the entry of Francis into Paris as the new king. She then joined the procession, riding with twenty of Brandon's men to attend the banquet at the palace. On the same day she wrote to Henry, adding her own account to the letter sent by Brandon. Mary was aware that this letter would be read by the Privy Council. In her letter she explains that when conversing with Francis she had:

> ... declar[ed unto him] the good mind [which] for divers consi[derations I] bear to my lord of Suffolk, asking him not only [to grant] me his favour and consent thereunto, but [also] that he would of his [own] hand write unto your grace, and to pray you to bear your like favour unto me, and to be content with the same; the which he granted me to do, and so hath done, according as shall appear unto your grace by his said [letters]. And, sire, I most humbly beseech you to take this answer which I have [made u]nto the French king in good part, the which [I did] only to be discharge[ed of t]he extreme pain and annoyance I was i[n, by reason] of such suit as t[he French kin]g made unt[o me not accordi]ng with mine honour, [the whi]ch he hath clearly left [off]. Also, sire, I feared greatly [lest, in] case that I had kept the matter from his knowledge, that he might have not well entreated my said lord of Suffolk, and the rather [for] to have returned to his [former] malfantasy and suits.[9]

Although she states that she only confessed, partly to avoid any further suitors being put forward by Francis, this is likely to appease the Privy Council rather than Henry. Another letter from Mary expresses her direct feelings on the matter; unfortunately due to fire damage we do not know the date so this could have been after the secret marriage took place but before it was revealed or once the secret was known by Henry. I have included a large portion of the letter as it gives incredible insight to how Mary used her writing skills as a weapon. Mary wrote to Henry:

> Sire, I beseech your grace that you will keep all the promises that you promised me when I took my leave of you by the w[ater s]ide. Sire, your grace knoweth well that I did marry for your pl[easure a]t this time, and now I trust that you will suffer me to [marry as] me l[iketh fo]r to do.[10]

Referring to Francis attempting to marry her off within France, Mary continues:

> I assure your grace that [my mi]nd is not there where they would have me, and I trust [your grace] will not do so to me that has always been so glad to fulfil your mind as I have been: wherefore I beseech your grace for to be good lord and brother to me; for, dire, an if your grace will have gran[ted] me married in any place, [sav]ing whereas my mind is, I will be there, whereas your grace not no other shall have any joy of me; for, I promise your grace, you shall hear that I will be in some religious house, the which I think your grace would be very sorry of, and all your realm. Also, sire, I know well that the king, that is [my so]n, will send to your grace by his uncle the duke of *** for to ma[rry me here. But I tru]st you[r grace *** I sha]ll never be merry at my heart, (for an ever that I d[o marr]y while I live). I trow your grace knoweth as well as I do, and did before I came hither, and so I trust your grace will be contented, unless I would never marry while I live, but be there where never [no] man nor woman shall have joy of me; wherefore I beseech your grace to be good lord to him and to me both, for I know well that he hath m[et ma]ny hindrances to your grace of him and me both. Wherefore, an your grace be good lord to us both, I will not care for all the world else, but beseech your grace to be good lord and brother to me, as you have been here aforetime, f[or in you] is all the trust that I have in this world after God.[11]

The last paragraph where she states 'be good lord to him' indicates this letter was written after the secret wedding and can only refer to Brandon. Whether

Henry knew of the intended marriage is a matter of opinion. Mary was well aware her letters would not be for private viewing; the Privy Council would certainly see this letter. To have a royal princess enter a convent when there was no heir to the throne would have been disastrous and Mary knew this. Francis had kept his promise to Mary and Brandon and wrote to Henry himself in support of the union, though he did of course omit to having pressured Mary to marry in France. He confirmed to Henry that he had asked Mary if she were inclined towards a second marriage, to which she 'confessed the great esteem she had for the Duke of Suffolk, and prayed him not only to give his own consent, but to write to Henry in Suffolk's favor, which he now does'.[12] Queen Claude and Francis' mother, Louise of Savoy, also wrote to Henry, giving their support to the union. He also allowed Mary to dismiss the French attendants and reinstate her English attendants. We cannot know why Francis changed his mind; maybe he realised it was a lost cause to force Mary to stay, or perhaps he took the opportunity to assist Mary thinking it would anger Henry and therefore get one over on him.

Following the letters of Mary and Francis, Brandon himself wrote to Henry. He took the opportunity to convince Henry that he could use the support of Francis as a way of consenting to the marriage, despite the opinions of the council. He asked Henry to write to Francis confirming his consent as he feared Francis would try and marry Mary to a French nobleman if Henry did not approve of the union. He went on to state that 'I know the queen had rather be out of this world than to abide. And, Sire, as for me, your grace not offended, I had rather be out of the world than to see her in that case'.[13] Mary had become fearful that Henry may be trying to entice her back to England and once there would marry her off to Charles of Castile; it was a possibility and her fears were perhaps not totally unfounded. But also the letters between Brandon and Wolsey indicate Henry knew the pair were keen to marry, although there is nothing that states Henry agreed they could marry in France. It is likely he expected the pair to return home and would then be married.

Mary was also aware that some of those at Henry's court were completely against the idea of Mary and Brandon marrying. Brandon reported an incident to Wolsey which he believed was a result of the opposing factor, led by Norfolk. He reports that Friar Langley had visited Mary and 'one day among the others, desired her to be shriven of him; whereunto she answered not to be disposed for that time. And then the said friar shewed her that he had the same day said mass; and he sware, by the Lord, that he had the same day consecrated, and that under benedictine he would shew her divers things which were of truth, ad of the which he had perfect knowledge, desiring her to give him hearing, and to keep the same to herself. And first, said unto her, that it was said in England that she should be married to [me] advising her to be aware of me, of all men; for he knew well that you and I meddled with the devil. And by the puissance of the said devil, we kept our master subject to all that [we could de]vise'.[14] That their opponents would take such measures would have been unnerving and whilst today it does not appear to be insulting, to the religious Tudors, being referenced as meddling with the devil was extremely insulting and even more worrying should this view spread. The prospect of being married against her will became too much for Mary.

With Henry still not having given permission, Mary took matters into her own hands and advised Brandon that if he did not marry her within the next four days, she would be lost to him forever. Brandon had a very big decision to make. He would later write his account of the conversation and states Mary was afraid that if she returned to England unmarried 'she should go into Flanders, to the which she said that she had rather to be torn in pieces than ever she would come there, and with that weeped. I never saw a woman so weep'.[15] Brandon explained that he had attempted to reason with Mary, explaining that if Henry consented, he would of course marry her but he made a promise to Henry before he left England that he would not do anything without his consent. Again this indicates that Henry knew what would happen, or at least knew of the couple's wish to marry, but perhaps Mary's fears were based on reality. Brandon continued that Mary had stated that if both kings had consented but Brandon wouldn't marry her, then the rumours that he was there to bring her back to England so she could be married off to Charles must be true. That Mary states both kings had consented is interesting as there is no record where Henry definitively consents, though he also does not reject the match.

In a small chapel within the Hôtel de Cluny, possibly on 3 March 1515, Mary and Brandon were married.[16] There were only ten people in attendance, including some of Mary's household whom she trusted, and an unnamed priest to conduct the ceremony. The ambassadors, Dr Nicholas West and Sir Richard Wingfield, were not informed nor were they present, possibly to avoid any opportunity of convincing Brandon not to go through with it, or to save them from any resulting consequences. In the final sentence of the aforementioned letter, Brandon ends with 'so she and I was married'.[17] When news of the secret union began to leak, Brandon was summoned by Francis who admonished him, 'I did not think you had been so base, and if I chose to do my duty, I should, this very hour, have your head taken off your shoulders; for you have failed in your faith; and, trusting to your faith, I have not had watch kept over you. You have secretly, without my knowledge married Queen Mary'. Brandon in response replied 'Sire, may it please you to pardon me; I confess that I have done ill, but, sire, I supplicate you to consider the love which has made me do so; I commit myself entirely to your compassion, praying you to have mercy upon me'.[18] Francis was not about to back down and advised he would not behead him, but would advise Henry of what had occurred and would wait upon his pleasure as to what to do with Brandon. This may have been absolutely terrifying for Brandon, except for the fact that Francis had attended the ceremony in secret, such a secret that his own court did not know about it. His threats were all for show but highlighted exactly what could have been the result of the actions taken by Mary and Brandon.

Brandon confessed to Wolsey in a letter dated 5 March 1515 that not only were they already married but they believed Mary to be pregnant. Although she was not in fact pregnant, the date of the letter casts doubt on the date of the marriage being two days prior, so perhaps the couple were attempting to confuse the timeline, or they thought the possibility of a pregnancy would impact the reaction of Henry and the Privy Council. It would, after all, be a Tudor heir. Wolsey's response would shatter any hope the couple had that their news would be joyfully received and accepted. Wolsey confirmed that although Brandon had asked him not to disclose the letter to Henry, he felt he had no choice as it impacted upon Henry's honour.

When shown the letter, Henry had reacted 'grievously and displeasantly, not only for that you durst presume to marry his sister without his knowledge, but also for breaking of your promise made unto his grace in his hand, I being present, at Eltham; having also such assured affiance in your truth that for all the world, and to have been torn with wild horses, you would not have broken your oath. Promise, and assurances made to his grace, which he doth well perceive that he is deceived of the constant and affirmed trust that he thought to have found in you. And for my part, no man can be more sorry than I am that you have so done, and so his grace would I should expressly write unto you, being so incholered [enraged] therewith that I cannot devise nor study by the remedy thereof, considering that you have failed to him which hath brought you up of low degree to be of this great honour, and that you were the man in all the world he loved and trusted best, and was content that, with good order and saving of his honour, you should have in marriage his said sister'.[19]

This letter indicates that Henry was hoping Brandon would bring Mary back to England and once there would allow them to marry but without evidence we cannot know if Mary's fears that this was a ruse to get her to return were well founded. Wolsey had not completely abandoned the despairing couple, he had suggested using Mary's dower and jewels to try and buy Henry's forgiveness. With the news spreading it was time for the couple to do damage control and seek the forgiveness of Henry.

Chapter Ten

Favourite Sister

Taking Wolsey's advice, Mary was swift to write to Henry, ensuring she took the blame rather than Brandon and also placing partial blame on the Privy Council:

> I assure your grace that I had never done [against your] ordinance and consent, but by the r[eason of the grea]t despair w[herein I was put] by the two fr[iars......] which hath certify[ed me] in case I come [to] En[gland] your council would never consent to the marriage between the said lord and me, with [ma]ny other sayings concerni[ng] the same promise, so that I verily [thought] that the said friar[s] would never have offered to have made me like ove[rture] unless they might have had charge from some of your council, the which put me in such consternation, fear, and doubt of the obtaining of the thing which I desired most in this world, that I rather chose to put me in your mercy accomplishing the marriage than to put me in the order of your council [knowing the]m to be otherways [minded]. Whereupon, sire, I put [my lord of Su]ffolk in choice w[hether he woul]d accomplish th[e marriag]e within f[our days, or else that he should never have] enjoyed me; whereby I know well that I constrained him to break such promises as he made your grace, as well for fear of losing of me as also that I ascertained him that by their consent I would never come into England.[1]

Mary is openly stating that she believes the friars were sent by someone on the council to dissuade her from marrying Brandon, and through their actions she came to believe they would never allow the union if she returned to England unmarried. She does not at any point blame Henry as she is relying on him to pardon the offence and allow them both to return. Interestingly, Mary ends her letters to Henry at this time with salutations such as 'By your loving sister, Mary', or 'By your loving and most humble sister, Mary'.[2] She omits her title, which is not omitted from her letters to Wolsey, perhaps in an effort to plead humility and a willingness to obey Henry. Whilst Mary was busy seeking forgiveness from her brother and writing a brief note to Wolsey in which she thanked him for his support, Brandon sought further assistance from Wolsey writing 'let me not be undone now; the which, I fear me, I shall be, without the special help of you'. He also asks Wolsey to deliver to Henry 'a diamond, with a great pearl; which you shall receive with this from the queen' and asks Wolsey to inform Henry that when Mary's dower is confirmed he can take his pick of everything.[3] Henry adored expensive clothing and gems so no doubt this would have been an enticing way of bribing him to forgive them and allow them home. It is possible that the item referred to is in fact the Mirror of Naples.

Wolsey's response (which has been noted in the previous chapter) whilst scathing also offered hope. 'It shall be well done that, with all diligence possible, you and the queen bind yourselves by obligation, to pay yearly to the king, during the queen's life, 4,000l. of her dower; and so you and she shall have remaining of the said dower 6,000l. and above to live withal yearly.'[4] He also added that they were to give Henry all of the plate of gold and jewels which Louis had received and ensure the 200,000 crowns which Francis owed to Mary as her dower was not only paid but handed to Henry. Wolsey warned Brandon to consider the danger they were in if they did not make reparation and the dangers of following alternative counsel on the matter. He also confirmed that he was writing in his own hand without the knowledge of anyone else. In this matter Wolsey was acting as their confidant and friend but it must be assumed that Henry knew exactly what was being communicated. Henry required a way to publicly forgive the couple, avoiding the death penalty for Brandon but satisfying his council who were urging him to behead his best friend and now brother-in-law.

Wolsey had also informed Brandon that there were rumours he had become an instrument of Francis, working for him rather than Henry. France had been the traditional enemy of England so the idea of this would have appalled both Brandon and Henry. There was no way Brandon would allow this rumour to continue and addresses it directly with Henry. Initially, he begs for forgiveness, 'Sire, for the passion of God, let it not be in your heart against me, but promise me rather death, prison, or otherwise, as may be your pleasure'. With regards to being an instrument of Francis, he states, 'Alas, Sire, that ever it should be thought or said that I should be so; for Sire, your grace not offended, I will make good against all the world, to die for it, that if ever I thought any such thing, or ever thought thing, or did thing, saving the love and marriage of the queen, that should be to your displeasure – I pray God, let me die a shameful death as ever did man'.[5]

Mary and Brandon were in an uncertain situation. They were out of favour with Henry, Brandon had expressed that Mary may be pregnant, but to the rest of Europe they were not technically married as the ceremony had been so secret. If Mary was pregnant, they could not risk the child being branded illegitimate so they now had to consider holding a public ceremony but were unsure if this would anger Henry even more. Brandon sought Wolsey's opinion as to whether he should ask Francis, Claude and Louise of Savoy to write once more. Louise of Savoy took matters into her own hands, writing to Henry on 12 March and commending Brandon for his loyalty to Henry.[6] Rather than an act of kindness, Louise of Savoy was likely attempting to have the matter resolved and Mary returned to England. On 31 March 1515, Mary and Brandon were married once more, this time in a more public ceremony. Louise of Savoy recorded the event in her journal, indicating that her previous letter had indeed been an attempt to rid France of Mary's presence as she referred to Brandon as a 'man of low condition'.[7]

Whilst waiting for Henry to respond, there were other matters for the ambassadors to resolve – the arrangements for a meeting between Henry and Francis and the future of Tournay. Francis commissioned John de Selva and Peter de la Guiche to treat with Henry on the renewal of the peace treaty and make arrangements for the payment of one million crowns which had been agreed by Louis XII in the previous treaty.[8] On 4 April, Henry likewise commissioned ambassadors to negotiate the peace treaty. Wolsey, the Duke of Norfolk, the Bishop of Winchester, and John Yonge were commissioned on Henry's behalf; the treaty was agreed the following day in London.[9]

Before they could leave France, Mary and Brandon not only required Henry's permission to travel to England but Mary's dower needed to be settled. On the face of it, due to the agreement made at Abbeville on 8 October 1514, this should have been a straightforward matter. The lands and their revenues settled upon Mary as her appointed dower could not be contested but there were aspects that Francis objected to – namely the gifts Louis had lavished upon Mary, and the items assigned for Mary's lifetime use. If the gifts of plate and jewels had been gifted to her as his wife, they were Mary's to retain, but if they had been gifted to her as queen, they were part of the crown jewels and therefore not Mary's to keep and should be returned to the crown. There was also an expectation that she would be responsible for part of any debts Louis had at the time of his death. With regards to the plate, furniture and other items that Mary was given the right to use for life, Francis opined that this was only if she remained in France and these items should not leave the country. Not willing to concede the plate and jewels and likely realising that Henry's forgiveness would partially be based upon the amount of gifts he would receive,

Brandon and the ambassadors convinced Francis to allow Mary to retain 'one half of the plate of gold, the which is in value 50,000 crowns – for the whole is but 100,000 crowns – and also he will be content to give her in jewels to the sum of 50,000 crowns, the which, by as far as I can perceive, shall be the one half of the jewels'.[10]

Francis had agreed to this as a favour, but at this point was not aware that Mary had already sent some of the jewels, including the Mirror of Naples, back to England. On 9 March, Mary had written and attached her seal to the following promise:

> Be it known to all manner persons that I, Mary Queen of France, sister unto the King of England, Henry the VIIIth, freely give unto the said King my brother all such plate and vessel of clean gold as the late King Loys of France, the XIIth of that name, gave unto me the said Mary his wife; and also, by these presents I do freely give unto my said brother, King of England, the choice of such special jewels as my said late husband King of France gave me: to the performation whereof I bind me by this my bill, whereto with mine howne hand and signed with my name, and to the same have set my sawlle.[11]

The final point of negotiation was Mary's expenses in travelling to Abbeville when she arrived in France. The agreement had stipulated that if Mary survived Louis the expenses incurred would be returned to Henry. Henry, in an effort to extort more money from Francis requested an extortionate amount which was rejected. The ambassadors were forced to accept a counteroffer made by the treasurer of 30,000 crowns which would cover the wages of servants and all other expenses incurred in the few days between Boulogne and Abbeville.[12] With everything agreed, all Mary and Brandon required was Henry's forgiveness, or so they thought. However, Francis found out about the gems sent to England and was furious. He demanded their return, particularly the Mirror of Naples. Francis stated that gem was worth 30,000 crowns alone and he refused to give Mary any other gems or plate until it was returned. Unfortunately for Francis, and fortunately for Henry, Mary had already given written consent that Henry could take his choice of her jewels and plate.

With the negotiations complete the ambassadors asked Francis when Mary could leave. He advised she was free to leave the Saturday after Easter and he himself would be leaving Paris the following Monday. Before Mary could leave she had to finalise her financial affairs. Now married her affairs were also a matter for Brandon and he gave Mary permission to sign the receipts required by Francis.[13] On 14 April she signed receipts for the 20,000 crowns assigned for travel expenses, which were to be paid at 10,000 per year, and 200,000 crowns for her dowry.[14] Two days later she also signed a receipt to confirm she had possession of the Mirror of Naples along with twenty other diamonds 'to serve as a headdress, 8 large pearls as buttons for the sleeves, 8 others for a carcanet, a large emerald, a large ruby and 2 large diamonds'.[15] The receipts were witnessed by the English ambassadors and French notaries. In addition, Mary acquiesced to the request of Francis to transfer the ability to nominate individuals to 'royal offices' within her dower lands to the grand master.[16] This would save Mary having to be concerned with appointments once she was back in England and allowed Francis to retain some measure of control over the lands.

Though Mary was out of favour with Henry and the French were now eager for her to leave, she was queen dowager and retained some degree of power. That others still perceived her as a woman of power and influence is evident in the receipt of a letter by Isabella of Aragon. Isabella was the widow of Frederick, king of Naples. He had lost his throne to Ferdinand and Louis and since his death Isabella and her children had fled their country and travelled around Europe relying on the hospitality of others. Her eldest son, also called Ferdinand, had been captured and was held prisoner in Barcelona and Isabella was relying on Mary's influence with Henry to have him released and returned to her.[17]

Mary finally left Paris on 16 April, travelling towards Calais. Louise of Savoy recorded Mary's departure in her journal, 'Marie d'Angleterre, widow of Louis XII, left Paris with her husband, the Duke of Suffolk, to return to England'.[18] Francis accompanied Mary as far as St Denis and some of the nobility were to escort her as far as Boulogne. Though Francis had promised Mary a parting gift, he was still unhappy about losing the Mirror of Naples and only gifted her four rings 'of no great value'.[19] On the day she left, the new peace treaty was proclaimed in Paris and bonfires were lit in celebration.[20]

Having still not received a response from Henry, Brandon wrote a further two letters. On 22 April he wrote from Montreuil, offering himself up for punishment, 'I will yield myself unto your grace's hands, to do with my poor body your grace's pleasure', but he cleverly makes an statement that he trusts Henry will not bend to the will of his council who Brandon is aware 'are clearly determined to tempt your grace that I may either be put to death, or be put in prison, and so to be destroyed'. Knowing Henry is not someone to be told what to do he plays on this trait by adding that he does not fear the malice of the council, 'for I know your grace of such nature, that it cannot be in their powers to cause you to destroy me for their malice; but what punishment soever I have,

I shall thank God and your grace of it, and think that I have well deserved it'.[21] Knowing Mary's skill in rhetoric, it is possible she assisted Brandon in penning this, ensuring Henry is reminded that he is the king, he makes the decisions, and the council cannot tell him what to do. This was an intelligent way of swaying Henry towards Mary and Brandon and away from his council purely because they were attempting to tell him what to do.

Mary and Brandon reached Calais on 30 April, where she wrote once more to her brother:

> Dearest brother, I doubt not but that you have in your good remembrance that whereas, for the good of peace and for the furtherance of your affairs, you desired me to marry with my lord and late husband, King Louis of France, whose soul God pardon; though I understood that he was very aged and sickly, yet for the advancement of the said peace, and for the furtherance of your causes, I was contented to conform myself to your said motion, so that, if I should fortune to survive the said late king, I might, with your good will, marry myself at my liberty, without your displeasure. Whereunto good brother, you condescended and granted, as you well know, promising unto me that in such case you would never provoke or move me, but as mine own heart and mind should be best pleased; and that wheresoever I should dispose myself, you would wholly be contented with the same. And upon that your good comfort and faithful promise, I assented to the said marriage, which else I would never have granted to, as at the same time I showed unto you more at large.[22]

Mary is effectively telling Henry that he made a promise and he needs to keep it. She is stating she would never have agreed to marry Louis without that promise and more so, there is a hint here that she had already told Henry where her heart really lay. She confirms to Henry that she is now in Calais awaiting his instructions and will make Calais her home until she hears from Henry and will not enter England without his permission. As Calais was under English jurisdiction, Henry could have had the pair arrested.

This letter is clearly one which would have been shared with the Privy Council and Mary dictated the letter to Brian Tuke, a secretary of Wolsey, knowing this. The existent letter is a draft which has been corrected by Wolsey, indicating his attempts to assist the couple in gaining forgiveness whilst also appeasing the council; Wolsey knew more than most how to construct letters suitable for the council. Mary does not specifically mention that she has already married Brandon and instead writes as if she is requesting permission to do so:

> Now that God hath called my said late husband to his mercy, and that I am at my liberty, dearest brother, remembering the great virtues which I have seen and perceived heretofore in my lord of Suffolk, to whom I have always been of good mind, as you well know, I have affixed and clearly determined myself to marry with him; and the same [I] assure you hath proceeded only of my own mind, without any request or labour of my said lord of Suffolk, or any other person. And to be plain with your grace, I have so bound myself unto him that for no cause earthly I will or may vary or change from the same.[23]

Mary is ensuring the council can in no way blame Brandon for the marriage. She accepts full blame but offers Henry an opportunity to grant his approval and welcome them home without admitting publicly that they had married without his consent. To entice Henry further to allow them home Mary confirms the debt they are willing to pay, as suggested by Wolsey, writing, 'I am contented and expressly promise and bind me to you, by these presents, to give you all the whole dote (dowry) which was delivered with me, and also all such plate of gold and jewels as I shall have of my late husband's. Over and besides this I shall, rather than fail, give you as much yearly part of my dower, to as great a sum as shall stand with your will and pleasure; and all the premises I promise, upon knowledge of your good mind, to make unto you sufficient bond.'[24] Henry finally relented and Mary and Brandon sailed from Calais to Dover on 2 May 1515. There must have been a real feeling of apprehension regarding the welcome they would receive.

Chapter Eleven

Duchess of Suffolk

Arriving in Dover, they travelled to meet Wolsey who then accompanied them to Birling for the face-to-face showdown with Henry. Henry rode out to meet the party and welcomed Mary 'as cordially and affectionately as he possibly could, rejoicing greatly in her honourable return, and great prosperity'.[1] This record comes from a set of instructions issued to Sir William Sidney which he was to convey to Francis, so of course it could be exaggerated, but Henry had not only gained the return of his best friend and favourite sister, but also a huge amount of wealth; he had every reason to rejoice. The party continued to Birling manor where they planned to stay overnight.

Whilst Mary may have been the favourite sister of Henry, this did not mean he completely forgave her, at least not as far as the Privy Council were concerned. Henry had to play the game and act like an incensed king and brother, otherwise every other courtier may think the rules no longer applied to them either. On 11 May an indenture was formalised regarding the financial obligations of Mary and Brandon towards Henry. The other details, which were previously agreed, were also formalised including the payment of the 200,000 crowns from Francis and the jewels and plate Mary had received from Louis. Brandon also resigned the wardship of Lady Lisle in favour of the Earl and Countess of Devon.[2] The indenture is recorded in June 1515, within the *Recognizances for the Repayment of Loans*. The entry states that: 'Mary the French Queen and Charles, Duke of Suffolk have indented with the King, that, for the release of 5,000l (£3,313,824) of the Duke's debts, the King or his assigns shall receive 1,000l (£662,764) in crowns of gold at Calais on 1 Nov., and 1,000l. on 1 May every year, till 24,000l. be paid: and the French Queen also gives the King 200 crowns, the moiety of her dowry'.[3] Mary's income from France as dowager queen provided the bulk of the couple's income, over double Brandon's yearly income.

It was determined that Mary and Brandon should be married yet again, this time in England. The previous ceremonies had been conducted either during Lent (which was forbidden without a licence) or performed without the banns being read, which also was forbidden without a licence from the Pope. A third ceremony, which would be solemnised correctly, with banns read and in the presence of witnesses would remove any future accusations of illegitimate children born to the union and would ensure Mary retained her honour. There was also the matter that although the courtiers would have all known of the marriage, the general population had no idea that their Tudor princess was once again married. The third ceremony gave Henry an opportunity to celebrate the union and be perceived as the kind, generous brother and monarch. Therefore, on 13 May 1515, in the presence of Henry VIII, Katharine of Aragon, and much of the nobility and ecclesiastical men of England, Mary and Brandon married once more at Greenwich. The wedding was celebrated with a tournament; both Henry and Brandon participating. Henry and Brandon were both excellent sportsman and often competed against one another or on the same team, Brandon's companionship in sports would have been another reason Henry would have been pleased to have his friend back.

Francis was reliant on the favour he had done for Mary and Brandon to influence Henry regarding the one million crowns he owed him, payable at 50,000 crowns per year. On 28 May 1515 he requested Brandon help him intercede with Henry and request he delay the next payment due to the financial constraints he was facing whilst in Italy.[4] Just as Francis hoped Brandon would assist him, Mary and Brandon in turn were reliant upon Francis for Mary's income from her French lands. The debt arrangement with Henry had been based on Wolsey's estimation that Mary would receive 10,000l per year. Paying Henry 2,000l a year would leave the couple with 8,000l. Unfortunately this was a gross over estimation, her revenues were actually approximately 6,000l per year, leaving them only 4,000l. The years between 1526 and 1533 were the most beneficial for Mary with regards to her dowager income. Mary was possibly receiving over 8000l per year inclusive of payments towards the arrears. This meant Mary's income as Dowager Queen of France was received regularly, unlike previous years when her income had been slow in arriving or simply stopped for a period of time. Being reliant on France would have made it difficult to keep up regular payments to Henry.

In an effort to ensure Mary had some independence regardless of her French income, Brandon settled upon Mary a life jointure on his lands held in Suffolk, which was ratified by parliament in 1515. The couple's fortunes would take a turn for the better when Brandon was granted some of the lands that had previously belonged to Anne Plantagenet, daughter of Edward IV. The lands had been held by her widower husband, the Earl of Surrey, until Henry settled the reversion of the lands upon Brandon.[5] Now settled back in England, Mary wished for her stepdaughters, Anne and Mary, to reside with them. As Anne was in the household of Margaret of Austria, Brandon wrote to Margaret on 30 May thanking Margaret for the placement and advised he had despatched Sir Edward Guildford and William Wodale to escort his daughter back to England.[6] Mary also retained some of those who had been in her service in France including one of the sisters of the Marquess of Dorset (Anne or Elizabeth, whilst the other remained in France); Lady Anne Jerningham; George Brooke; and Richard Manners. As theirs was a royal household, others flocked to try and join their service. One of those was the future Lord Stourton, William, who declares himself as 'Mary's servant', though he was employed within the Brandon household; this shows his respect for Mary.[7]

Although there is only a little evidence available regarding the relationship between Mary and her elder sister, Margaret, Queen of Scots (by this time queen dowager), once back in England Mary did make an effort to assist her sister who was struggling to protect herself and her children against John Stewart, 2nd Duke of Albany, who allegedly had his sights set on the throne of Scotland as the nearest male relative to the young king. Margaret's eldest son was now King James V of Scotland though still a minor, therefore Margaret had initially been appointed as regent until she married Archibald Douglas, 6th Earl of Angus, in 1514. This marriage alienated much of the nobility and also lost her the regency as the will of James IV stated she was to act as regent only whilst she remained a widow. Albany was chosen to replace Margaret as regent. Margaret had been requesting assistance from Henry since at least January 1515 and Henry had responded by threatening war upon Scotland. Margaret had also lost her right to supervise her sons but she did not take that lightly and took her children to Stirling Castle, refusing to hand them over. Albany arrived in England from France on 17 May 1515 and sought custody of the two young boys. Margaret refused but he took the boys away from her anyway and denied Margaret regular access to the king and prince. Henry had been urging Margaret to secretly leave and travel to England with her sons but now she had no access to her sons he urged her to come alone.

Having met Albany during her time in France, Mary took the initiative to write to him requesting he treat her sister and nephews kindly. She also encouraged Brandon, now back in favour with Henry, to do the same. Mary did receive a favourable response, 'touching the queen of Scotland your sister, I swear to you by my faith that for my part I have done and will do her all the pleasure and service by me possible'.[8] That would not be the end of the matter. A couple of months later, in July, Henry agreed that Scotland be included in the peace treaty between England and France but refused to accept Albany as regent as this was detrimental to his own sister.[9] He was also aware that Albany, having grown up in France, was under the influence of Francis and therefore would be biased against England. This put Mary in a precarious position; she could not afford to upset Francis but obviously would want the best for her sister. Henry would also have been aware that by rejecting Albany he was risking Mary's income and as a result the ability for Mary and Brandon to repay their debt.

Mary and Brandon were still at court during May 1515. It is apparent Henry was enjoying having the pair back, Brandon for his sportsmanship, and Mary as the jewel of the court who had always partnered Henry in dancing and entertainments. Henry, Katharine of Aragon, Mary and Brandon, amongst other courtiers, celebrated May Day with a picnic on Shooter's Hill where they were entertained by Robin Hood and his Merry Men. That summer whilst Henry went on royal progress, Mary and Brandon spent time visiting their own residences in Suffolk. This would have been the first opportunity Mary had to see her new places of residence and show herself to the local residents. The local people of Yarmouth were pleased to welcome Mary, so much so that Mary stayed for three days and promised to influence Henry to visit the town. June of this year also saw Brandon granted a new appointment which would increase his income by 6l 13s 4d a year. He was appointed as steward of the manors of 'Snytterfeld, Budbroke, Hampton-super-Montem, Haseley, and Hatton', as well as possessions across various counties which were previously owned by Richard Beauchamp, Earl of Warwick, and were now in the possession of the crown.[10]

As summer ended and Henry returned from progress, Mary and Brandon returned to London to stay at Bath Place, a property in the possession of Wolsey. Henry, occupied by ship building, aroused French suspicions and they questioned who the target was of Henry's ships. Brandon managed to diffuse the situation explaining that Henry's new ship was purely for his own interests and to entertain the queen and Mary. In support of this, Mary accompanied Henry and Katharine on a ship to Greenwich in October. Mary was also given the honour of christening Henry's new ship on 1 November 1515. Henry, ever the entertainer, took to the role of galley master, dressing as a sailor. He had a gold whistle that when he used it, musicians began to play, after which all those on board observed Mass performed by the Bishop of Durham. Following Mass, Mary was led forward by Henry and she gave the ship the name of 'The Virgin Mary'. It is no wonder the French were concerned; the ship boasted 207 guns and could carry up to 1000 men.[11]

In the meantime, Margaret was almost eight months pregnant and had requested permission from Albany to travel to Linlithgow for her confinement, which he approved. He would come to regret that decision as Margaret had secretly made plans with Henry that she would leave there after a couple of days with only a few unknowing servants and seek safety in England, with Lord Dacre meeting her at the border. Margaret successfully reached Harbottle

Castle but went into labour prematurely, giving birth on 7 October 1515. The child was a daughter, named Margaret Douglas, the future mother-in-law of Mary, Queen of Scots. Albany wrote to Margaret offering her the restitution of her jewels if she returned to Scotland but she declined and remained at Harbottle until she was sufficiently recovered to travel to Morpeth to await Henry's summons.[12]

Whilst Margaret was recovering from childbirth, Mary was the centre of attention at court. Wolsey received his cardinal's hat and in celebration hosted a magnificent banquet at Hampton Court Palace on Sunday, 18 November 1515. Mary and Brandon were both guests and enjoyed a lavish feast and a series of entertainments courtesy of the newly elected Cardinal of York. Mary herself was pregnant at this point as was her sister-in-law, Katharine of Aragon. Wolsey offered his Bath Place residence to Mary for her confinement. As the couple were in London in November it is likely they spent Christmas and New Year with Henry and Katharine of Aragon.

On Tuesday, 11 March 1516, between 10:00 and 11:00 p.m., Mary gave birth to her first child. The baby was a boy named Henry, providing a male heir for Brandon and despite the birth of Henry's daughter, Mary (the future Mary I), just a month earlier on 18 February 1516, the newborn Brandon heir also placed them even closer to the throne, a fact that would not have gone unnoticed by Henry and Brandon. Despite Mary and Brandon achieving Henry's greatest desire, he does not appear to have reacted negatively and not only attended the christening on 20 March but accepted the role of godfather to his nephew. The christening took place at Bath Place and the event was recorded in detail. The hall from the nursery to the chapel was hung with arras and cloth of gold, whilst 100 torchbearers lined the sides of the hall and a further twelve gentlemen stood inside bearing torches. The altar was draped with embroidered cloth of gold and a set of steps placed in front of it with cushions for the godparent's comfort when kneeling. A crimson satin canopy embroidered with the sun in splendour emblem of York, the Tudor rose, and Mary's arms, was held over the font which contained the holy water that was kept lukewarm by two esquires:

> ... the young lord was conveyed to the porch from the nursey, with many noblemen as esquires, knights and lords. Then followed the basin, borne by Thomas Bourser, the taper borne by Anthony Saint Amand, the slat borne by lord Cobham, and my Lady Elizabeth Gray bearing the chrisom; my Lady Anne Gray bearing the child, the young lord, was assisted by the Lord Dacres, chamberlain to the French queen, and the Lord Edward Gray; the Lord Dacres at the head, and the Lord Gray at the foot, and the train borne

> by Sir Humphrey Banister, the chamberlain, and four torches borne about the young lord by four esquires. Then followed the Lady Shelton, lady mistress, and the nurse somewhat behind her. And so after them, other ladies and gentlemen, every one of them in their degree, to the number of forty; they all well and richly apparelled; the king's grace, the lord cardinal, the Lady Catherine, godfathers and godmother at the font – the Bishop of Durham, godfather at the bishoping, the king giving the name Henry. The bishop that did the ceremonies at the christening was the Bishop of Rochester, assisted with divers other prelates.[13]

Lady Catherine was Catherine of York, the Countess of Devon. She was the daughter of Edward IV and therefore aunt to Mary and Henry. Gifts were offered by the churchmen and godparents including, 'the king's gift borne next afore the child by Sir John Peter, that is to say, a salt of gold and a cup of gold; the lord cardinal's gift borne by his steward, which was two flagons of silver and gilt; the Lady Catherine's gift borne by her chamberlain, the which was two plain pots of silver and gilt; the Bishop of Durham's gift borne by his own serjeant, which was two pounsed pots of silver and gilt'.[14] After the ceremony, those in attendance were served spiced wine before they returned to the nursery where Mary was waiting having not attended the service as per the custom at the time. Although we do not have any details, Mary would have followed the common practices of the time which saw women with the financial ability to do so, remain resting in their chambers for a few weeks after childbirth. This was known as lying-in.

Mary recovered sufficiently in time to return to the court a few weeks later, when the three Tudor siblings were reunited. Mary had not seen her sister for thirteen years since she had left for Scotland on 24 June 1503. Henry finally summoned her from Morpeth on 8 April 1516; he was urged to do so as Margaret was growing frustrated and was beginning to listen to Albany and considering returning to Scotland. On 3 May 1516, Margaret arrived at Baynard's Castle and was conveyed from there to Greenwich where, according to Hall, she was 'receaved joyously of the kyng, the quene, the Frenche quene her syster'.[15] The royal court would have witnessed three queens together, possibly with their three young children. In honour of Margaret, Henry arranged a magnificent feast on the day of her arrival followed by two days of jousting, beginning on 19 May. Henry, Brandon, the Earl of Essex and Nicholas Carew defended against all comers, after which they all retired to Katharine's chambers to feast. Margaret spent almost the next year in England, dividing her time between Baynard's Castle and wherever the court was staying but when she finally left England, the sisters would never see each other again. It was alleged that Margaret was left in almost poverty whilst Mary was treated very kindly and lovingly by Henry, but it should be noted that Mary had her own residence, income and would attend court largely when Henry was entertaining so she was not around him all of the time incurring expenses. Mary and Brandon left court and retired to their estates in Suffolk shortly after the entertainments to welcome Margaret were concluded.

On 13 June 1516, Mary arrived at Butley Priory for the first (at least the first recorded) of many visits. Mary travelled without Brandon but with a retinue of servants and her chaplain. Religious houses at the time were expected to offer hospitality; to have royalty visit them would increase their reputation and encourage others to visit and offer patronage. Privileged and honoured by her visit, the abbey kept a record of the visit. Mary is noted as 'the most excellent Lady Mary, Queen of France, the most beautiful and beloved sister of our most invincible King Henry VIII, and wife of the most excellent Charles Brandon, Duke of Suffolk'. The record then goes on to describe how Mary was received:

> First, a stool was placed with a silken covering and two silken cushions, opposite the gates of our cemetery: then the prior and convent, in silken capes, preceded by the cross-bearer, taper-bearer, and incense-bearer, marched to the said stool; where, when the prelate had arrived, he first knelt down with his servants, then sprinkled holy water over her chaplain, then over himself, and lastly, over the said queen.[16]

After hearing Mass, Mary offered a gold noble to the abbey before retiring to an apartment within the convent accommodations that had been made ready for her use. The following day Mary departed but not before hearing Mass once more and offering another golden noble. Mary had made a good impression on those at the abbey and likewise they had also gained an influential and powerful supporter.

Mary returned to court towards the end of the summer but would soon be seeking to leave again. Henry, up to this point had not pressed the matter of the repayments but as he himself needed money to fill the treasury coffers, he wanted to call in debts. Brandon was top of the list as not a single payment had been made towards their debts.[17] He had also borrowed 200l from George Talbot, 4th Earl of Shrewsbury and had to apologise for only being to repay half of the debt due to having to pay Henry but he vowed to pay as soon as he received the money owed from France. In an effort to reduce expenses incurred from staying at court, Mary and Brandon sought to retire to their estates but unfortunately Mary fell ill and could not travel. Accommodations at court were planned and co-ordinated meticulously. Unless serving, or approved by Henry, those residing at court had to pay for their upkeep. The numbers of those at court also impacted the planning of food, drink and other necessities. Food, drink and other allowances such as candles, the number of servants, horses, and dogs one could bring were all dependent upon rank. To change plans for leaving court would need to be communicated and that is what Brandon had to do. Writing to Wolsey he explained that 'the French queen's grace cannot depart from the court so soon as was appointed; for, Sir, it hath pleased God to visit her with an ague, the which has taken her grace, every third day, four times very sharp; but by the grace of God she shall shortly recover; for, Sir, the king's grace's physicians takes marvellous good heed unto her grace, and also specially his grace comforts her, so like a good and loving sovereign lord and brother, that it takes away a great part of her pain'.[18] This 'ague' appears to be one which would become recurring for the remainder of Mary's life. As she was not in good health, it is doubtful Henry would have enforced charges on her to stay at court and it appears he spent time comforting Mary, despite his dislike of illness.

It appears Henry was initially unhappy with the fact Mary and Brandon could not afford the repayments and both had stayed away from court since Mary was able to travel but Henry requested Brandon's presence in September 1516. Mary, grateful for Henry's request to see Brandon, wrote to him from the priory of Letheringham in Suffolk. Mary does not indicate if she is visiting the priory for enjoyment or for respite. She communicates that Brandon is 'marvellously rejoiced, and much comforted that it hath liked your grace so to be pleased; for the which your special goodness to him, showed in that behalf, and for sundry and many other your kindness, as well to me as to him, showed in divers causes, I most humbly thank your grace'. Mary flatters Henry but it should also be noted that to be away from court was a risk, there were few opportunities to be gained being away from Henry's presence so it would have been a relief to be called into his presence. She noted that Henry was going to be at Brandon's manor of Donnington and Brandon was to join him there, and states, 'if it had been time convenient, and your grace had been therewith pleased, I would most gladly have accompanied my said lord in this journey'. She ends by asking beseeching 'our Lord to send unto you, my most dearest and best beloved sister, the queen's grace, and to the Queen of Scots, my well beloved sister, trusting that I be ascertained from your grace of the prosperous estate and health of my dearly beloved niece the princess, to whom I pray God send long life'.[19] The self-imposed exile must have affected Henry as he agreed to reduce the repayments and also agreed that they only had to pay when Mary was receiving her revenues from France.[20] Due to the infrequency of payments this would have been a relief for the couple.

There is no record of Mary returning to court over the next few months but in March 1517, Mary and Brandon were entertaining Mary's sister-in-law, Katharine of Aragon. Katharine wished to make a pilgrimage to Our Lady of Walsingham and the couple chose to meet the queen and accompany her. Brandon met with Katharine at Pickenham Wood whilst Mary met the party a little further along the route. Unfortunately, on the way to Walsingham, there would be an event that found Brandon once more seeking the advice of Wolsey and anticipating that he would be blamed by Henry. Brandon reports that on 16 March, Mistress Jerningham had been in the presence of Mary before Katharine arrived. Afterwards she called her daughter-in-law, Lady Anne Grey and John Berkeley, heir of Lord Berkeley and had them betrothed. Lady Anne Grey was a lady-in-waiting to Mary and had been with her in France and remained with her on her return. John Berkeley was a ward of the crown and had been placed with Brandon 'to put him to my rule and guiding.'[21] As a royal ward, Henry's consent was required for Berkeley to marry and Brandon would have been fearful that the blame would be placed firmly at his feet for allowing this to happen within his household. Luckily for Brandon, Henry did not blame him and in fact requested his company for the May day celebrations. Brandon responds that he would be content to participate but advises that he is 'somewhat unprovided of such things as belong to that busines'. It is possible he is referring to jousting equipment. He then requests that 'if it may stand with your grace's pleasure, I would bring up the queen your sister against Easter, to both plays, and then to remain, till she and I may know you grace's further pleasure'.[22] With permission granted the couple travelled to court.

A couple of months later in May, Mary and Brandon were once more under pressure. The relief offered in regard to their debt repayment a few months earlier was snatched away from them when not only were the repayments reinstated but Brandon was ordered to pay a further 500 marks per year regardless of whether or not Mary was receiving her income from France. The usual forty-day allowance to pay was also reduced to two weeks. Their court expenses of 600l were added to the total and Mary had to promise not to return her dower to Francis upon her death and all her remaining jewels and plate were to be inherited by the crown.[23] Mary sent Henry 2,000l worth of jewels and plate which seemed to placate him, at least for a while. In the same month Mary used her influence, along with Margaret who was still at court and Katharine of Aragon, to intercede with Henry on behalf of rebels who committed crimes on 'evil May-day'.[24] Riots had broken out in London and the businesses, homes and persons of 'foreigners' were attacked. Having three queens beg for their pardon was too difficult to ignore and Henry acquiesced pardoning the majority, though a few were hung for their offences.

The following month, Henry hosted entertainment at Greenwich in honour of the ambassadors present in England to celebrate the new treaty between Emperor Maximilian, Prince Charles and himself. The ambassadors were welcomed by Henry, 'The King was dressed in stiff brocade in the Hungarian fashion, having a collar of inestimable value around his neck. The Queens, (Katharine of Arragon and Mary Tudor, Queen Dowager of France), the Dukes, the Marquis (of Dorset), and other barons all arrayed in cloth of gold, with chains around their necks; everything glittered with gold.'[25] The ambassadors were maintained at court at Henry's expense and invited to dinner daily by various men of the court. The main entertainment was the joust held on 7 July, a few days after their arrival.

Apostolic nuncio, Francesco Chieregato, recorded the event in a latter to Isabella, Marchioness of Mantua:

> The place where the jousts were held is a tiltyard made expressly for such exhibitions, three times the size of the Piazza di San Pietro at Mantua, enclosed with a wall, and having stands (poggioli) for the spectators. At one end of the yard two spacious tents of cloth of gold were pitched side by side, and the first person who appeared was Sir Edward Gylforde, the brother of him who went to Mantua. He and his horse were sumptuously arrayed in cloth of gold with a raised pile, and he wore a chain worth upwards of 2,000 ducats; he was accompanied by 40 footmen, all dressed alike, in a livery of silk. This individual was superintendent of the joust; and 24 trumpeters followed him, all clad alike, in frocks of cloth of silver with a raised pile, and caps of white velvet. Next came 40 gentlemen in similar frocks and caps; every one of them, however, wearing a gold chain of five fingers' breadth around his neck, upwards of 2,000 ducats having been melted to make each of these chains, whose design presented an H and a K, the initial letters of the King and Queen. The horses were all white, and all caparisoned alike, having cost the King a mint of money, as during the last four months all the London goldsmiths have wrought nothing but these trappings. The bridles, pectorals, girths, and cruppers of the horses, together with the pommels of the saddles, were of pure silver, on which were chiseled all the royal emblems, none of the materials being either of leather or silk.
>
> These 40 gentlemen carried the King's spears, and were followed by 14 jousters, great personages, whose horses were preciously caparisoned, each with new fashions different from the

others. Each jouster was accompanied by 24 running footmen, dressed in silk livery. Then came 12 heralds, also in white frocks, with their tabards as usual, preceding 100 running footmen, also clad in white cloth of silver with a raised pile, in the midst of whom was the King in armour, with his helmet on his head. His surcoat of cloth of silver, with a raised pile, was wrought throughout with emblematic letters, the stop to every letter consisting of a pearl, each of which was worth from 30 to 40 ducats. The bridle and pectoral were studded with jewels, valued at 300,000 ducats.

The King having made the usual display in the lists, the Duke of Suffolk entered from the other end of them, with well nigh equal array and pomp, accompanied by 14 other jousters, all great person-ages, in rich array, like those on the King's side. After they had made their procession, the King wanted to joust with all of them; but this was forbidden by his Council, which moreover decreed that each jouster was to run six courses and no more, so that the entertainment might be ended on that day, by reason of the speedy departure of the ambassadors.

The competitor assigned to the King was the Duke of Suffolk aforesaid; and they bore themselves so bravely that the spectators fancied themselves witnessing a joust between Hector and Achilles. The others then jousted in succession, according to their rank, until the close; when the King, accompanied by the Duke, and by his company of running footmen, went to disarm; after which he was reconducted into the lists with the trumpeters, followed by 24 pages, who, as well as their horses, were clad in one livery, half gold brocade with a raised pile, and the other half blue velvet, both halves being embroidered with little bells. The King appeared with a similar frock (saglio) on a tall white horse, trapped from head to foot with little bells, as aforesaid, without any more brocade, and on his head a very large feather (penacchio) quite full of jewels. All these horses were very handsome and big, including those given by the Marquis [of Mantua]. On arriving in the lists the King presented himself before the Queens and the ladies, making a thousand jumps in the air; and after tiring one horse, he entered the tent and mounted another of those ridden by the pages; doing thus constantly, and reappearing in the lists until the end of the joust.[26]

Another report states that Brandon honoured Mary by having him and his companions dressed in 'white velvet and crimson satin, lozenged, and set full of the letters C. M.', for Charles and Mary, embroidered in gold.[27] Later that day the guests were welcomed to a banquet where Mary and Katharine of Aragon flanked Henry at the head table, the Duke of Luxembourg was honoured with the position on Mary's left, whilst Wolsey took the left of Katharine. Chieregato continues with compliments of the English court, 'In short, the wealth and civilization of the world are here; and those who call the English barbarians appear to me to render themselves such. I here perceive very elegant manners, extreme decorum, and very great politeness'.[28] Mary was part of that image, not only in her appearance and attire but her position as dowager queen of France. The account of the apostolic nuncio goes on to conclude that after the banquet, Henry and the guests 'danced with the ladies until daybreak'.[29] Being pregnant, we do not know how much Mary participated in the dancing but as she regularly partnered Henry, it is doubtful she chose to sit out and miss all the fun. Mary was still at court on 1 August but as Henry and Katharine were departing on progress the following day due to the sweating sickness being in London, it is likely Mary also left the next day.[30] The royal family escaped the sweating sickness but Wolsey did not, though he was extremely lucky to survive something that killed so many.

After the entertainments Mary left, travelling towards Walsingham Priory, likely to pray for a safe birth. On her way she had to call into the home of the Bishop of Ely, Nicholas West, at Hatfield due to her labour starting. On Thursday, 16 July 1517, only a few days after leaving court, Mary gave birth. This time it was a baby girl named Frances in honour of her birth day – St Francis' Day – and possibly as a recognition of Francis I and the assistance he had provided the couple, or at least an attempt to remain amicable with the French king, and therefore encourage him to maintain payment of Mary's revenues. Another magnificent christening took place to honour the new royal child. Once more a canopy depicting Mary's arms, Tudor roses, the sun in splendour, and fleur-de-lis was suspended above the font and the walls were hung with tapestries featuring Hercules and Holofernes. The baby was carried by Lady Verney with the assistance of Lord Powys, who were preceded by those bearing the chrisom, tapers, and basin, whilst eight gentlemen bearing torches surrounded Lady Verney. The remainder of the procession of ladies and gentlemen followed. Inside the church, eighty yeomen lined the way bearing torches.[31] The service was officiated by Sir Oliver Poole with the assistance of chaplains in Brandon's service. On this occasion, Henry was not asked to be godfather, instead the Abbot of St Albans was given the honour. Being a girl, Frances was required to have two godmothers and one godfather (her brother had one godmother and two godfathers). The godmothers of Frances Brandon were Katharine of Aragon and her daughter, Princess Mary. Neither could attend and sent Lady Elizabeth Grey in place of Princess Mary and Lady Boleyn in place of Katharine of Aragon. This is believed to have been Elizabeth Boleyn, mother to Mary and Anne Boleyn, or possibly Anne Boleyn, wife of Edward Boleyn.[32]

The following month, Brandon was still in favour, Henry granted him the wardship of two boys whose father had been their friend, Sir Thomas Knyvet.[33] Knyvet had died at sea fighting the French in 1512. The wardships were sold to Brandon at a low cost indicating Henry's favour and also increasing the income of the Brandon household. The remainder of the year appears to have been spent away from court. Plague was reported in London in November and much of the court business suspended until after Christmas, though Henry was still meeting with ambassadors outside of the city. It is likely Mary and Brandon spent Christmas at their own estates away from London.[34] Even though she was not with Henry, she did send New Years' gifts including a gift for her niece which Henry paid 20s to 'The French Queen's servant, bringing a pomander of gold to the Princess'.[35]

In March 1518, there were reports that Henry intended to betroth Princess Mary to the Dauphin of France, son of Francis I, also named Francis.[36] The following month, Easter was spent at Abingdon with Henry. Their departure from court was delayed once more due to Mary's health and as summer started, they were staying at Elmswell, the manor of Bury St Edmunds Abbey. Mary remained there when Brandon was called away to Enfield on business towards the end of July 1518. Brandon then travelled to the estate of Wanstead where he was the appointed keeper. Henry was staying there and when asked by Wolsey to return to London, Brandon refused stating Henry wished him to remain.[37] By August, Henry was back in Lambeth where it is thought negotiations were ongoing with France relating to the betrothal and the return of Tournai; the terms being that Henry would pay 300,000 crowns as a dower for Princess Mary and King Francis would pay the same for Tournai in annual payments of 25,000.[38]

More ambassadors arrived from France in July, this time with a proposal of marriage. After initial negotiations, Francis despatched a more senior delegation. The French embassy was led by Bonnivet, Lord High Admiral of France, who entered London on 23 September 1518. They travelled to Greenwich two days later for an audience with Henry, to discuss the proposed marriage between Princess Mary and the Dauphin of France. Whilst the ambassadors were busy with Henry and his council, the rest of the court 'danced and passed the time in the queen's chamber, with ladies', no doubt including Mary who had travelled to Greenwich with Brandon.[39] The peace treaty was proclaimed on 3 October at St Paul's Church. Wolsey gave Mass, after which the articles of the treaty were read and sworn to by both parties. After the ceremonies, all went to dine before further festivities later in the day at the home of Wolsey – York Place. The guests were entertained with a masque featuring twelve ladies and twelve gentlemen dressed in 'green satin, decorated with cloth of gold'.[40] The pairs removed their masks after performing several dances. The leading gentleman was of course Henry, and the leading lady, Mary, whilst Brandon accompanied Lady Daubeney. The dancers then sat to dine before the whole party was provided with dice and money to gamble and the dancing recommenced for the remainder of the evening.

The betrothal of Princess Mary took place on 5 October at Greenwich. The attendees were greeted by Henry standing in front of his throne, once more flanked by Katharine and Mary whilst Princess Mary stood in front of her mother, 'dressed in cloth of gold, with a cap of black velvet on her head, adorned with many costly jewels'.[41] After an oration by Cuthbert Tunstall, Henry and Katharine gave permission for the marriage and Mary was presented with a ring by Wolsey before she was blessed. Mass was then sung before the court went to feast. Henry accepted the expenses on this occasion for Mary and her household as it was to his benefit to have her presence at court.[42] A celebratory joust was held two days later, followed by another sumptuous banquet. Mary sat to the left of Henry with Cardinal Campeggio to her left. After feasting on comfits, swans, larks, peacocks, eggs, and other dishes, a pageant began. Katharine retired as she was pregnant but Mary remained for the entertainment. The pageant was full of symbols about the union between France and England.[43] For Mary, it must have brought memories of her reception in France.

A further indenture was recorded in 1518, possibly whilst Mary was at court for the ongoing proceedings of the betrothal of her niece. The indenture is recorded as: 'for 24,000l. due by them at Calais; 600l. for their diets in the King's house; also, 2,301l. 1d.: whereof 20,000l. is the "proper debt" of the French Queen, and 6,901l. 1d. the debt of the Duke. The King has received from them, in jewels, 1,666l. 13s. 4d.; and will receive the rest by instalments of 1,000 marks at Mich., and the same at Easter each year, "if the French Queen so long shall live and the Duck togeders"'.[44]

The following March, Henry hosted another entertainment for the French who were in England as hostages to ensure Francis made the agreed payments. The group, including Mary, were entertained by a comedy of Plautus before Henry, Mary and Brandon left the chamber. Eight ladies with masks entered the chamber 'in blacke veluet bordred about with gold, with hoopes tro the wast douneward, and sleues ruffed and plited at the elbowe and plain in the middes, full of cuttes, plucked out at euery cutte with fine Camericke, and tired like to the Egipcians very richely'.[45] Eight men then entered, all being masqued. After dancing, the sixteen removed their masks to reveal Mary, Henry and Brandon as part of the entertainers, much to the delight of the court. The following day was another joust; Henry and eight of his companions fought against Brandon and another eight men, all being commended by the French hostages.

The records for the remainder of 1519 are quiet on Mary but it is thought she gave birth to her second daughter, Eleanor Brandon, sometime in 1519. Unfortunately little is known about the birth or christening though it can be assumed the christening followed a similar pattern to that of Frances Brandon two years earlier. By early 1520, Mary is at Croydon and unwell, causing concern to Brandon who wrote to Wolsey regarding his absence from court. In his letter of 16 March he explains that Mary has been visited by a number of physicians but is not yet restored. He continues that on the two occasions he had travelled to London to visit Wolsey, Mary had recalled him home but now she was recovering, he hoped to visit within the next few days.[46] In a further undated letter we witness Brandon's clear affection for his wife when he explains to Wolsey that Mary is now worse than before and 'has taken such a phantasy that she thinks that she should not do well, without she should come up to London for remedy; insomuch that she weeps everyday and takes so on that I am afraid it should do her harm'. Brandon continues to explain that he wishes to bring Mary to court and almost desperately asks 'as to be means unto the king's grace, that she may have a lodging in the court;- an it be but one chamber, – because it shall not be said that she is now in worse favour than she was at her departing'.[47] Mary herself sent a letter with Brandon's but hers was to her brother, to whom she confirms her illness, writing, 'so it is that I have been very sick, and ill at ease, for the which I was fain to send for Master Peter the physician, for to have holpen me of the disease that I have. Howbeit, I am rather worse than better'. She then makes the same request that she be permitted to travel to court, 'I would be glad to see your grace, the which I do think long for to do; for I have been a great while out of your sight, and now I trust I shall not be so long again; for the sight of your grace is to me the greatest comfort that may be possible'.[48] Mary did not remain unwell for long and was back in the spotlight by May 1520.

Maximilian, Holy Roman Emperor, died on 12 January 1519. Mary's former betrothed, Prince Charles was elected as the successor to the Imperial crown, becoming Charles V. It was arranged for him to visit Henry and his aunt Katharine of Aragon whilst he was on his journey to claim his crown and he landed in Dover on 26 May 1520. As royalty, Mary was expected to attend the court and meet with Charles. Henry went to meet him at Dover to escort him back to Canterbury where the court had arrived the previous day. This would be the first time Mary had met the man she was supposed to marry if it were not for his family continually delaying the matter. Whilst the rest of the court danced and enjoyed themselves, Charles allegedly refused to dance and sat moodily watching Mary dance, entranced by her beauty and angered at his loss.[49] For her part, Mary had ensured her wardrobe was replenished and she and her ladies wore new or amended garments intending to dazzle their visitor. Attending Mass on Whit Sunday, Mary wore a gown in the Milanese fashion 'dressed in silver tissue, in strips, after the Italian fashion, joined throughout with gold cords, at the extremeties of which were fine pearls as aiglettes'.[50] It is possible Mary wanted him to know what he had missed when his family had snubbed her, even if it were not Charles himself who had done this.

Charles remained for four days and the day he departed was the same day Henry and his court, including Mary, made the journey across the Channel to attend the Field of Cloth of Gold. The event was the result of lengthy negotiations to arrange a meeting between Henry and Francis and was to be held just outside Calais. Wolsey had been busy for months planning the spectacular event. Every detail had to be managed including the number of servants each person could take with them. Wolsey had made enquiries with Brandon regarding his and Mary's requirements, Brandon responded with a list of individuals Mary intended to accompany her, which unfortunately hasn't survived, but we do know Brandon took eleven gentlemen, fifty-five servants, and five chaplains. He also took thirty horses. Likely the chaplains and servants would share duties for the couple. Mary's accommodation at the event was within the temporary structure that had been created to look like a palace. She was allocated three large rooms adjoining the chambers of her sister-in-law, Katharine of Aragon. A brick gatehouse separated her chambers on the other side from those of Wolsey, whose chambers adjoined those of Henry and a passage was created to allow Henry to visit Katharine out of public view.[51] Mary had access to a chapel, banqueting house and a gallery leading to the bridge out of the structure. A tiltyard was purposefully built with a scaffold for Katharine and the other ladies to watch the jousting.

The two kings spent their time together feasting and various other pastimes, including visiting each other's camp. Henry spent time being entertained by Queen Claude whilst Francis spent time in the company of Katharine of Aragon. The two kings did not visit each other's camp whilst the other was present unless both camps were feasting together. The accounts of the Field of Cloth of Gold refer to 'Queen Mary, in a litter of cloth of gold, wrought with lilies, and two letters, namely, an L and an M joined together and covered with porcupines, the emblems of King Louis. Three waggons followed, one covered with cloth of gold, one with cloth of gold on crimson, and the other with cloth of gold on azure, crowded with ladies, the rest of whom were on palfreys; they were handsome and well arrayed'.[52] Mary displays the perfect act of diplomacy by honouring Louis in the presence of the French.

On the final day, 24 June, Mary, with a group of courtiers, accompanied Henry to Ardres where the French camp was situated. The siblings rode on horses trapped in velvet of yellow and white; Henry dressed as Hercules whilst Mary was attired in the Genoese fashion of 'white satin, ornamented with crimson satin and cloth of gold, with a square head tire and flowing veil'.[53] As they travelled to visit Claude, Francis and his courtiers passed them on his way to Guisnes to visit Katharine but neither group stopped to speak or acknowledge one another. Once at Ardres, the group spent time feasting and dancing before returning to their own camp in the evening where once more they passed Francis. This time the two kings did stop to speak and exchanged parting gifts, a signal that ended the most spectacular event the Tudor court had witnessed.

The English court travelled to Calais the following day, 25 June 1520. Whilst many left for England, Henry and his primary courtiers, including Mary and Brandon, remained in Calais for a couple of weeks before leaving on 10 July to Gravelines. They were visiting Margaret of Austria and Charles V. Margaret had been one of those responsible for delaying the marriage of Mary and Charles and also had an interesting history with Brandon, so one must wonder if there had been tension at the meeting with all four parties present. Despite any feelings, the group spent time together at Gravelines before they all returned to Calais and spent a further couple of days together before Henry and his court returned home. The French were not happy about Henry's additional excursion, causing risk to Mary's income.

Mary received her revenues from France as usual in December 1521 but frustrated at the lack of consistent payment from France, Mary's chancellor and treasurer undertook the objective to arrange the payments. By this time, despite Mary handing over jewels, in terms of monetary repayments to Henry, Mary and Brandon had not even paid a years' worth of payments, having only paid 1,334l 6s 4d. The efforts to obtain Mary's income would prove difficult. In May 1522 she received a small payment and by 1523 Francis had diverted her revenues to his own household to fund his military ambitions.[54] Without a regular income Mary had little choice but to spend the majority of her time away from court at her estates. Mary likely chose to remain away from court as her son, Henry died at some point in 1522. Brandon had lost his heir and between Henry VIII and Mary there were now only female children.

Chapter Twelve

Family, Friends and Friars

As a princess, dowager queen and duchess, there was a standard of life Mary was accustomed to. When attending court, Mary used to reside in Henry's household, eating with him and joining in his entertainments but it was unusual for a woman at court to stay in the king's household and after a period of time she began to reside in Katharine of Aragon's household instead.

Despite the death of her son and an inconsistent income, Mary did attend some festivities at her brother's court in 1522. One of these was the celebrations prior to Lent, beginning with a tournament at Greenwich on 1 March and culminating with a masque hosted by Wolsey at York Place on 4 March. The pageant was named 'Chateau Vert' and featured a wooden castle complete with towers and battlements covered with green foil. Inside the castle were eight ladies, named for the female virtues led by Mary as Beauty. The other virtues were Honour (Countess of Devonshire), Perseverance (Anne Boleyn), Kindness (Mary Boleyn), Constancy (Jane Parker), Bounty, Mercy and Pity. The ladies were dressed in the Milanese fashion of white satin gowns, with gold embroidery, their Venetian gold cauls and Milanese bonnets covered in jewels and their respective virtue embroidered upon them. Choristers dressed as ladies in the Indian fashion and named Danger, Disdain, Jealousy, Unkindness, Scorn, Malebouche (evil tongue), and Strangeness waited at the foot of the castle ready to hold it against any attackers. Eight male virtues were led by Ardent Desire (likely William Cornish, master of the children) who asked the ladies at the foot to hand over the castle. With Scorn and Disdain refusing the eight male virtues, Amorous (Henry), Nobleness, Youth, Attendance, Loyalty, Pleasure, Gentleness and Liberty attacked the castle, throwing fruit whilst avoiding missiles of sweetmeat and rose water from the ladies. The virtuous ladies were soon left to defend themselves after the other ladies escaped. Mary and her companions left the castle to dance with their male partners before unmasking. The pageant was followed by a sumptuous banquet. The expensive gowns and cauls remained in the possession of the ladies afterwards.[1]

When not at court, Mary spent most of her time at one of her and Brandon's many properties. Their primary household consisted of two knights, one esquire, forty male servants including one French man, and seven female servants. This does not include ladies-in-waiting or the young ladies Mary would have taken into her household to educate. The annual expense for wages was 327l in 1516.[2] Westhorpe is mostly remembered as Mary's residence but it was of course not their only residence. On their return from France, Brandon began the work of rebuilding a house in Southwark, that had belonged to his uncle, Sir William Brandon. Brandon named the property Suffolk Place.

Building during the Tudor era was not a quick process and the works on Suffolk Place were almost complete seven years later in 1522, when Henry VIII and Charles V, Holy Roman Emperor visited. Brandon had also leased a large park adjoining the estate which provided good hunting, something Henry would certainly have been attracted to and approved of. It is reported that the property, constructed of brick, was 'a large and most sumptuous house' and had fashionable terracotta adornments.[3] Henry was obviously impressed with the property as the following year he gave Brandon another property in exchange for the Southwark manor. We do not know Mary's thoughts on the exchange but it must have been difficult to refuse Henry when he wanted something, as Wolsey found out when he gave Henry Hampton Court Palace. During the period when they did occupy Suffolk Place, it offered a prime location for their time spent in London, particularly if they did not wish to pay the costs of staying at the royal court.

Of the many properties owned by Brandon, we know that he also spent time at Ewelme Castle, Wingfield Castle, Wyverstone, Walsham and Henham Hall. He built a hunting lodge at Hook Norton which held eighty red deer. The lodge was intended for use when staying at Ewelme Castle and with records stating Brandon paid £1000 on repairs at the castle it must have been another lavish property, one which Mary would also have spent time at.[4] Westhorpe was the jewel of Brandon's property portfolio. When Brandon was granted the reversion of the majority of the de la Pole estates on 1 February 1515, his servants went on their way to purchase all of the properties that he did not own outright but that formed the estate. This was a long and expensive process. The location of Westhorpe offered him access to many of his other properties which formed a large part of his income. Though they did visit and make use of the property, they did not use it as their primary residence until the 1530s meaning Mary only spent the last years of her life there. It was used prior to that for ducal business including the mustering of troops in August 1523. Records indicate that it is possible they did not use the estate primarily due to the renovation and building works between the mid-1520s and 1530. Historian and biographer of Brandon, S. Gunn, notes that in 1528 the title of the bailiff at Westhorpe was changed to 'keeper of the place and gardens' and his salary was increased, indicating his work was becoming more substantial, possibly as the family began to use the property more extensively.[5] In June 1531, a merchant from Antwerp was owed

£2000 from Mary and Brandon which Gunn opines may have been to complete the building work at Westhorpe. As Mary's income at that time was received on a regular basis it would not have been a problem to repay this, making the couple comfortable in sourcing a loan to finalise the work.

Brandon later claimed to have spent an enormous 12,000l (£6,240,295) on Westhorpe, though what portion of the renovation work was a result of Mary's influence is unknown.[6] Unfortunately, the manor no longer exists but we are fortunate enough to have records of the estate. Mary certainly had some influence, the gardens were in the Franch fashion, probably installed and maintained on Mary's orders. Westhorpe was a moated courtyard property built in brick, with a reported internal measurement of 126 x 126 foot. If that is the size of the courtyard, one can only imagine the sheer size of the building surrounding it.

There are small pieces of evidence and records that help provide a glimpse of the estate that Mary would call home. When Westhorpe was destroyed, eyewitness Thomas Martin reported seeing terracotta adornments, stained glass and a marble statue of Hercules with a lion.[7] The house was pulled down in the eighteenth century but we cannot be certain the statue or other adornments he noted belonged to Mary and Brandon. It should be noted there are terracotta Tudor roses that survive from the demolishment of Westhorpe, so it can be assumed it was opulent. On the western approach to Westhorpe, visitors would cross a brick bridge over the moat and be greeted by a three-storey gatehouse with corner towers. The western bridge still exists but it is believed to have been lavish in its time. There are terracotta panels and stone pillars, on top of which likely featured statues of royal beasts. Sir Nicholas Vaux, brother of Lady Guildford, requested to borrow terracotta beasts from Brandon in 1520, though these were likely those from Suffolk Place rather than Westhorpe. A surviving terracotta panel, originally from the gatehouse, now sits above the entrance of the property that is now situated on the former site of Westhorpe. The panel features Brandon's heraldry and that of his later wife, Katherine Willoughby, though it is entirely possible that Katherine's heraldry replaced that of Mary's following Mary's death and their marriage.[8]

On the ground floor of the gatehouse a porter's lodge as well as a chamber with a fireplace and a privy could be found whilst on the upper floors were chambers leading to inner chambers and garderobes, all of which benefitted from fireplaces, making it apparent Mary and Brandon cared for their servants comfort.[9] Passing through the gatehouse, one would come across a three-story building, the ground floor comprising of a gallery, chambers, a privy, and access to the upper floors. The next floor also had a gallery which led to chambers and the house of office. The upper floor consisted of gables and garrets. All the chambers across the three-storeys had windows with a view of the courtyard and featured fireplaces throughout. Opposite this building, on the other side of the courtyard, was the lower range. The range housed the ewery as well as another gallery leading to four chambers, three of which had inner chambers featuring yet more fireplaces and as with the other building, windows facing the courtyard. Windows were expensive during the Tudor era so having so many windows was an indication of wealth.

Finally the fourth façade of the courtyard was the hall, boasting a large bay window facing the courtyard and an oriel window looking outwards from the estate. The hall was served by the kitchens, pantry, buttery, cellar and scalding house from one end. Above these rooms were two storeys of chambers, providing a total of twenty-six chambers across two floors for the servants, all with individual fireplaces and a shared privy.[10] As providing this level of accommodation and comfort for servants was not common practice, I am of the opinion that this was Mary's influence. Access to the servants' quarters and this part of the estate could be accessed via a different bridge, making it almost like a worker's entrance where it is likely deliveries were made to.

The upper floor held the great chamber, featuring two bay windows, the full height of the room. From the great chamber you could access the private dining room of Mary and Brandon, which they would have used when not entertaining, or for more intimate meals. A separate kitchen served the private dining room which was also adjoined to a tower. The first floor of the tower hosted a series of rooms leading to one another. Just like in the royal court, the more intimate you were with the host determined how far into the rooms you could go. Mary was a duchess and dowager queen, therefore a standard of etiquette and privacy is to be expected. The windows of the entrance chamber overlooked the enclosed privy garden. The following rooms were all elaborately panelled and contained fireplaces and a privy, indicating these were the private chambers of Mary and Brandon.

From the tower and the great chamber, you could access the vestry and the private chapel of Westhorpe. When Westhorpe was destroyed there was a reference to stained glass in the report by Martin – it is likely the glass featured in the chapel and possibly the oriel window. Adjoining the chapel was a room where you could access the courtyard and therefore provide access directly to the chapel for the household without going through the private chambers of Mary and Brandon. From the descriptions of the galleries and adjoining rooms it appears that each side of the courtyard was accessible without going outdoors, a perfect feature in adverse weather. The brick walls are reported to have been 'decorated with plaster cheker wise white & blake'. One of Mary's favoured priories, that of Butley, had similar decoration so it is possible Mary's influence was at work here.[11] There was also the parish church, St Margaret's, within walking distance of Westhorpe where Mary would attend services, sitting in her reserved pew.

Before Westhorpe became their primary residence, Mary and Brandon stayed at a variety of places. West Stow Hall was another of the Brandon properties they visited regularly. The property no longer exists with the exception of Mary's arms which feature in the current porch. They travelled their estates, stayed with friends and spent periods staying at abbeys and priories. Fairs were held annually at St Edmundsbury and Mary was a regular visitor; she was received in state and many came to see their beautiful duchess and pay homage to her. This also gave Mary a connection to the Abbey of St Edmund.

Mary and Brandon used their influence to excuse others who were absent from court. They stayed with their friend Thomas Grimpson, who Wolsey had summoned but Brandon wrote to Wolsey explaining that they had just arrived to visit and did not know the area so could not manage without their host.[12] One of the factors influencing their time away from court was the costs; another was likely the birth of her second son in 1523, also named Henry after the death of her firstborn.[13] Perhaps as a way to celebrate the birth of his nephew, assist his sister and encourage them back to court, Henry granted Mary and Brandon further properties in 1523. He settled various manors in Suffolk on the couple and their heirs, increasing their portfolio and income. Only a month later, in August 1523, Brandon was ordered to lead an army into France. War with France would be difficult for Mary, not only had her revenues ceased due to the war but now her husband was being sent to fight. Unfortunately for Brandon, he would once more anger Henry. Due to the difficult weather conditions in France, which cost the lives of many men, Brandon had begged for permission to disband the army but by the time Henry responded promising aid, the army was already largely on their way home. Brandon did attempt to reassemble the men but on realisation of the situation he withdrew to Calais on 12 December. Henry was furious and Brandon found himself for a second time waiting in Calais for permission to return to England. Mary and friends of Brandon had to use their influence on Henry to have Brandon returned home and even when Henry relented, Brandon was not allowed in his presence and retired from court where he remained until Henry's temper had subsided.[14]

Brandon finally returned to court in March 1524 to participate in the jousting held on 10 March. Henry had commissioned new armour and harness of his own design and wished to test it; he likely also must have been missing his favourite jousting partner. On this occasion, the two who had jousted together and against each other many times over the years were almost met with disaster. Henry had failed to lower his visor. When running at each other, Brandon could not see the fault, due his own vision impairing visor and through the thunderous noise of the horse hooves, failed to hear the spectators shouting for him to 'hold'. Brandon's lance 'strake the kyng on the brow right vnder the defece of y hedpiece' and splintered.[15] Any lower and Henry would have taken the full force to the face.

On realisation Brandon was distraught and he fell at Henry's feet, vowing never to run against his monarch and friend ever again. Luckily Henry was unharmed and blamed himself, lowering his visor and choosing to ride again. In that split second Mary could have lost her brother and as a result, possibly her husband.

Although Brandon had inferred the costs of staying at court were a factor in them retiring from court, it is also entirely possible that Mary and Brandon enjoyed their time together away from court and may have relied on their debt as an excuse to spend more time together. They also had their children to think about. Mary had her stepdaughters and her own children to care for. As per the custom, although we do not have records of the names, Mary, as royalty, would have used a wetnurse for her children and employed nursery staff such as rockers, nurses, and possibly a governess. Her son, Henry, was brought to court where on 18 June 1525 he was created Earl of Lincoln, on the same day her illegitimate nephew, Henry Fitzroy, was created Duke of Richmond and Somerset, and Earl of Nottingham. Being so young, at only 2 years old, he had to be carried by Sir John de Vere.[16] Unfortunately, we do not know if Mary was present, but Brandon certainly was as he was given the honour of escorting Fitzroy to Henry for the ceremony. The elevation of Fitzroy and others was celebrated with a banquet but given that Mary's son was only a toddler at the time, it is unlikely he participated.[17] Another event took place in 1525 which Mary most certainly would have been involved in and likely influenced – the marriage of her stepdaughter, Anne Brandon. Anne was married to Edward Grey, 3rd Baron Grey of Powys. Mary would not live to see the scandal of her stepdaughter leaving her husband in 1537 for a relationship with Randal Haworth, whom she would later marry. Although Brandon did take action on behalf of Anne to ensure she received an annuity from her husband he did omit her from his own will.

The same year, Mary's income was once more at risk. Francis had been captured following a resounding defeat by Emperor Charles at Pavia in February. With Francis imprisoned, there was no way France would allow her payments to be made. Thankfully for Mary, it would only be a matter of months before the matter was resolved. Henry had instructed his ambassadors to, 'Remember the matter of the queen's dower, taking such order that special clauses may be passed for that purpose as well as for the yearly payments in time to come, as for the arrears passed in these wars; alleging therein that, neither by law, honour, nor conscience, she may be avoided from her said dower, considering that she is in no blame or fault of any war depending between the two realms, and that also the same was granted peaceably, to enjoy into what place or country soever she do divert unto'.[18]

Mary wrote in her own hand to Wolsey on 3 August whilst she was residing at Wingfield Castle. She stated, 'I trust my said causes shalbe brought to suche good conclusion and ordre now that I shal from hensfurthe enyoie my rightes there in as ample wise as I have donne heretofore'.[19] Later that same month, with Louise of Savoy acting as regent during the incarceration of Francis, she agreed the Treaty of More in August 1525. The treaty made agreement for Mary's revenues to be reinstated, and the payments that had been withheld were all to be paid.[20] Wolsey also made further arrangements for Mary and Brandon to receive additional funds. The French ambassadors were so grateful they actually thanked Mary for her intercession in bringing about the treaty to which Brandon replied on her behalf that they would do their best to uphold it.[21]

It was also determined that for the ongoing continuation of her revenues, it would be beneficial for Mary to have men resident in France to act on her behalf. For this task Mary chose her trusty almoner, Dr Denton, to act alongside a servant of Brandon's, Francis Hall. By this time Mary was at Leystone Abbey from where she wrote to Wolsey on 10 September 1525, recommending the men for the commission:

> Where it hath pleasid the king, my deriest brother, and you to be contented that I shuld send by sufficient Auctorite certeyn trusty persons in to Fraunce as well for surveying of my dotte and dowery there asfor Redressing of such enormytees as ar or may unto theym appere to be within the same, I entend as now to send thidder by vertue of commyssion Doctor Denton my Chauncelor and my trusty servant Fraunces hall for thordering of my said causes there. Nevertheles for asmuch as your lordship hath alwaies taken peynn in all my causes and have advertisid me evermore with your best advyse and counsaill in the same which I have alwayes gladly folowed to my great comfort and so entend to doo. And for that it lieth in you muche to prefer myn honor and profit in this bihalf. I have sent unto you my said servant Fraunces hall Which bicause the hole Commyssion were to tedious for your lordship shall enforme you of theffect of the same commyssion to whome I pray you to give credence.[22]

With the approval of Denton and Hall given, Mary issued letters patent authorising them to go to France on her behalf.[23] Louise of Savoy kept to the agreement; Mary received 5000 crowns on 12 October 1525 with the agreement that 5000 would be received each November and May going forwards until the accumulated debt of 220,000 livres had been paid. In an additional act of goodwill, Brandon was granted a French pension for the value of 875 crowns per year. It certainly looked like the financial concerns of Mary and Brandon were finally over. Possibly in gratitude for his diligence on her behalf, Mary bestowed two manors upon the Ipswich college founded by Wolsey.

Mary was back at court in May 1526 and enjoying the entertainments of her brother's court. On this occasion she got to share the enjoyment with her young niece, Princess Mary, who at aged 10 was now old enough to participate. The court enjoyed a banquet at Greenwich which featured a 'large ornamental tower of spicery' which apparently took six days to construct.[24] Francis was released by Charles in early 1526 and Mary wrote from Southwark in May, 'I have thanked the Almighty for the grace that He has given you to deliver you from this anxiety and to bring you back in good health into your kingdom where I find so much honesty and goodness in my lady and my good cousin, your mother, that I do not know how to thank you enough'.[25] The praise for Louise of Savoy and Francis is likely an effort on Mary's side to ensure he did not discard the arrangements made by his mother and maintained the payments that had been agreed. It was almost expected of Mary as the dowager queen of France to maintain decorum even when she had been treated badly by France.

Mary spent time the following year and 1529 at Ely where she was welcomed and entertained honourably. Between this time, Mary was also busy with the marriage arrangements for her stepdaughter, Mary Brandon. Mary married Thomas Stanley, 2nd Earl of Cumberland around 1526. Mary also returned to Butley Priory for another visit where she enjoyed the hospitality of the monks and later that year, Mary and Brandon spent time in Letheringham Priory, Mary remaining when Brandon returned to court. Letheringham was under the patronage of the Wingfield family, two of whom were ambassadors for Henry and had worked closely with Brandon. On this occasion Brandon had asked Henry if Mary should come and although we have no reply, it must be assumed there was either no reply or that Henry refused as Mary was left behind. Whilst Brandon was away, Mary kept herself busy with the friars and entertaining herself. On 5 August she visited a neighbour, Sir John Glenham, and stayed overnight before returning. Once back at the priory she asked for her meal to be served outdoors in the garden and this became a regular pastime for Mary to eat outdoors. Mary was still there on 21 August when a storm caused the party to seek shelter within the church. Mary left the following day after hearing Mass but not before she gifted presents to the friars and monks. Mary gave monetary gifts as well as a rich canopy and later despatched a chest embroidered with cloth of gold for them to keep their vestments safe.[26]

With her visits to religious houses throughout the years, Mary had become a guest of honour and was treated accordingly. She clearly enjoyed her time in seclusion, particularly at Butley, where she repeated visits throughout the years, spending weeks at a time residing there.

Chapter Thirteen

Queen of Hearts

Although Mary appears to have spent much time travelling between different properties, it is doubtful she visited all of the Brandon properties but it appears she was happy in her last years spent at Westhorpe. From here, she spent time with her children and stepdaughters and continued to hold a place in the hearts of her friends and allies. Throughout her life, Mary habitually used her influence to patronise people and used her influence to obtain positions and favours for those she cared for. She continued to use the title 'Queen of France' for the rest of her life, as this placed an expectation of honour and obeisance on those from whom she sought favour.

Her friend of many years, Jane Popincourt, finally left England in 1516 to return to France in order to take possession on an inheritance. Henry VIII rewarded her with a payment of 100l (£66,276) for her service.[1] Regardless of how Louis XII felt about Jane, the fact that she and Mary kept in contact and Henry awarded such a large sum indicates that they thought highly of her. Her companionship to Mary as a young lady would have been invaluable to her. Nobody would have predicted Mary would become the queen of France but the skills she developed in the language can partially be attributed to Jane.

John Palsgrave can also be credited with Mary's French language skills. Sometime after his appointment to tutor Mary in 1512, he began writing *L'eclaircissement de la langue Francaise*. Though it was not published until 1530 it is thought his lessons with Mary formed the basis of the text. He dedicated the work to Henry VIII with the epistle:

> Desirous to do some humble service unto the nobilite of this victorious realme, and universally unto all other estates of this my natyfe country, after I was commaunded by your nost redoubted hyghnesse to instruct the right excellent princes, your most dere and most entirely beloved suster quene Mary douagier of France in the French tonge.[2]

Mary clearly left an impression on Palsgrave and she continued to patronise him and sought benefits for her former tutor and secretary. In April 1515, on hearing that two benefices had become vacant upon the promotion of Dr West, she wrote to Wolsey 'beseeching you, my lord, at mine instance, and for my sake, to be so good lord unto my servant John Palsgrave, master of art, which hath done unto me right good and acceptable service, to his and his friends' great charge, and on my part as yet hitherto unremembered, as by your good wisdom and provision to find the means that he may have one of the said benefices'.[3] Palsgrave also notes that it was Mary and Brandon that encouraged him to continue with his work in writing the French text. He reports that he had shown them the first two volumes and as a result of their support he went on to produce the third volume which expanded on the previous two, improving the guidance on grammar and vocabulary.[4]

Even whilst she was expected to be in mourning following the death of Louis XII, Mary did not cease attempting to assist those she cared for. On 18 February she wrote to Wolsey on behalf of her almoner, Dr Denton, who had not received a benefice intended for him. Mary admonished Wolsey, 'you desired the king my brother to give unto my trusty and well-beloved almoner, Doctor Denton, the prebend in St. Stephen's, which as then the dean of his chapel, and now bishop of Lincoln, had in possession, as then the king's grace shewed me in your presence that he should have it, and also you promised me the same, and to solicit the king my brother for the performance of his promise. Nevertheless, I am credibly informed that my almoner is disappointed of the said prebend, and that your chaplain hath it, of the which I marvel greatly; forasmuch as my said almoner hath done me good service in this country, to the great honour of the king my brother, and mine also, and that the promise was made undesired of my behalf, for you were the person that only moved the king to give it unto my almoner, and I am assured that his grace would not have varied without he had been persuaded to the contrary'.[5] Mary goes on to say that she wishes Wolsey to obtain the resignation of his chaplain so Dr Denton can have the promised prebend but that she will seek a promotion worth double for the chaplain as restitution. Unbeknownst to Wolsey she had also written to Henry expressing displeasure at Wolsey's actions in depriving Denton of the prebend. Dr Denton was a valuable member of Mary's household and she retained him in her service even upon her return to England and for many years afterwards.

In a letter dated 27 September, Mary wrote from Butley Priory and reminds Wolsey of a promise he made to 'shew your gracious favours in all the causes reasonable' to a man named Anthony Savage, the brother of Mary's servant Susan.[6] It appears Wolsey did not act as Mary wrote again, this time a little more scathing in her tone, 'I think you have forgotten your said promise herein, but in consideration of his long and painful suit that he hath had and sustained, to his utter undoing; whereby he is so far impoverished that he hath not whereby to live; nether, without some gracious remedy may be shortly for him provided, he shall never be able to live, in time to come. I am so bold to desire you, of your goodness, to have him in your good remembrance, and to have remorse and pity unto him on this behalf'.[7] Unfortunately, we do not know the outcome of Mary's petitions but as there is no letter to Henry on this matter, it is possible that Wolsey relented before Mary involved her brother, who did genuinely seem to care for his younger sister and her happiness. She had previously involved Henry in securing a prebend in the collegiate church in Tamworth for her almoner John Golde.

Henry was not the only one Mary used her influence on. When she returned to England, she brought Antione du Val with her. He had been in service to Louis as clerk of the closet but Mary wished to retain him in her household which she dutifully did. He would later return to France and Mary wrote in January 1528 to the Grand Master of France requesting that he 'will be pleased, at this my request, to cause to be given to him the first vacant office of clerk of the closet, in the household of the said lord, and to hasten to him the letters of retaining, placing him speedily in attendance, so that on the occurrence of the vacancy, none may step in but himself. And what moves me to write to you is, that you have the power to do this, and also that I verily believe you will not refuse me, I as I place confidence in you, as well in this as in greater affairs; praying you very kindly to let him understand that this present, according to my request, has been of service to him'.[8]

Surprisingly, Mary was unsuccessful but she did not let the matter drop. She sent two further letters in December 1528 and June 1529. Remaining unsuccessful, Mary decided to take matters further. She enlisted the assistance of Jane Popincourt, 'my good friend', who was back residing at the French court. The letter gives insight into the relationship that continued after Jane left England. Mary thanks her friend for headdresses sent for her children and requests she remember the past, referring to Jane as 'one of my own relatives'. She then makes her request:

> I am disposed to employ you, that you may, in my name, ask the Grand Master to have in his very good recommendations, Antione du Val, who formerly was my clerk of the closet; and that, from regard to me, he will procure for him the like situation, in the establishment of the king my son-in-law, as I wrote to him more fully; and I pray you not to be negligent in this matter, but continually to urge it, so that I may obtain my request concerning him; and from time to time may be advertised by you of his reply.[9]

Despite the anger of her brother in relation to her marriage to Brandon, Henry never really enforced the debt they owed him. There are multiple indentures recording the amount they had repaid and any changes to the arrangement. The final indenture in December 1526 states that Mary and Brandon offered certain jewels left to Mary in partial payment of the debt and specified that should Mary die without repaying the full amount, remaining plate and jewels should go to Henry.[10] The marriage of Mary to Brandon was not the only dispute with Henry. Mary was openly opposed to Henry's relationship with Anne Boleyn. Mary had a long and loving relationship with her sister-in-law, Katharine of Aragon, and she could not bear to see her treated so badly by her brother. In 1517, Katharine had gifted Mary a gold ring with a heart shaped diamond surrounded by rubies, indicating her friendship and love for Mary.[11] Mary in return had shown her love and respect for Katharine when, in 1526, Lord Willoughby de Eresby died. He was the husband of Katharine's closest lady-in-waiting, Maria de Salinas, and they had a daughter named Katherine (likely named after Katharine of Aragon) who was now the sole heiress. The young Katherine became a ward of Mary and Brandon, made official in 1529. Katherine joined Mary's household and was treated like a member of the Brandon family.

With Anne Boleyn now queen in all but name, Mary chose to largely stay away from court. In April, her 15-year-old niece, Margaret Douglas, arrived in England as a result of the Treaty of Berwick. Mary invited her niece to stay with her at Westhorpe rather than at the court, possibly because she did not wish her niece to be in the presence of Anne Boleyn or perhaps just because she wished to spend quality time with her. Mary must have taken Margaret with her when she spent two months at Butley Priory, arriving on 19 June, where she had been allocated an apartment within the main residence. We may thank Mary for the popularity of picnics. She spent her time hunting and enjoying picnics on the grounds of the priory and within the little gardens of the differing friars.[12] From the priory she could partake in hunting at Staverton Park or Scuttegrove Wood which were fairly close by. Brandon would often join her but would be regularly called away on business, leaving Mary to enjoy the hospitality of the priory with her ladies and servants. During a fox hunt at Sholsgrove wood a royal messenger arrived to summon Brandon to court as Cardinal Campeggio had arrived with the task of hearing the argument for Henry's divorce from Katharine of Aragon. This greatly distressed Mary, who sided with her sister-in-law. Brandon left Butley on 28 September and Mary remained until 16 November when she made gifts to all the friars and monks she had spent so much time with. Margaret moved from Mary's household in December to enter the household of Princess Mary, as chief lady of the privy chamber. By this time she had developed a close relationship with her aunt and Katherine Willoughby.[13]

Brandon, on the other hand had less choice about conducting Henry's bidding, at least to an extent. During proceedings, when Henry was seeking an annulment from Katharine of Aragon, Brandon appeared to have forgotten the friendship Wolsey had shown him following his marriage to Mary. Frustrated with Wolsey and Cardinal Campeggio, brought to England to determine the matter, Brandon declared that 'It was never merry in England whilst we had cardinals among us', to which Wolsey responded, 'Sir, of all men within this realm ye have least cause to dispraise or be offended with cardinals, for if I, simple cardinal, had not been, you should have had at this present, no head upon your shoulders wherein you should have a tongue to make any such report in despite of us'. After imploring Brandon to understand the position of the cardinals, acting on behalf of the Pope, he ended by saying, 'ye know what friendship ye have received at my hands, the which I never revealed to any person alive before now, neither to my glory, nor to your dishonour'.[14] Whilst Brandon was at court, Mary chose to visit her friend Sir John Glenham once more, heading to his residence directly from Butley and remaining there until 23 November when she made her way to court to spend Christmas at Greenwich in the company of Brandon, Henry and Katharine of Aragon. The queen 'made no great joye of nothing, her mynd was so troubled'.[15] It must have been incredibly difficult for Mary to see her sister-in-law in such a difficult position and know that she could do little to change the circumstances. After Christmas of 1531, Mary spent very little time at court, and instead retired, though she did send Henry a New Years' gift in 1532 of a gold writing whistle and a writing table; in return she would receive gilt plate.[16]

Brandon was not always able to hide his feelings about Henry's relationship with Anne Boleyn and allegedly in 1531 had accused her of having some kind of relationship with Thomas Wyatt. Brandon was banished for this but not long afterwards Anne made her counterattack, accusing Brandon of 'having connection with his own daughter'.[17] Mary's reaction is not known but she did speak out publicly against Anne Boleyn the following year, in 1532. The dispute between Mary and Anne was picked up by the men of Norfolk and Brandon and it was reported that in April 1532:

> At the moment of his arrival at the Court, one of the chief gentlemen in the service of said Duke of Norfolk, with 20 followers, assaulted and killed in the sanctuary of Westminster Sir (D'no) William Peninthum [*sic*] chief gentleman and kinsman of the Duke of Suffolk. In consequence of this, the whole Court was in an uproar, and had the Duke of Suffolk been there, it is supposed that a serious affray would have taken place. On hearing of what had happened, he [Suffolk] was on his way to remove the assailants by force from the

> sanctuary, when the King sent the Treasurer [Thomas Cromwell] to him, and made him return, and has adjusted the affair; and this turmoil displeased him. It is said to have been caused by a private quarrel, but I am assured it was owing to opprobrious language uttered against Madam Anne by his Majesty's sister, the Duchess of Suffolk, Queen Dowager of France.[18]

Despite all the goings on, Mary had not fallen foul of Henry completely. He still sent her New Years' gifts, including gilt bowls in 1533, but largely Mary avoided the court. Her daughter, Eleanor, was betrothed to Henry Clifford, the heir of Henry Clifford, 1st Earl of Cumberland in March 1533. She did not attend the ceremony creating Anne Boleyn Marchioness of Pembroke, did not travel to Calais when Henry and Anne travelled to meet Francis, and did not attend Anne's coronation on 1 June 1533, even though her son-in-law, Monteagle, was made a Knight of the Bath at the ceremony. Being his sister, Mary likely escaped the wrath of Henry; Brandon could not risk that and abided by all Henry's wishes, leaving Mary at home. Throughout the last months of Mary's life, Brandon was recalled home due to her illness. One of Mary's last public appearances was in May when she witnessed her eldest daughter, Frances, marry Henry Grey, Marquess of Dorset. The marriage took place at Suffolk Place with Henry in attendance. Again, Mary was likely very influential in the arrangements of this marriage. Unfortunately Mary would not live to see the birth of her granddaughters who would later become the focus point of Tudor drama.

That year, in May 1533, Mary was still using her influence for the benefit of others. One of Mary's last known letters was to Arthur Plantagenet, 1st Viscount Lisle, Lieutenant of Calais, requesting his assistance:

> ... you will be so good lord unto John Williams, this bearer, as to admit him into the room of a soldier in Calais, with the wages of eightpence by the day; assuring you, cousin, in your so doing you shall shew unto us full good and acceptable pleasure, which we shall right willingly acquit at your desire in time coming, trusting the conditions, haviour [behaviour], and personage of the said John be such as you shall be contented with the same.[19]

Unfortunately, we do not know if Williams was accepted into service of Lord Lisle. It is also unfortunate that Lord Lisle would not have the opportunity to call in the favour when he most needed help in 1540.[20] Lord Lisle was the illegitimate son of Edward IV and was therefore related to Mary through her mother, Elizabeth of York.

Chapter Fourteen

La Volonté de Dieu Me Suffit

Mary Tudor, Princess of England, Queen of France, and Duchess of Suffolk died at her home in Westhorpe on 26 June 1533 between 07:00 a.m. and 08:00 a.m.

Mary was embalmed then laid in a lead coffin; her entrails are believed to have been buried at the parish church of Westhorpe. She was then taken to the chapel at the manor where a pall of richly embroidered blue velvet was used to cover the coffin. The chaplains sang divine service daily, tapers burned and attendants took turns in honour of their mistress, for almost a month before it was finally time for her funeral. Those wishing to attend or pay their respects arrived on 20 July and a dirge mass was sung. In honour of her rank, the French sent a herald to assist in the ceremonials. The final requiem Mass took place on 21 July. The chief mourner was her daughter, Lady Frances Brandon, who entered the chapel flanked by her little brother, the Earl of Lincoln, and her husband, the Marquess of Dorset. The trio were followed by other mourners, walking in pairs: Lady Eleanor Brandon and Lady Katherine Willoughby; Mary's stepdaughters, Anne and Mary, with their husbands; Lady Chelston and Lady Wingfield; Lady Glenham and Lady Corbett. After Mass the mourners broke their fast in the great chamber whilst final preparations were made for the procession.

Six gentlemen carried the coffin from the chapel to the funeral carriage, which was drawn by six horses, trapped in black velvet embroidered with Mary's arms. The carriage was also draped in black velvet and on each corner was a flag bearing Mary's arms. On reaching the carriage, two ushers knelt bareheaded at each end awaiting the arrival of the coffin. A pall of black cloth embroidered with cloth of gold and featuring a black cross on a white background, with an embroidered representation of Mary dressed in state robes and holding a sceptre and wearing a crown, was draped over the coffin.[1]

The procession to Mary's resting place was led by one hundred poor men carrying tapers and dressed in black hooded gowns. The clergy of the chapel at Westhorpe followed carrying a cross and behind them rode the aristocracy and the officers of Mary's household; Lord Powys, Mary's chamberlain, Clarencieux Garter Kings of Arms, riding on horses trapped in black. The funeral carriage came next surrounded by one hundred burning torches. As chief mourner, Frances Brandon rode behind the carriage, flanked by the Marquess of Dorset and Lord Clifford. Ten ladies rode behind, each attended by a bareheaded page to show their respect. Two mourning chariots followed behind, in front of Mary's female attendants who walked rather than rode. Lastly came the remainder of Mary's servants, yeomen and all those from her estates who had chosen to attend to pay their respects. Along the way to the Abbey of St Edmund, people came to offer their respects from various parishes and offer a tribute on behalf of the parish. Each delegation was given a monetary gift to offset their expenses.

The procession reached St Edmundsbury around 2:00 p.m. on the same day where it was met by the clergy 'in their best ornaments, doing such ceremonies as to the same appertaineth'.[2] Proceeding towards the abbey, the procession was met at the first gate by the abbot and monks of St Edmundsbury. At the following gate the Bishop of London and a number of clergymen waited for Mary. The coffin was removed from the carriage and placed in a hearse which was covered by a cloth of black sarcenet with gold fringes and bore Mary's arms and motto 'La Volonté de Dieu me Suffit' (God's will is enough for me), embroidered in gold. Those bearing torches moved to surround the hearse and the procession began its final part of the journey to the abbey church. The route from the gate all the way to the high altar was lined with black cloth and escutcheons of Mary's arms.

On reaching the altar, the mourners filed into their places before a solemn dirge was chanted by the clergy. The French representative claimed 'Pray for the soul of the right high excellent princess, and right Christian Queen, Mary, late French queen, and all Christian souls'.[3] After this short ceremony the procession were led into a large chamber where supper was provided. The mourners who chose to remain were accommodated overnight whilst a select few were chosen to stay with the coffin overnight before the final funeral service took place the following day. Two masses were said before breakfast the following morning.

The service began after breakfast when the procession were led to the chapel of the abbey for a requiem Mass. Mary's daughters, Frances and Eleanor, along with her stepdaughters, Anne and Mary, were given the opportunity to approach the coffin and make an offering. Lady Katherine Willoughby, then a ward of Charles Brandon, also participated in making an offering. The ladies received palls of cloth of gold which they carried to Mary's coffin and handed to the Garter King who respectfully laid them across the coffin. After the offerings, a sermon was read by the Abbot of St Bennetts, concluding the Mass. Frances and the other mourners returned to the large chamber used the previous day. This was not usual protocol; it was normal for the mourners to wait until the melancholy rites had been completed before departing but it is possible the death of their mother had become too much for the young ladies to bear, especially as their father, as per custom, was not present. It may have particularly been overwhelming for Frances in her position of chief mourner. After the rites were completed, the coffin was carried to the grave which had been dug and covered with a canopy and banners. Once lowered into the grave, Mary's officers of the household broke their staves of office and dropped them into the grave of their mistress, signalling the end of their tenure. With the funeral service complete, the mourners retired to eat before departing to their respective residences. Residents of Bury St Edmunds were also invited to partake in food at four different locations around the town and given a small monetary token. The officers and heralds were all paid for their service and the costs of their funeral attire was all paid for. As well as the funeral, Henry VIII ordered a funeral service for his beloved sister at St Paul's and at Westminster.

Almost immediately after Mary's death, Brandon faced trouble when his beloved home came under the threat of none other than his brother-in-law. In a debt settlement, Henry had demanded that Westhorpe revert to him if Brandon had no male heirs. Although his marriage to Mary appears to have been his happiest and had left him with a male heir, it was not the last and he married for the final time in September 1533. This may appear disrespectful after such a short period of mourning following Mary's death but his new spouse, Katherine Willoughby, 12th Baroness Willoughby de Eresby, was a wealthy heiress, originally Brandon's ward and intended to be the spouse of his heir, Henry Brandon, 1st Earl of Lincoln. Brandon had a successful career under the reign of his closest friend Henry VIII. Within two years (1511–1513) Brandon was granted 'The offices of keeper of the park of Wanstead, ranger of the new forest, steward of the royal castles and manors in Wales, steward of the lands of the Earl of Warwick, now in the king's hands'.[4]

Brandon did have two more heirs, the sons of Katherine Willoughby, but unfortunately both died only six years after their father. As a result the estate was surveyed which provides us with the details of the extent of Westhorpe as Mary would have known it.[5] Henry was not totally unsympathetic and did cancel a portion of Brandon's debt and on 19 July 1533 he cancelled all of Mary's debt, but the loss of Mary's dower was a significant blow to Brandon's income. He still owed a huge 6700l (£2,158,000) and opted to give Henry plate and jewels worth 4360l.[6] He also made arrangements to exchange some properties and lands in an effort to improve his landholdings and income.

After Brandon's death in 1545 the estate remained empty until 1553, when it was granted to Anne of Cleves, though she never resided there. Brandon died on 22 August 1545; his loss was keenly felt by Henry who insisted on paying for his friends funeral. Brandon was laid to rest in a place of prominence and very near to where his master and best friend would join him only a two years later: St George's Chapel, Windsor.

Chapter Fifteen

Legacy

There is no doubt Mary Tudor left behind a legacy that is still talked about today. Her granddaughter, Lady Jane Grey, features prominently in Tudor history. Henry himself had decided that after his own heirs, it should be the children of Mary to succeed to the throne before those of his elder sister, Margaret. During the tumultuous period of Henry seeking a divorce from Katharine of Aragon, Mary had become fearful for her own marriage and sought a papal bull assuring the legitimacy of her marriage and her children as well as her stepdaughters. Brandon's previous wife, Lady Mortimer, was still alive at the time and Mary feared she would have her children and marriage declared illegitimate. It could be said, however, that the declaration that Mary had so desired ultimately brought about the destruction of her granddaughter. Had there been doubt as to the legitimacy of both Frances Brandon and her daughter, Jane, then Jane would never have been a viable candidate for the throne.

Although Mary had witnessed the marriages of her stepdaughters and one of her daughters, Mary died before her daughter, Eleanor, married. Eleanor, though contracted in March 1533, did not marry her betrothed until June 1535. Her uncle, Henry VIII did attend, making it a more prominent event than it may have otherwise been. When Mary died she left behind a male heir who sadly died on 1 March 1534. The loss of Henry Brandon would impact the Tudor succession following the death of his cousin, Edward VI.[1]

It is unfortunate that there are very few remaining contemporary portraits of Mary but those we do have do support the records that she was a beautiful woman. In one account by a Venetian recorder, he states 'her eyes and eyebrows too light; for the rest it appears to me that nature optime suplevit: she is slight, rather than defective from corpulence, and conducts herself with so much grace'.[2] That her eyes and eyebrows were 'too light' suggests Mary was either blue or grey-eyed with fair hair, possibly even the golden red we associate with the Tudors. In the media she is often dismissed to the sidelines or removed completely. *The Tudors* TV show went as far as combining her and her sister Margaret into the same character, naming the character Margaret but using Mary's life events, such as her marriage to a foreign king (in this case the King of Portugal) and Brandon.

Possibly the most well-known portrait is that held in The National Gallery but this has been disputed as to who the sitter is. The portrait is marked on the back indicating it is Mary but this was a nineteenth-century addition. The portrait was believed to have been painted by Jehan Perréal for Louis XII at the time of her marriage to the French king. However, it has since been thought that the sitter may in fact be Mary's sister-in-law, Katharine of Aragon or even Isabella of Castile. The gown is in the Spanish style supporting the argument for the latter but there is nothing to say that Mary did not own a Spanish gown; she was after all very close to her sister-in-law. My own view is that the portrait is Mary, painted as Mary Magdalen as a sign of her piety ahead of her marriage to the French king.

The supposed marriage portrait is also very well-known and was initially thought to have been painted around 1515 following the third marriage ceremony at Greenwich. However, recent studies considering the fashions featured in the painting have suggested that this portrait was actually painted in 1532.[3] Mary's marriage to Louis is believed to be depicted in a beautiful tapestry currently held at Hever Castle, Kent. The origins of the tapestry are unfortunately lost, but if you do go to Hever, it is a beautiful item and you can determine for yourself if you believe it to be a true depiction of Mary.

Mary's beauty and ancestry should not be her only legacy; she was clearly a highly competent letter writer, using her skill to get her way and protect herself and those she cared about. Mary has become the focus of romantic stories, remembered for her beauty and features in literature both past and present. In a poem which is believed to have been printed by Wynkyn de Worde in 1507, Mary is mentioned for her beauty and virtue:

> Durynge the moneth of June every sonday
> Two chalengers in blewe dyde them assaye
> Of horse and man fyrst day was theyr araye
> Sarcenet blue
> And theyr armoure paynted of the same hue
> At the felde ende was pyght for to say true
> A pauyllyon on the grasse fresshe and nue
> Wherein these twayne
> Chalengers for to arme them dyde remayne
> When they were armed at ease without payne
> They yssued to begyn with all theyr mayne
> Theyr challenge there
> Ageynst all defendauntes that wolde appere
> After the entre as is the manere

About the felde they were brought euery where
That was all playne
Without a tylte abydynge tyme certayne
By the kynge assigned our prynce souerayne
With spores sharoe two courses to sustayne
In blanke armure.
Ageynst eche comer that lyst to aduenture
The courses done with swerdes sherpe and sure
Saue onely of theyr poyntes rebature
Thay dyde tourney
Full strokes syx eche other to assaye
And eche man dyde his best I dare well say
Eueryche of theym thought to bere the pryce away
Theyr strokes done
The defendaunt presented hym selfe soone
Before a pryncesse that of this region
Hath to fader Kynge and Emperoure alone
Whose victory
Hye majesty with tryumphaunt regally
And noble fame of prudent policy
Knowen is in euery realme vulgarely
To his honoure
And to oures of whome he is gouernoure
Frome this royall reed rose and stately floure
And frome the whyte of all virtue myrroure
This Yonge lady
This comfortable blossome named Mary
Spronge is to all Englondes glory
With bothe roses ennued moost sweetly
By dame nature
That euery thynge lynynge hath in her cure
But whan she made this propre portraiture
She dyde that might be done to creature
And not onely
For excellent byrthe but surmountynge beauty
In the worlde of her aege moost womanly
Lyke to be to princesses exemplary
For her virtue
Vnto whiche pryncesse the defendauntes dyde sewe
Besechynge her grace to haue syx strokes newe

To whose request this pryncesse fresshe of hewe
Ryght soone dyde graunte.[4]

This may have been the first reference made to Mary in poetic literature but would certainly not be the last. The poem makes reference to the red rose of Lancaster and the white rose of York. It is possible that the poem was produced as a pamphlet to celebrate the jousts where Mary was clearly the lady of honour. Mary is also the focus of a stanza which is believed to have been written by Brandon and shows his understanding of the disparity between their ranks:

Cloth of gold, do not despise,
Though thou be matched with cloth of frieze;
Cloth of frieze, be not too bold,
Though thou be matched with cloth of gold.[5]

The relationship between Mary and Brandon has become the focal point of romantic tales, woven into poetry, fiction and even tapestries. It is reported that in the inventory of King Charles I there are six pieces of arras tapestries depicting the life of Brandon; it must be assumed his marriage to Mary would have featured somewhere on this seventy-yard tapestry.[6]

During the dissolution of the monasteries, the Abbey of St Edmund would not be exempt, though Mary's body was removed before the abbey was destroyed. In 1539 Mary's body and tomb were transferred to the nearby St Mary's Church, Bury St Edmunds, and placed in the north side of the sanctuary. Over 200 years later in 1784, Mary was disturbed again. Her tomb was dismantled and her coffin opened. Locks from her hair were cut and taken as trinkets. One of these, can be seen in the Moyse's Hall Museum, Bury St Edmunds, having previously been in the possession of the family of Reverend Ashby. Another is kept at Knowsley Hall, having been taken by Horace Walpole. There have been attempts to use Mary's hair to solve one of the biggest historical mysteries: were the skeletons of the two children found in the White Tower at the Tower of London the Princes in the Tower? Unfortunately, the testing was inconclusive but that does not mean Mary's hair won't provide answers in the future.[7]

Mary was reburied in her current location and a stone placed above it with the engraving 'Mary, Queen of France 1533'. A few years later, Mary was disturbed once more when there were plans to pave the chancel with marble but upon realising that it was in fact Mary's grave and not just a cenotaph, her coffin was left alone and the tomb replaced. For those who visit Mary's tomb and feel it should be more extravagant for a Tudor princess and Queen of France, imagine if the beautiful white marble surround was not there. The marble kerb was not installed until 1907 following a visit by Edward VIII in 1904, who ordered a kerb to be added.

The tomb itself is fairly plain but Mary is commemorated in the exquisite Mary Tudor window in the South Chapel of St Mary's. The window was created in memory of Mary to be gifted to Queen Victoria. The upper tracery of the window depicts the arms of Mary and the men she had been closely linked with during her life: her brother, Henry VIII; her betrothed, Prince Charles of Castile, Holy Roman Emperor; first husband Louis XII of France; and lastly her second husband Charles Brandon, Duke of Suffolk. The rest of the window tells Mary's story in a series of nine individual images. The story begins in the small panels of the upper panels, left to right: Sir Thomas More and Desiderius Erasmus visiting the children at Eltham Palace in 1500; the proxy betrothal of Mary and Prince Charles in 1508; Mary saying goodbye to Henry VIII and Katharine of Aragon when leaving for France from Dover in 1514. The story then continues on the upper panels: Mary's marriage to Louis XII in October 1514; Mary's entry into Paris for her coronation in November 1514; Mary meeting Charles Brandon, Duke of Suffolk who was in attendance as Henry VIII's ambassador. Mary at this point in January 1515 was a widow. The final panels on the bottom row tell the last part of Mary's story: her marriage to Charles Brandon, Duke of Suffolk in March 1515; receiving forgiveness from Henry VIII in May 1515; and lastly, Abbot John Reeve conducting Mary's funeral service in the Abbey of St Edmund in July 1533. It should be noted that if visiting Mary's resting place you can also visit the grave of Abbot Reeve nearby. There is also a beautiful print portraying the size and pomp of the funeral procession to the abbey. There is something very poignant about the window and Mary's tomb. Mary now rests alone, in a peaceful church with the beautiful carved angels of the nave roof close by to watch over her.

Mary Tudor, Princess of England, Duchess of Suffolk, and Queen of France is mostly remembered for her marriage to Charles Brandon, 1st Duke of Suffolk. Her marriage is portrayed as one of the most romantic stories of the era. Ballads, poems and plays portray them as star-crossed lovers that managed to obtain their happy ending. Whilst they do appear to have had a happy marriage, Mary was so much more than one half of a couple who managed to survive the wrath of Henry VIII. It is interesting to wonder if they would have had the same success if events had occurred when Henry VIII was older and not opposed to sentencing friends and family to death.

When reading Mary's own letters it becomes apparent that not only was she extremely intelligent but she was an accomplished writer, using her quill to play her part in situations in whichever way she felt would be effective in accomplishing her objectives. If she were required to play the damsel in distress, she could. Her words would imply she was a feeble female in need of the protection of those whom she addressed, encouraging the men in her life to act as the heroes, protecting her and displaying the ideals of chivalry as expected during the time. On other occasions she used her writing to make the receiver well aware they were dealing with a woman of power and influence. Erin A. Sadlack opines that Mary and Charles Brandon co-operated when writing letters following their secret wedding.[8] Their prose is similar in its content, though it is apparent Mary is the more eloquent. Mary knew how to flatter, particularly her brother, who was happy to receive such compliments. Through her letters it becomes apparent that Mary's education was much more impressive than she is given credit for. Her younger female relatives , such as Lady Jane Grey and Elizabeth I are credited as being highly intellectual but it is possible Mary was just as intelligent. She made full use of her letter writing skills and learned from writers such as Ovid, Chaucer and Christine de Pizan. Mary was well aware that words were powerful and could evoke differing reactions in readers and used her knowledge to beget the reaction she desired. A portion of this credit must go to John Palsgrave who clearly took his work with the princess seriously and introduced her to a number of texts that would not only serve her in her short tenure as queen but for the remainder of her life.

Mary's first marriage to Louis XII of France can be interpreted as a brother forcing his sister to do his bidding in order to secure him an advantage – but Mary was no fool. She was well aware at the time that Louis was aging and was often reported as suffering from illness. Mary may well have considered that it was doubtful her French husband would survive for long. As queen, Mary would be the most powerful woman in France. But if Louis died, Mary would retain a measure of power as dowager queen. If she had a son, her power would be much the greater during his minority. If she did not bear a child, she would still remain influential, wealthy and by the terms of the treaty could return to England with her goods and jewels when she chose. These were all things to consider for Mary. It does in fact appear that the marriage between her and Louis was a content union. Mary stayed with her husband even when he was sick, nursing him herself. Mary appears to have genuinely cared about the French king and although he may not have been her choice, she made the most of the situation. Mary retained the title of the French Queen for the remainder of her life; it brought her influence and prestige and she was well aware of how to use it.

Mary managed to survive not only marrying without the consent of her king but also openly criticised his decision to marry Anne Boleyn. I do not believe any other person could have survived these actions, but not only did she survive, she thrived and remained his favourite sister throughout her life. She is often just a footnote in the stories of others but Mary's beauty dazzled the courts of sixteenth century Europe. Nevertheless, she is much more than a pretty face. Mary wielded the arts of chivalry and rhetoric in a patriarchal society, using these skills as weapons to ensure she retained her role and power whilst also using them for the benefit of those she loved. Mary is thoroughly deserving of her own story, which I hope I have portrayed with justice.

Timeline

28 January 1457 – Birth of Henry Tudor (Henry VII) at Pembroke Castle
11 February 1466 – Birth of Elizabeth of York at the Palace of Westminster
22 August 1485 – Battle of Bosworth
30 October 1485 – Coronation of Henry Tudor at Westminster Abbey
18 January 1486 – Marriage of Henry VII and Elizabeth of York
20 September 1486 – Birth of Arthur Tudor at Winchester Priory
28 November 1489 – Birth of Margaret Tudor (Queen of Scots) at the Palace of Westminster
28 June 1491 – Birth of Henry Tudor (Henry VIII) at the Palace of Placentia (Greenwich)
2 July 1492 – Birth of Elizabeth Tudor at Sheen
14 September 1495 – Death of Elizabeth Tudor at Eltham Palace
14 March 1496 – Birth of Mary Tudor at Sheen Palace
June 1498 – First recorded request for Mary's hand in marriage: Ludovico Sforza, Duke of Milan for his son Massimiliano, Count of Pavia
21 February 1499 – Birth of Edmund Tudor at Greenwich Palace
19 June 1500 – Death of Edmund Tudor at Hatfield House
2 October 1501 – Katharine of Aragon arrives in England
12 October 1501 – Mary, with her sister Margaret and other relatives, watch Katharine of Aragon enter London
14 November 1501 – Arthur Tudor and Katharine of Aragon marry at St Paul's Cathedral
2 April 1502 – Death of Arthur Tudor at Ludlow Castle
24 January 1503 – Betrothal of Margaret Tudor and James IV of Scotland
2 February 1503 – Birth of Catherine Tudor at the Tower of London
11 February 1503 – Death of Elizabeth of York at the Tower of London
18 February 1503 – Death of Catherine Tudor at the Tower of London
8 August 1503 – Margaret Tudor and James IV of Scotland marry
25 September 1506 – Death of Philip I of Castile
21 December 1507 – Treaty of Perpetual Peace signed by Henry VII, Maximilian, Holy Roman Emperor and Prince Charles. Treaty agrees betrothal of Mary Tudor and Prince Charles

17 December 1508 – Proxy marriage of Mary Tudor and Prince Charles at Richmond Palace
21 April 1509 – Death of Henry VII
23 April 1509 – Henry VIII proclaimed king
11 June 1509 – Henry VIII and Katharine of Aragon marry at the Friar Observant's Church
24 June 1509 – Coronation of Henry VIII and Katharine of Aragon
29 June 1509 – Death of Margaret Beaufort
15 October 1513 – Treaty signed by Henry VIII and Margaret of Austria (on behalf of Maximilian). Treaty instructs Mary Tudor and Prince Charles to be married before 15 May 1514
1 February 1514 – Charles Brandon created Duke of Suffolk
30 July 1514 – Mary Tudor renounces betrothal to Prince Charles
7 August 1514 – Treaty of 'Peace and Friendship' signed between England and France
13 August 1514 – Proxy marriage of Mary Tudor and Louis XII of France; Duke de Longueville acts as proxy for Louis
14 September 1514 – Proxy marriage of Louis XII of France and Mary Tudor; Earl of Worcester acts as proxy for Mary
23 September 1514 – Mary leaves London for Dover
2 October 1514 – Mary leaves Dover sailing for Boulogne
4 October 1514 – Mary arrives in Boulogne
5 October 1514 – Mary reaches Montreuil
7 October 1514 – Mary travels to Abbeville. Meets Louis XII for first time by 'accident' whilst travelling
8 October 1514 – Mary's retinue approved by Louis XII
9 October 1514 – Marriage of Mary Tudor and Louis XII of France at the Hôtel de la Gruuthuse
10 October 1514 – Much of Mary's retinue dismissed, including Lady 'Mother' Joan Guildford
31 October 1514 – Marry arrives at St Denis
5 November 1514 – Coronation of Mary Tudor, Queen of France at the Cathedral of St Denis
6 November 1514 – Mary makes her entry into Paris as queen of France
1 January 1515 – Death of Louis XII of France
2 January 1515 – Mary retires to the Hôtel de Cluny for mourning period
25 January 1515 – Coronation of Francis I
3 March 1515 – Secret wedding of Mary Tudor and Charles Brandon
31 March 1515 – Public wedding of Mary Tudor and Charles Brandon
5 April 1515 – Peace treaty ratified between England and France

16 April 1515 – Mary and Brandon leave Paris for Calais
2 May 1515 – Mary and Brandon arrive at Dover
13 May 1515 – Formal wedding of Mary and Brandon
18 February 1516 – Birth of Mary Tudor, the future Mary I of England at the Palace of Placentia
11 March 1516 – Birth of Henry Brandon at Bath Place
3 May 1516 – Arrival of Margaret Tudor in London; she is reunited with her siblings
16 May 1516 – Margaret Tudor leaves London; the sisters will never meet again
16 July 1516 – Birth of Frances Brandon at Hatfield
1519/20 – Birth of Eleanor Brandon
26 May 1520 – Mary meets Charles V, her former betrothed
31 May 1520 – Mary leaves Dover for France for the Field of Cloth of Gold
7 June – 24 June 1520 – Field of Cloth of Gold
1522 – Death of Henry Brandon
1523 – Birth of Henry Brandon, 1st Earl of Lincoln
March 1525 – Mary's stepdaughter, Anne Brandon, marries Edward Grey, Lord Powys
1527/29 – Mary's stepdaughter, Mary Brandon, marries Thomas Stanley, Lord Monteagle
March 1528 – Charles Brandon purchases wardship of Katherine Willoughby
1529 – Marriage of Mary and Brandon formally legitimised via a papal bull
31 May 1529 – Proceedings begin at Blackfriars concerning Henry VIII's annulment from Katharine of Aragon
29 November 1530 – Death of Cardinal Thomas Wolsey
6 June 1530 – Eustace Chapuys, Spanish ambassador reports that he believes Mary and Brandon would oppose the marriage of Henry VIII and Anne Boleyn
23 April 1532 – Mary speaks publicly against the marriage of Henry VIII and Anne Boleyn
May 1532 – Marriage of Frances Brandon and Henry Grey
25 January 1533 – Marriage of Henry VIII and Anne Boleyn
1 June 1533 – Coronation of Anne Boleyn
25 June 1533 – Death of Mary Tudor, Queen of France at Westhorpe Hall
10 July 1533 – Requiem Mass at Westminster Abbey for Mary, ordered by Henry VIII
21 July 1533 – Funeral procession of Mary
22 July 1533 – Burial of Mary at the Abbey of St Edmund
7 September 1533 – Brandon marries Katherine Willoughby

1 March 1534 – Death of Henry Brandon, 1st Earl of Lincoln
June 1535 – Marriage of Eleanor Brandon and Henry Clifford, 2nd Earl of Cumberland
19 July 1535 – Debts in Mary's name are cancelled
29 January 1536 – Death of Katharine of Aragon
19 May 1536 – Death of Anne Boleyn
October 1537 – Birth of Lady Jane Grey
1539 – Mary's body is moved from the Abbey to St Mary's Church, Bury St Edmunds
25 August 1540 – Birth of Lady Katherine Grey
18 October 1541 – Death of Margaret Tudor, Queen of Scots
20 April 1545 – Birth of Lady Mary Grey
22 August 1545 – Death of Charles Brandon, Duke of Suffolk
28 January 1547 – Death of Henry VIII
27 September 1547 – Death of Eleanor Brandon
12 February 1554 – Death of Lady Jane Grey
23 February 1554 – Death of Henry Grey
1 March 1554 – Marriage of Frances Brandon and Adrian Stokes
21 November 1559 – Death of Frances Brandon
6 September 1784 – Mary's coffin opened and locks of hair taken; reburied in the sanctuary
1881 – Mary Tudor window presented to Queen Victoria in memory of Mary at St Mary's Church, Bury St Edmunds
1904 – Visit by Edward VIII and a kerb ordered to be placed around her grave
1907 – Marble kerb added to Mary's grave

Appendix One

Excerpt of the Will of Henry VII

ALSO whereas for the more affured confervacion and encreace of the ftate, and honour of us, our Herres and Succeffours, and of our Reame, and th'advacement of the profperitie, vtilitie and comoditie of our Subgiects, it is by our conducte and moyne couvenanted, accorded and concluded, betwixt us on the oon partie, and the mooft facrede Prince Maximilian, elect Emperour, afwel for himself and in his owen name, and as then King of Romains, as alfo as graundfader, tutor and governour, of the perfone, lands and countries, of the right high and mighty Prince Charles Prince of Spayne, Archiduc of Aufrich, Duc of Bourgoyne, Brabant etc. and Counte of Flandres etc. his nepheu, and the fame Charles Prince of Spayne, by th'affent of his faid tutour, and the right noble Princeffe the Lady Margarete Ducheffe of Savoie, Awnte to the faid Princeon th'oder partie, for marriage by Godds grace to be had, and folempnely in the face of the Churche to be contracted, betwixt the faid Prince of Spaine, and our mooft dere doughter the Lady Mary, at fuche tyme as the faid Prince of Spaine fhall be of fuch perfite and full age, as the lawes of the Churche require for that porpofe, vnder fuch maner and fourme, and in fuche tyme and place, and with fuche condicions, as in the treatie thereupon paffes and concluded betwixt the Commiffioners of bothe fides, and afterward afwel by us as by the faid Emperour, Prince of Spayne and Ducheffe, by our and their feveral Letters Patents, under our and their greate feals, fubfcribed with our and their hands, ratified and confermed, it appereth more ample and at length; according whereunto fpowfells by words of the prefent requifite due and concenient in that behalve, by oure moynes, and at our right grete coft and charges, have been folempnely and openly contracted betwixt the faid Prince of caftell, by his Proctour in that parte fufficiently conftituted, ordeigned and deputed on the oon partie, and our faid doughter in her perfone on th'oder partie, in our Manour of Richemount, the [blank] daie of the moneth of Decembre, in the xxiiii yere of our Reigne, our felf in our perfone, and th'Ambaffadours of the faid Prince of Caftell, with many other of the mooft honorable Lords Spirituall and Temporall, Laidies, and other Nobles of our Royme in a grete nombre then being prefent, with diverfe and many mooft folempne and honourable Jufts, Touneys, Fefts, and other triumphes and ceremonies, to fuch an acte convenient and requifite, enfuying the faid contractie of efpoufellis, and by a long fpace of tyme contynuying and enduring.

AND whereas we for the Dote and mariage of our faid doughter, over and above the coft of her traduccion into the parties of Flandres, and furnifshing of Plate and other her Arraiments for her perfone, Juelxs, and garnifshing of her Chambre, which wol extende to no little fome nor charge, muft paie and content to the faid Prince of Spaine, the fome of fity thoufand pounds in redy money, at certaine termes expreffed n thr faid Treatiel for the whiche paiement, by th'advife of our Counfell, we have by our Letters vnder our great Seale fubfcribed with our hande, bounden our felf, our heires and Succeffours, Reames, Lands, Countreis, and all other goods moevable and immovable, and in like wife the perfonesand goods of all and every our Subgects, movables and imovables where foever thei fhall be founden; and that in like wife the Maire and Fellifhip of our ftaple of Calais, have at our defire bounden theim and their fucceffours, for the paiement of the faid Some; we vndoubtedly trufte and have our full confidence, that the thre Eftats of our reame, according to the laws and auncient cuftumes provided, and inviolably tyme out of mynde obferved and ufed, for the mariage of the Kings children of the Reame, fhall and wol by auctiritie of Parliament, fufficiently ordeyne and provide for the full paiement and contentacion of the faid L.M, to the faid Prince of Spayne, according to the porpointe of the faid treatie; and fee us of our faid Staple difcharged of the faid bands and obligacions. Confidering fpecially, that the perfection of the faid mariage, fhall redounde to the gretteft honour, fuertie, tranquillitie, refte, peace, prouffite and commoditie, vniverfally and particularly of our said bande as before is faied ftande bounden for the fame.

AND in cafe it foo fortune, as God defebde, that the faide mariage, by the dethe of the faid Prince of Caftile, or by any other chaunce or fortune whatfoever it be, take not effect, but vttrely diffolve and breke, or that our faid doughter be nat narried by us in our life, nor after the fame have fufficient provifion for her Dote and mariage by the faid thre Eftates; we then wol, that our faid doughter Mary have for her mariage, fift thoufand poundes paiable of out goods, yf fo moch remaigne after the performance of fuch things and charges as in our Wille is above and before exprefed and fpecified, which things and charges, we wol furft and before all other matiers be doon and performed, of and with our faid goods as farre as thei wol extende; and that doon and fully performed, yf any thing then remayne of our faid goods, we wol then that they for the payment of the faid L.M take of the faid goods as farre as thei wol goo. And if the faid goods wol not perfourme the faid L.M, we then wol that that lakketh and cannot be levied of our faid goods for the paiement of the faid L.M, bee levied of the faid rentes, revenues, prouffits and emoluments, by the hands of our Executours, foo and in noon other wife, that in her faid mariage the be ruled and ordred by th'advife and cofent of our faid Sone and Prince, and our faid Executours, and foo that fhe be married to fome noble Prince out of this our Reame.

(The Will of Henry VII, p. 38–42. (Bryson, S., *Mary Tudor*, p.69–72.)

Appendix Two

Turpyn's Chronicle of Calais

Preparations to be made in Calais on that occasion for her reception, and for the Emperor, Margaret, Henry VII and Charles.

The below is an excerpt. The full inventory, including the names of servants and household, can be found in Turpyn's *Chronicle* p.54–66. *Italics* appear to be in the handwriting of Henry VII. Date is the last year of his reign.

'For the transporting of my Lady the Princess of Castill, 1507'

Hereafter ensueth suche stuff as is needed to be provided for my lady the princesse of [Castille], and as welle for her wardobe of beddes as [for] her stable, against the solemnizations of her Mariage.

All these parcels to be had out of the kinges wardop, or, in default thereof, in London;

Firste, her bedde chambur to be hanged with clothe of golde, *with a bordre embroidered with hir bages, or som other devise*.

Item, for the said chambur a large trussing bedde, with celor, testor, and counterpoint of the same clothe of golde, with curteyns of damaske.

Item, a chayar of clothe of golde.

Item, iiij. Longe and large carpettes to cover the floure of the same chambur.

Item, v. cossions of fine clothe of golde, i. *richer then the other*, iij. Longe and ij. Shorte.

Item, smale carpettes for windowes borde and cobordes, v. at the lest, *of velet of cramosyne*, and as many carpettes of wolle for everyday.

Item, a fethirbed of fine downe, with a bolster, ij. pillowes of, and v. small pillowes, for to take the say, and for every of them iij. pilowe-beers off fyne holland clothe.

Item, iiij. peir of fyne shetes, and ij. peir of fustians for the said trussing bedde.

Item, a palet be *of feddurs* with bolster, furnisshed with shetes iij. payr, fustians *oon payre*, and counterpoint *oon*, for the gentilwomen that shall lie in the said chambur.

This must be provided in Flaunders:

For the second chambour.

First, a riche story of Aras golde and silke of *iiij yerdes* depe, with a bordor of her armys and bagies for a remembraunce, *of ij. feet de. Depe, price the Flemmyshe elme xx, and that the same storye conteigne in toto.... Flemish elnes.... The bordor.*

Item, a large sparver of clothe of golde *and cramosyn vellet perpale, the vellette embrodred with her bages and other devise*, with a counterpoint of the same, the curteyns of the same sparver to be of *dowble sarcenet, perpaled with the colours that the clothe of golde and vellet shalbe.*

Item, a chaiar of clothe of golde for the same chambour, with v. cossions of clothe of golde, iij. longe and ij. shorte.

Item, a fetherbedde of fyne downe, with a bolster and ij. pilowes with shetes, fustians, and pillowe beers as is appointed for the trussing bedde.

Item, a longe large carpet for the *borde under the fote, and iiij. for windowes and cupboard.*

Item, a traverse of cramosyn sarcenet.

For the iij chambour

First, a hangynge of *fyne tapessheryre*, with bagies and armys in the bordour *of vj. C. Flemmysshe elnes in toto.*

Item, a bedde of astate with a counterpoint *of clothe* of velvet and clothe of golde of her colours purpale.

Item, a chaiar of clothe of *cramosyn vellet embrodred*, and v. cossions of the same.

Item, a large fedderbed, with a bolster for the said bedde of astate.

Item, a large and longe carpett, and iiij. smale carpettes for the said chambur.

Item, a charriet for herre or her principalle ladies, covered with clothe of golde, with iiij. cossions of the same, and the horse harneis in likewise.

Item, ij. other charrietts for ladies or gentilwomen, covered with crymsyne velvet, and for every chariot iiij. cossions of the same, and the horse harneis in likewise.

Item, a large and a goodlie palfray to be ledde in hande, with a sadill and pillion, covered with riche clothe of golde, the bordres richelie imbrodred, orels of goldsmith worke, and the harness of the same.

Item, another goodlie palfray, with a like riche side-sadille, for the said ladie princesse to ride alone; the harneis like.

Item, viij. Other palfrais to folowe her with side-sadils richelie covered with clothe of gold, orels imbroderred upon velvet, with harness of the same.

Item, iij. or iiij. fotemen with riche cotes of goldsmyth worke to goo aboute her litter, or about her palfray.

Item, a pase to lifte her upon her palfray, covered with silver plates gilte, as the qwene is grace is.

Item, a chaunge for the said palfrays, that is to say, as well pilions, sadils, and harneis, and also coveringes for the said litter chariottes, to cover them when it is foule wedder, and a chaunge of harneis for every of the horsis of the said litter and ladies chariottes.

Item, a closed carre for her warderobe of the robes, and ij. chariottes for the warderobe of the robes, ij. large cannavas and ij. berehides for the said chariottes to save the stuf drie.

Item, a bottell horse and sadell for her flagons.

Item, a sumpter horse for her trussing bedde.

Item, another for her cofers.

Item, a male horse.

Item, another horse for the grome of the stables.

Item, the said palfrais to be provided for the betymes, and in likewise horses for the litter, the ladies chariottes, and for all other cariages befor specified.

The document continues with requirements for Maximilian, Margaret, Charles and Henry VII (not included here).

The inventory then goes on to list specific items for Mary including jewels, furniture and plate such as a list of jewels for her wedding day:

Furste, a cronelle for her hedde, of golde and stone, in the day of her marriage.

Item, a goodlie devise for her necke, set with stone and perle.

Item, a goodlie gurdille of goolde, of as goodly facion as may be devised.

Item, ij braselettes of golde, set with stone and perle.

Mary's household are also included, totalling 101 persons, not including any servants those individuals were permitted to take.

Appendix Three

Mary's Wardrobe

Some excerpts taken from the princess's inventory of robes, dated 1514, are shown here. (Norris, H., *Tudor Costume and Fashion*, Dover Publications, Mineola, 1997.)

Robes in the French mode

- One velvet robe of purple colour, lined with yellow cloth of gold on satin.
- One robe of cloth of gold decorated with baudekyn damask and furred with ermine.
- One robe of cloth of silver damask lined with crimson velvet embossed in gold.
- One robe of figured cloth of gold in a kind of damask furred with pampilion.
- One other robe of crimson cloth of gold damask of Italian work furred with mink.
- One robe of purple cloth of gold tissue furred with sable.
- One robe of crimson satin lined with green cloth of gold damask.
- One robe of crimson satin embossed in gold and worked with birds' eyes, lined with purple two-pile velvet embossed in gold.
- One robe of crimson double-pile velvet lined with crimson cloth of gold damask in a design of cuttes.
- One black velvet robe lined with ermine.
- One robe of purple satin lined with purple cloth of gold of damask.
- One crimson satin robe embossed in gold of baudekyn furred with Romaine.
- One robe of grey satin embossed in gold in the manner of birds' eyes, lined with crimson velvet.
- One robe of yellow velvet lined with Romaine.
- One robe of yellow velvet trimmed with skins of black coneys.

Cottes in the French mode

- One gray satin cotte embossed in gold with birds' eyes.
- One cotte of purple cloth of gold in the manner of Camelot.

- One other of crimson satin.
- One other cotte of crinkled white cloth of gold, figured in white.
- One cotte of silver cloth of Venetian baudekyn.
- One cotte of gold satin broché on gold in the colour of green birds' eyes.
- One cotte of crimson cloth of gold damask of baudekyn.
- Seven pairs of sleeves suitable for the said cottes.

Robes in the English style

- One crimson satin robe edged with cloth of silver damask lined with black taffeta.
- One satin broché robe on silver baudekyn lined with lamb.
- One robe of satin broché in crimson on gold in the new fashion, and bordered with velvet and lined with black taffeta.
- One robe of black velvet bordered with black satin and lined with black taffeta.
- One robe of black velvet lined with marten.
- One robe of black velvet bordered with mink and lined with calaber.
- One robe of yellow velvet bordered with figured cloth of gold in white and lined with taffeta.
- One robe of cloth of gold figured in figures and white tissue, furred with ermine.
- One robe of satin embossed with silver bordered with gold and lined with white taffeta.

Cottes in the English style

- One silver cotte in the manner of Camelot bordered with crimson velvet.
- One cotte of green satin bordered with cloth of gold.
- One cotte of black satin tissue on gold bordered with crimson velvet.
- One cotte of crimson satin bordered with cloth of gold.
- One cotte of purple satin edged with cloth of gold.
- One cotte of white satin edged with crimson velvet.
- One cotte of yellow satin bordered with crimson velvet.
- Seven pairs of sleeves suitable for the said cottes.
- One robe of silver cloth in a kind of damask of baudekyn, bordered with cloth of gold lined with white taffeta.

Robes in the Milanese style

- One robe of green satin lined with cloth of silver damask and bordered with cloth of silver damask.
- One robe of cloth of gold embroidered in circles, lined with green velvet and green taffeta and bordered with crimson satin.

Milanese 'bonets'

- Three bonets, the first of crimson velvet, another of black velvet, and the other of crimson satin.

Aiglettes for robes in the Milanese style without laces. The aiglettes are attached to the robe

- Twenty-eight large aiglettes in Venetian gold and twelve small.
- Twenty-eight large aiglettes made of gold and crimson silk and twelve small.
- Twenty-eight large aiglettes of gold and green silk and twelve small.

Mantle, capes

- One scarlet mantle, two capes of black velvet. Twelve pieces belonging to the capes.

Appendix Four

Mary and Brandon as the Central Characters of Romantic Literature

Drayton, Michael (1563–1631), Ovid (43 BC–17 or 18 AD), *England's heroical epistles, written in imitation of the stile and manner of Ovid's Epistles with annotations of the chronicle history* (p.166 onwards).

Mary the French Queen TO Charles Brandon Duke of Suffolk

The ARGUMENT.
Mary, the Daughter of that Renowned Prince King Henry the Seventh, being very young at her Father's death, was after by her Brother King Henry the Eight, given in marriage to Lewis King of France, being a man old and decrepit; This fair and beautiful Lady, long before had placed her Affections on Charles Brandon Duke of Suffolk, a brave and couragious young Gentleman, and an especial Favorite of the King her Brother, and a Man raised by him. King Lewis the Husband of the beautiful Queen died not long after he was married, and Charles Brandon having Commission from the King to bring her back to England, but being delayed by some sinister means, the French Queen writeth this Epistle to hasten the Duke forward on his intended voyage to France.

Such health from Heav'n my self may wish to me,
Such health from France Queen Mary sends to thee.
Brandon, how long mak'st thou excuse to stay,
And know'st how ill we Women brook delay?
If one poor Channel thus can part us two,
Tell me (unkind) what would an Ocean do?
Leander had an Hellespont to swim,
Yet this from Hero could not hinder him;
His Bark (poor Soul) his Breast; his Arms his Oares,
But thou a Ship to land thee on our Shores:
And opposite to famous Kent, doth lie

The pleasant Fields of flowry Picardy,
Where our fair Callice, walled in her Sands,
In kenning of the Cliffy Dover stands.
Here is no Bedlam Nurse, to pout nor lour,
When wantoning, we revel in my Towre,
Nor need I top my Turret with a Light,
To guide thee to me, as thou swim'st by Night;
Compar'd with me, wert thou but half so kind,
Thy Sighs should stuff thy Sails, though wanting Wind:
But ah thy Breast's becalm'd, thy Sighs be slack,
And mine too stiff, and blow thy broad Sayls back.
Perhaps thou'lt say, that I should blame the Flood,
Because the Wind so full against thee stood:
Nay blame it not, that it did roughly blow,
For it did chide thee that thou wast so slow;
Think not it came to keep thee in the Bay,
T'was sent from me, to bid thee come away:
But that thou vainly let'st occasion slide,
Thou might'st have wasted hither with the Tide.
If when thou com'st, I knit mine angry Brow,
Blame me not, Brandon, thou hast broke thy Vow;
Yet if I meant to frown, I might be dumb,
For this may make thee stand in doubt to come:
Nay come, sweet Charles, have care thy Ship to guide,
Come, my sweet Heart, in Faith I will not chide.
When as my Brother and his lovely Queen,
In sad Attire for my depart were seen,
* The utmost date expired of my stay,
* When I from Dover did depart away;
Thou know'st what Woe I suff'red for thy sake,
How oft I fain'd, of thee my leave to take;
God and thou know'st, with what an heavy heart
I took my farwel, when I should depart;
And being ship'd gave signal with my Hand
Up to the Cliff, where I did see thee stand;
Nor could refrain, in all the peoples view,
But cry'd to thee, Sweet Charles, adieu, adieu.
Look how a little Infant, that hath lost
The thing wherewith it was delighted most,
Weary with seeking, to some corner creeps,

And there (poor Soul) it sits it down and weeps;
And when the Nurse would fain content the mind,
Yet still it mourns, for that it cannot find:
Thus in my careful Cabbin did I lye,
When as the Ship out of the Road did flie.
Think'st thou my Love was faithful then to thee,
When young Castle to England su'd for me?
Be judge thy self, if it were not of power,
When I refus'd an Empire for my Dower.
To Englands Court, when once report did bring,
How thou in France didst revel with the King,
When he in triumph of his victory,
Under a rich imbroid'red Canopy,
Entred proud Tournay, which did trembling stand,
To beg for mercy at his conqu'ring hand;
To hear of his endearments, how I joy'd?
But see, this calm was suddenly destroy'd.
When Charles of Castile there to banquet came,
With him his Sister, that ambitious Dame,
Savoy's proud Dutches, knowing how long she
All means had try'd to win my love from me;
Fearing my absence might thy vows acquite,
To change thy Mary for a Margarite,
When in King Henries Tent of Cloth of Gold,
She often did thee in her Arms enfold;
Where you were feasted more deliciously,
Than Cleopatra did Mark Anthony,
Where sports all day did intertain your sight,
And then in Masks you pass'd away the night.
But thou wilt say, 'tis proper unto us,
That we by nature all are jealous:
"I must confess 'tis oft found in our Sex,
"But who not love, not any thing suspects:
"True love doth look with pale suspitious eye,
"Take away love, if you take jealousie.
Turwin and Turney when King Henry took,
For this great change who then did ever look?
When Maximilian to those wars addrest,
Wore Englands Cross on his Imperial breast,
And in our Army let his Eagle flie,

That view'd our Ensigns with a wond'ring Eye,
Little thought I when Bullen first was won,
Wedlock should end, what angry War begun.
From which I vow, I yet am free in thought,
But this alone by Wolseies wit was wrought.
To his advice the King gave free consent;
That will I, nill I, I must be content.
My Virgins right, thy state could not advance,
But now enriched with the Dower of France;
Then, but poor Suffolk's Dutchess had I been,
Now, the great Dowager, the most Christian Queen.
But I perceive where all thy grief doth lie,
Lewis of France had my Virginity,
He had indeed, but shall I tell thee what,
Believe me, Brandon, he had scarcely that:
Good feeble King, he could not do much harm,
But Age must needs have something that is warm;
"Small drops (God knows) do quench that heatless fire.
"When all the strength is only in desire.
And I could tell (if Modesty might tell)
There's somewhat else that pleaseth Lovers well;
To rest his Cheek, upon my softer Cheek,
Was all he had, and more he did not seek;
So might the little Baby clip the Nurse,
And it content, she never a whit the worse:
Then think this, Brandon, if that make thee frown,
He on my Head, for Maydenhead, set a Crown.
Who would not change, a Kingdom for a Kiss?
Hard were the Heart that would not yield him this;
And time yet half so swiftly doth not pass,
Nor yet full five Months elder then I was.
When thou to France conducted wast by Fame,
With many Knights which from all Countries came,
To see me at Saint Dennis on my Throne,
Where Lewes held my Coronation;
Where the proud Dolphin, for thy valour sake,
Chose thee at Tilt his Princely part to take;
When as the Staves upon thy Cask did light,
Grieved therewith, I turn'd away my sight,
And spake aloud, when I my self forgot,

'Tis my sweet Charles, my Brandon, hurt him not:
But when I fear'd the King perceived this,
Good silly Man, I pleas'd him with a Kiss,
And to extoll his valiant Son began,
That Europe never bred a braver Man;
And when (poor King) he simply praised thee
Of all the rest I ask'd which thou shouldst be?
Thus I with him dissembled for thy sake,
Open confession now amends must make,
Whilst this old King upon a Pallat lies,
And only holds a combat with mine Eyes;
Mine Eyes from his, by thy sight stoln away,
Which might too well their Mistress Thoughts bewray.
But when I saw thy proud unconquer'd Launce
To bear the Prize from all the flow'r of France;
To see what pleasure did my Soul embrace,
Might eas'ly be discerned in my Face.
Look, as the Dew upon a Damask Rose,
How through that liquid Pearl his blushing shows,
And when the gentle air breaths on his top,
From the sweet Leaves falls eas'ly drop by drop;
Thus by my Cheek, distilling from mine Eyes,
One Tear for Joy anothers Room supplies.
Before mine Eye (like Touch) thy shape did prove.
Mine Eye condemn'd my too too partial Love;
But since by others I the same do try,
My Love condemns my too too partial Eye.
The precious stone, most beautiful and rare,
When with it self we only it compare,
We deem all other of that kind to be
As excellent, as that we only see;
But when we judge of that, with others by,
Too credulous we do condemn our Eye,
Which then appears more orient, and more bright,
Having a Boyl whereon to shew its light.
Alanson, a fine timb'red Man, and tall,
Yet wants the shape thou art adorn'd withal;
Vandome good Carriage, and a pleasing Eye,
Yet hath not Suffolk's Princely Majesty;
Couragious Burbon, a sweet Manly Face,

Yet in his Looks lacks Brandon's Courtly Grace.
Proud Longavile suppos'd to have no Peer,
A man scarce made was thought, whilst thou wast here.
The Count Saint-Paul, our best at Arms in France,
Would yield himself a Squire, to bear thy Lauce.
Galleas and Bounarm, matchless for their might;
Under thy towring Blade have couch'd in fight.
If with our Love my Brother angry be,
I'le say, to please him, I first fancied thee,
And but to frame my liking to his mind.
Never to thee had I been half so kind,
Worthy my love, the Vulgar judge no man.
Except a Yorkist or Lancastrian;
Nor think, that my affection should be set,
But in the Line of great Plantaginet.
I mind not what the idle Commons say,
I pray thee Charles make hast and come away.
To thee what's England, if I be not there?
Or what to me is France, if thou not here?
Thy absence makes me angry for a while,
But at thy presence I should gladly smile.
When last of me, his leave my Brandon took,
He sware an Oath (and made my Lips the Book)
He would make hast which now thou do'st denie;
Thou art forsworn: O wilful Perjury!
Sooner would I with greater sins dispence,
Than by intreaty pardon this Offence.
But then I think, if I should come to shrive thee,
Great were the Fault that I should not forgive thee,
Yet wert thou here, I should revenged be,
But it should be with too much loving thee.
I, that is all that thou shalt fear to taste;
I pray thee Brandon come, sweet Charles make hast.

Charles Brandon Duke of Suffolk TO Mary the French Queen

BUT that my Faith commands me to forbear;
The fault's your own, if I impatient were;
Were my dispatch such as should be my speed,

I should want time your loving Lines to read.
Here in the Court, Camelion-like I fare,
And as that Creature only feed on Air;
All Day I wait, and all the Night I watch,
And starve mine Ears, to hear of my dispatch.
If Dover were th' Abydos of my Rest,
Or pleasant Calice were my Maries Cest,
You should not need, bright Queen, to blame me so,
Did not the Distance, to Desire say no:
No tedious Night from Travel should be free,
Till through the Seas, with swimming still to thee,
A snowy Path I made unto thy Bay,
So bright as is that Nectar-stained Way.
The restless Sun by travelling doth wear,
Passing his Course, to finish up the Year;
But Paris locks my Love, within the Main,
And London yet thy Brandon doth detain.
Of thy firm love thou put'st me still in mind,
But of my Faith, not one word can I find.
When Longavile to Mary was affy'd,
And thou by him wast made King Lewis's Bride,
How oft I wish'd, that thou a Prize might'st be,
That I in Arms might combate him for thee!
And in the madness of my love distraught,
A thousand times his Murther have fore-thought:
"But that th' all-seeing Pow'rs, which sit above,
"Regard not Mad-mens Oaths, nor faults in Love,
"And have confirm'd it by the grant of Heaven,
"That Lovers sins on Earth should be forgiven;
"For never Man is half so much distress'd,
"As he that loves to see his Love possess'd.
Coming to Richmond after thy depart,
(Richmond, where first thou stol'st away my heart)
Me thought it look'd not as it did of late,
But wanting thee, forlorn and desolate,
In whose fair walks, thou often hast been seen,
To sport with Cath'rine, Henries beautious Queen,
Astonishing sad Winter with thy sight,
So that for thee the day hath put back night;
And the small Birds, as in the pleasant Spring,

Forgot themselves, and have begun to sing.
So oft as I by Thames go and return,
Me thinks for thee the River yet doth mourn,
Whom I have seen to let his Stream at large,
Which like an Hand-maid waited on thy Barge;
And if thou hap'st against the Flood to row,
Which way it eb'd, it presently would flow,
Weeping in Drops upon the labouring Oares,
For joy that it had got thee from the Shoares.
The Swans with musick that the Rowers make,
Ruffing their plumes, came gliding on the Lake,
As the swift Dolphins by Arions strings,
Were brought to Land with Syren ravishings;
The flocks and heards that pasture near the Flood,
To gaze on thee, have oft forborn their food,
And sat down sadly mourning by the brim,
That they by Nature were not made to swim.
When as the Post to Englands Royal Court,
Of thy hard passage brought the true report,
How in a storm thy well-rigg'd Ships were tost,
And thou thy self in danger to be lost:
I knew 'twas Venus loath'd that aged Bed,
Where Beauty so should be dishonoured;
Or fear'd the Sea-Nymphs haunting of the Lake,
If thou but seen, their Goddess should forsake.
And whirling round her Dove-drawn Coach about,
To view the Navy then in lanching out,
Her ayrie Mantle loosely doth unbind,
Which fanning forth a rougher gale of wind,
Wafted thy Sails with speed unto the Land,
And ran thy Ships on Bullins harb'ring strand.
How should I joy of thy arrive to hear?
But as a poor Sea-faring passenger,
After long travail, tempest torn and wrack'd,
By some unpitty'ng Pyrat that is sack'd;
Hears the false Robber that hath stoln his wealth,
Landed in some safe Harbour, and in health,
Inrich'd with the invaluable store,
For which he long had travelled before.
When thou to Abvile held'st th' appointed day,

We heard how Lewis met thee on the way;
Where thou, in glitt'ring Tissue strangely dight,
Appear'dst unto him like the Queen of Light;
In Cloath of Silver, all thy Virgin Train,
In Beauty sumptuous, as the Nothern Wain;
And thou alone the foremost glorious Star,
Which led'st the Team of that great Waggoner.
What could thy Thought be, but as I did think,
When thine Eyes tasted what mine Ears did drink?
A cripple King, layd bed-rid long before,
Yet at thy coming, crept out of the door:
'Twas well he rid, he had no leggs to go,
But this thy Beauty forc'd his Body to;
For whom a Cullice had more fitter been,
Than in a golden Bed, a gallant Queen.
To use thy Beauty, as the Miser Gold,
Which hoards it up but only to behold;
Sill looking on it with a jealous Eye,
Fearing to lend, yet loving Usury:
O Sacriledge (if Beauty be divine)
The prophane Hand to touch the hallowed Shrine!
To surfeit sickness on the sound mans Diet,
To rob content, yet still to live unquiet.
And having all, to be of all beguil'd,
And yet still longing like a little Child.
When Marquess Dorset, and the valiant Grays
To purchase Fame, first crost the narrow Seas,
With all the Knights that my Associates went,
In honour of thy Nuptial Tournament;
Think'st thou I joy'd not in thy Beauties pride,
When thou in Triumph didst through Paris ride?
Where all the Streets, as thou didst pace along,
With Arras, Biss, and Tapestry were hung;
Ten thousand gallant Citizens prepar'd,
In rich Attire thy Princely self to guard:
Next them, three thousand choice Religious Men,
In golden Vestments follow'd on agen;
And in Procession as they came along,
With Hymen sweetly sang thy Marriage Song,
Next these, five Dukes, as did their places fall,

With each of them a Princely Cardinal;
Then thou, on thy Imperial Chariot set,
Crown'd with a rich impearled Coronet;
Whilst the Parisian Dames, as thy Train past,
Their precious incense in abundance cast.
As Cynthia, from her wave-embattel'd Shrowds,
Op'ning the West, comes streaming through the Clouds,
With shining Troops of Silver-tressed Stars,
Attending on her, as her Torch-bearers;
And all the lesser Lights about her Throne,
With admiration stand as lookers on;
Whilst she alone, in height of all her pride,
The Queen of Light along her Sphere doth glide.
When on the Tilt my Horse like Thunder came,
No other Signal had I, but thy Name;
Thy Voyce my Trumpet, and my Guide thine Eyes,
And but thy Beauty, I esteem'd no prize.
That large lim'd Almain of the Giants Race,
Which bare strength on his Breast, fear in his Face,
Whose sinew'd Arms, with his steel-temper'd Blade,
Through Plate and Male such open passage made,
Upon whose Might the Frenchmens glory lay,
And all the hope of that victorious day;
Thou saw'st thy Brandon beat him on his Knee,
Off'ring his Shield a conquer'd Spoil to thee,
But thou wilt say, perhaps, I vainly boast,
And tell thee that which thou already know'st.
No sacred Queen, my Valour I deny,
It was thy Beauty, not my Chivalry:
One of thy tressed Curls there falling down,
As loath to be imprisoned in thy Crown,
I saw the soft Ayr sportively to take it,
And into strange and sundry forms to make it;
Now parting it to four, to three, to twain,
Now twisting it, then it untwist again;
Then make the threads to dally with thine Eye,
A Sunny Candle for a golden Fly.
At length from thence one little tear it got,
Which falling down as though a Star had shot,
My up-turn'd Eye pursu'd it with my Sight,

The which again redoubled all my Might.
'Tis but in vain, of my Descent to boast;
When Heav'ns Lamp shines, all other Lights be lost;
Faulcons seem poor, the Eagle sitting by,
Whose Brood surveyes the Sun with open Eye:
Else might my blood find Issue from his force,
Who beat the Tyrant Richard from his Horse
On Bosworth Plain, whom Richmond chose to wield
His glorious Ensign in that conqu'ring Field;
And with his Sword, in his dear Sov'reigns sight,
To his last breath stood fast in Henries Right.
Then, beautious Empress, think this safe delay,
Shall be the Even to a joyful Day:
"Fore-sight doth still on all advantage lye,
"Wise-men give place forc'd by necessity;
"To put back ill, our good we must forbear,
"Better first fear, then after still to fear.
'Twere over-sight in that, at which we aim,
To put the Hazzard on an after-Game;
With patience then let us our Hopes attend,
And till I come, receive these Lines I send

Notes

Abbreviations

CSPM: Calendar of State Papers and Manuscripts in the Archives and Collections of Milan 1385–1618
CSPS: Calendar State Papers Spain
CSPV: Calendar of State Papers Relating to English Affairs in the Archives of Venice
E101: Exchequer, King's Remembrancer, Various Accounts
FQL: The French Queen's Letters
L&P: Letters and Papers Illustrative of the Reigns of Richard III and Henry VII
LPFD: Letters and Papers Foreign and Domestic in the Reign of Henry VIII
LPE: Lives of the Princesses of England from the Norman Conquest
LRIL: Letters of Royal and Illustrious Ladies of Great Britain
PPE: Privy Purse Expenses

Introduction

1. Amin, N., *The House of Beaufort*, Amberley, Stroud (2018), p.156.
2. Ashdown-Hill, J., *The Wars of the Roses*, Amberley, Stroud (2017), p.48.

Chapter One – A Tudor Rose

1. There are different opinions on Mary's year of birth. It should be noted that during that time the Julian calendar was in use meaning that the new year began on 25 March. The Gregorian calendar was adopted in 1752. Where reference is made to Mary's birth on 18 March 1495, the new year had not yet begun. Therefore, using the modern calendar Mary would have been born in 1496.
2. LPE, Vol. V, p.2, fn. 1. The reference in Green is given in Latin and reads 'Anne Skeron nutrici dominae Marie pro quarterio unius anni finiti ad festum Sancti Johannis Baptisae ultim. Johannae Skidmore et Aliciae Bywimble, cuilibet earum, pro attendiciis suis, nutrici ducis Eboracensis et

sororum suarem, per medium annum…' Translation: 'Anne Skeron nurse of the lady Mary for the quarter of one year ending at the feast of St. John the Baptist last. Joan Skidmore and Alice Bywimble, to each of them, for their attentions, to nurse the Duke of York and his sisters, for half a year…' The original reference is from Calendar Privy Seal Bills Henry VII, Rolls House.

3. E101/414/6 fol. 49v (Payments), 1496.
4. Gairdner, J. (ed.), *The Spousells of the Princess Mary*, The Camden Society, London (1893), p.17.
5. CSPV, Vol. 1, 790. The letter is dated 3 March and declares Mary as 3 years old but she would have not been 3 for another couple of weeks.
6. CSPM, 593 – November 1498.
7. CSPV, Vol. 1, 790.
8. L&P, Henry VII, Vol. 1, p.400.
9. LPE, Vol. V, p.2.
10. Ibid.
11. McElroy, A., *Educating the Tudors*, Pen and Sword, Barnsley (2023), p.6.
12. PPE, Elizabeth of York, p.12.
13. BL Add MS 59899 fol. 82r viewed via Tudor Chamber Books online.
14. LPE, Vol. IV, pp.62–63.
15. LPE, Vol. IV, p.62.
16. LPE, Vol. IV, p.64.
17. LPE, Vol. IV, pp.64–65.
18. PPE, Elizabeth of York, p.22.

Chapter Two – 'A blossome named Mary'

1. CSPS, Vol. 1, 398.
2. CSPS, Vol. 1, 406.
3. PPE, Elizabeth of York, p.23.
4. Perry, M., *Sisters to the King*, André Deutsch Ltd, London (2002), p.57.
5. FQL, p.11.
6. FQL, p.36.
7. LPE, Vol. V, p.3.
8. Ibid.
9. L&P, Vol. 2, pp.146–147.
10. LPE, Vol. V, p.4. Printed in LPE as a modernised version from Cotton. MS. Vespacion C. xii. f. 239 b.
11. CSPV, 883.
12. CSPV, 885.

13. Gairdner, J. (ed.), *The Spousells of the Princess Mary*, The Camden Society, London (1893), pp.viii–x.
14. FQL, p.27
15. CSPV, 887.
16. CSPS, Vol. I, 488.
17. CSPS, Vol. I, 499.
18. This is an excerpt from *The Justes of the Moneths of May and June*. Unfortunately there is no author recorded for the poem but it is believed to have printed by Wynkyn de Worde in 1507. The whole poem can be read in Carew Hazlitt, W. (ed.), *Remains of the Early Popular Poetry of England*, John Russell Smith, London (1866), pp.113–120.
19. A larger excerpt can be found in Appendices: *The Justes of the Moneths of May and June*. Unfortunately there is no author recorded for the poem but it is believed to have printed by Wynkyn de Worde in 1507. The whole poem can be read in Carew Hazlitt, W. (ed.), *Remains of the Early Popular Poetry of England*, John Russell Smith, London (1866), pp.109–130.
20. CSPS, Vol. I, 556.
21. LPE, Vol. V, p.6.
22. LPE, Vol. V, pp.7–8.
23. LPE, Vol. V, pp.8–9.
24. CSPS, Vol. I, 579.
25. CSPS, Vol. I, 594.
26. CSPS, Vol. I, 586.
27. CSPS, Vol. I, 587.
28. CSPS, Vol. I, 594.
29. The details are recorded and printed in *The Spousells of the Princess Mary*, The Camden Society, London (1893). The original was printed by Pynson in two versions: one English and one Latin. The original Altin version is thought to have been written by Peter Carmelianus, Latin Secretary to Henry VII. Gairdner has managed to collate the two into one volume. There are large sections of the original English version which were unfortunately lost and the English is much shorter, possibly in an effort to produce something that more people could read. Where the English is missing or appears much shorter in comparison, I have attempted to translate the Latin version where required. Any errors are my own.
30. Gairdner, J. (ed.), *The Spousells of the Princess Mary*, The Camden Society, London (1893), p.3–4.
31. This has been translated from the Latin as the English text is missing — any errors are my own. Gairdner, J. (ed.), *The Spousells of the Princess Mary*, The Camden Society, London (1893), p.8.

32. Ibid., p. 9.
33. Gairdner, J. (ed.), *The Spousells of the Princess Mary*, The Camden Society, London (1893), pp.14–15.
34. Ibid., p.12.
35. Ibid., p.13.
36. This has been translated from the Latin as the English text is missing — any errors are my own. Gairdner, J. (ed.), *The Spousells of the Princess Mary*, The Camden Society, London (1893), p.17.
37. Gairdner, J. (ed.), *The Spousells of the Princess Mary*, The Camden Society, London, (1893), p.17.

Chapter Three – Princess of Castile

1. This has been translated from the Latin as the English text is missing — any errors are my own. Gairdner, J. (ed.), *The Spousells of the Princess Mary*, The Camden Society, London (1893), p.17.
2. Ibid., p.18.
3. LPE, Vol. V, p.12.
4. Gairdner, J. (ed.), *The Spousells of the Princess Mary*, The Camden Society, London (1893), pp.21–22.
5. This has been translated from the Latin as the English text is missing — any errors are my own. Gairdner, J. (ed.), *The Spousells of the Princess Mary*, The Camden Society, London (1893), pp.18–19.
6. LPE, Vol. V, p.13.
7. Gairdner, J. (ed.), *The Spousells of the Princess Mary*, The Camden Society, London (1893), p.25.
8. Ibid., pp.29–30.
9. This has been translated from the Latin as the English text is missing — any errors are my own. Gairdner, J. (ed.), *The Spousells of the Princess Mary*, The Camden Society, London (1893), pp.34–35.
10. LPE, Vol. V, p.14.
11. The full inventory can be read in the Appendix or Turpyn, R., *The Chronicles of Calais in the Reigns of Henry VII and Henry VIII, to the Year 1540*, The Camden Society (1846), pp.54–66.
12. This letter is given the date of 1513 in L&P, Henry VIII, Vol. 1, 4606. However, James Gairdner argues that there is no evidence of de Bergh (referred to specifically in the letter) being present at the English court in 1513. Gairdner also makes reference to the childish appearance of Charles'

signature in comparison to his signature at 16 years old. Gairdner, J. (ed.), *The Spousells of the Princess Mary*, The Camden Society, London (1839), pp.xi–xii.
13. LPE, Vol. V, p.15.
14. CSPS, Vol. II, 1.
15. LPE, Vol. V., p.15.
16. *The Will of King Henry VII.* Printed for *The Editor*, London, 1775, pp.41–42.
17. CSPS, Vol. II, 9.
18. *Hall's Chronicle*, p.509.
19. *Hall's Chronicle*, p.510.
20. This is equivalent to £1331 in 2017; conversion courtesy of the National Archives Currency Converter. The King's Book of Payments, LPFD, Vol. II, 1509–1515, pp.1441–1444.
21. King's Book of Payments, LPFD, Vol. II, 1509–1515, pp.1444–1449.
22. Conversion courtesy of the National Archives Currency Converter based on 2017.
23. Revels, LPFD, Vol. II, pp.1490–1518.
24. *Hall's Chronicle*, p.514.
25. LPE, Vol. V, p.16.
26. *Hall's Chronicle*, p.516.
27. According to *Hall's Chronicle*, p.516, the godparents were William Warham, the Earl of Surrey and Catherine, Countess of Devonshire, daughter of Edward IV.
28. LPFD, Vol. I, 671.
29. *Hall's Chronicle*, p.517.
30. The 1511 Westminster Tournament Roll was commissioned by Henry VIII to record the joust. It is almost 60ft long and is held at the College of Arms.
31. LPFD, Vol. I, 678.
32. Revels, LPFD, Vol. II, pp.1490–1518.
33. Revels, LPFD, Vol. II, pp.1490–1518.
34. *Hall's Chronicle*, pp.517–518.
35. Revels, LPFD, Vol. II, pp.1490–1518.
36. *Hall's Chronicle*, p.519.
37. King's Book of Payments, LPFD, Vol. II, 1509–1515, pp.1449–1453.
38. Ibid.
39. Ibid., pp.1453–1458.
40. LPFD, Vol. I, 1027.
41. King's Book of Payments, LPFD, Vol. II, 1509–1515, pp.1458–1463.
42. Ibid., pp.1453–1458.
43. Revels, LPFD, Vol. II, pp.1490–1518.

44. Ibid.
45. Ibid.
46. *Hall's Chronicle*, p.526.
47. King's Book of Payments, LPFD, Vol. II, 1509–1515, pp.1458–1463.
48. FQL, p.31.
49. King's Book of Payments, LPFD, Vol. II, 1509–1515, pp.1458–1463.
50. It is thought Mary also owned a set of these tapestries.
51. LPFD, Vol. I, 2867
52. King's Book of Payments, LPFD, Vol. II, 1509–1515, pp.1458–1463.
53. LPE, Vol. V, p.21.
54. The full list can be found in Appendix or Turpyn, R, *The Chronicles of Calais in the Reigns of Henry VII and Henry VIII, to the Year 1540*, The Camden Society (1846), pp.54–66.
55. *Hall's Chronicle*, p.567.
56. King's Book of Payments, LPFD, Vol. II, 1509–1515, pp.1458–1463.
57. LPFD, Vol. I, 2779.
58. *Hall's Chronicle*, p.568.
59. LPFD, Vol. I, 1866
60. LPE, Vol. V, p.25.
61. LPFD, Vol. I, 2768.
62. The translation is my own, the wording translated directly provides male titles reading as follows: Most Serenely, to Prince Mary, Archduke of Austria, Prince of Spain and Duke of Burgundy, our dearest daughter. I changed the translation to female titles for ease of reading. Any mistakes are my own. LPFD, Vol. I, 2895.
63. King's Book of Payments, LPFD, Vol. II, 1509–1515, pp.1463–1466.
64. LPFD, Vol. I, 2924
65. LPFD, Vol. I, 3041.
66. LPFD, Vol. I, 3074.
67. LPFD, Vol. I, 3093.
68. LPFD, Vol. I, 5282.

Chapter Four – 'Nymph from Heaven'

1. LPFD, Vol. I, 2958.
2. LPFD, Vol. I, 2955.
3. CSPV, Vol. II, 436.
4. CSPV, Vol. II, 415.

5. *Hall's Chronicle*, p.569.
6. LPFD, Vol. I, 3009.
7. LPFD, Vol. I, 2976.
8. LPFD, Vol. I, 2972
9. LPFD, Vol. I, 2992.
10. LPFD, Vol. I, 2982.
11. LPFD, Vol. I, 3027.
12. LPFD, Vol. I, 3009.
13. LPFD, Vol. I, 3098–3100.
14. CSPV, Vol. II, 440.
15. LPFD, Vol. I, 3109.
16. LPFD, Vol. I, 2957.
17. LPFD, Vol. I, 2958.
18. CSPV, Vol. II, 466.
19. LPFD, Vol. I, 5282.
20. LPFD, Vol. I, 3134.
21. Henry refers to Mary as 13 years old. In December 1508 she was only 12 years old. CSPV, Vol. II, 487.
22. CSPV, Vol. II, 482.
23. CSPV, Vol. II, 505.
24. LPFD, Vol. I, 3146.
25. CSPV, Vol. II, 482.
26. CSPV, Vol. II, 505.
27. LPFD, Vol. I, 3171.
28. King's Book of Payments, LPFD, Vol. II, 1509–1515, pp.1463–1466.
29. LPFD, Vol. I, 3147.
30. FQL, p.79.
31. CSPV, Vol. II, 482.
32. Ibid.
33. LPFD, Vol. I, 3186.
34. LPFD, Vol. I, 3180. See images.
35. LPFD, Vol. I, 3187.
36. LPFD, Vol. I, 3199.
37. CSPV, Vol. II, 473.
38. CSPV, Vol. II, 475–476.
39. LPFD, Vol. I, 3207.
40. LPFD, Vol. I, 3153.
41. CSPV, Vol. II, 505.
42. Italics are my own. CSPV, Vol. II, 500.

Chapter Five – The French Queen

1. CSPV, Vol. II, 465.
2. CSPV, Vol. II, 490.
3. LPFD, Vol. I, 3155.
4. LPFD, Vol. I, 3156.
5. LPFD, Vol. I, 3191.
6. LPFD, Vol. I, 3201.
7. LPFD, Vol. I, 3202.
8. LPFD, Vol. I, 3224.
9. LPFD. Vol. I, 3225. The letter is in French and is mutilated but reads '[gr]ant co[ntentement le soin que] vous aves pris a ... [l]a pais, et vous prie [tenir] main a lentretenemen[t] dicelle ainsy que j'ay en vo[us conf] iance; car de mon co[eur je] la desire sur toutes ... [en]tretenir; et au su[rplus fai]ctes mes recommand[ations a]u Roy mon bon frer[e ton] maistre et luy dicte[s] je luy prye menvoye[r sa] seur le plus tost q[ue] faire se pourra et qui[l] fera en ce faisant singulie[r ... mon cou[sin] ... de Longueville vous ... re plus au long.' (Translation: [gratefully grateful for the care that] you have taken in... [the] country, and beg you to [keep] hand in the maintenance[t] of this so that I have [you] confidence in it; for with my heart I desire it above all... [to] maintain it; and in addition make my recommendations to King my good brother your master and dictate to him I ask him to send me to his sister as soon as possible and who[l] will in doing so singular[r... my cousin[sin]... of Longueville... re more at length).
10. LPFD, Vol. I, 3208.
11. LPFD, Vol. I, 3230.
12. LPFD, Vol. I, 3233.
13. LPFD, Vol. I, 3232.
14. LPFD, Vol. I, 3246–3247.
15. LPFD, Vol. I, 3264.
16. LPFD, Vol. I, 3240.
17. Ibid.
18. LPFD, Vol. I, 3252.
19. LPFD, Vol. I, 3257.
20. LPFD, Vol. I, 3262.
21. LPFD, Vol. I, 3266.
22. LPFD, Vol. I, 3321.
23. LPFD, Vol. I, 3323.

24. Descriptions of the gowns Mary had can be found in the appendices or Norris, H., *Tudor Costume and Fashion*, J. M. Dent & Sons, London (1997), pp.209–211.
25. LPFD, Vol. I, 3326.
26. LPFD, Vol. I, 3325.
27. Norris, H., *Tudor Costume and Fashion*, J. M. Dent & Sons, London (1997), p.355.
28. LPE, Vol. V, p.35.
29. King's Book of Payments, LPFD, Vol. II, 1509–1515, pp.1466–1469.
30. LPE, Vol. V, p.35.
31. LPFD, Vol. I, 3326.
32. LPE, Vol. V, p.36.
33. CSPV, Vol. II, 511.
34. LPFD, Vol. I, 3295.
35. LPFD, Vol. I, 3269.
36. CSPV, Vol. II, 496.
37. LPE, Vol. V, p.60.
38. Further receipts for sums received by those appointed to accompany Mary can be found in the September section of LPFD, Vol. I, particularly 3320 and grant no. 33.
39. LPFD, Vol. I, 3268.
40. LPFD, Vol. I, 3294.
41. LPFD, Vol. I, 3325.
42. Norris, H., *Tudor Costume and Fashion*, J. M. Dent & Sons, London (1997), p.209.
43. LPFD, Vol. I, 3324, grant no. 8.
44. King's Book of Payments, LPFD, Vol. II, 1509–1515, pp.1466–1469.
45. LPFD, Vol. I, 3348. Also FQL, p.101. Sadlack refers to Elizabeth Howard being the Duchess of Norfolk but the first wife of the 2nd Duke of Norfolk, Elizabeth Tilney, died in 1497. Thomas Howard married Agnes Tilney the same year, therefore it cannot have been Elizabeth Howard in attendance. However, it may have been Elizabeth Stafford who had married Thomas Howard, Earl of Surrey, in 1513, and daughter-in-law to the 2nd Duke of Norfolk. Sadlack also states it was the sister of the Duke of Norfolk who was the Countess of Oxford at the time, however, Anne Howard, the sister of the 2nd Duke of Norfolk died in 1474. Thomas and Agnes did have a daughter named Anne who was married to the Earl of Oxford. The marriage was declared invalid in May 1514 but appears to have been recognised to the extent that she was still referred to as his widow when he died in 1526. It appears the reference to the

Duke of Norfolk is referring to the 3rd Duke of Norfolk who was an earl at the time and did not achieve dukedom until 1524 upon the death of his father. The 2nd Duke of Norfolk most certainly accompanied Mary. Leland simply refers to the Duchess of Norfolk and her daughter the Countess of Oxford, therefore I am of the opinion it was Agnes and her daughter Anne who attended, possibly in addition to Elizabeth Stafford.

46. LPFD, Vol. I, 3294.
47. LPFD, Vol. I, 3331.
48. LPFD, Vol. I, 3320.
49. CSPV, Vol. II, 500.
50. CSPV, Vol. II, 500.
51. LPE, Vol. V, pp.60–61.
52. CSPV, Vol. II, 503.
53. FQL, p.64.
54. LPFD, Vol. I, 3513.
55. Although the record notes January 1515, it is of course the payment for taking Mary to France and is recorded as paid at a later date, possibly when the pilot returned to England. King's Book of Payments, LPFD, Vol. II, 1509–1515, pp.1466–1469.

Chapter Six – 'She is a Paradise'

1. Turpyn, R., *The Chronicles of Calais in the Reigns of Henry VII and Henry VIII, to the Year 1540*, The Camden Society (1846), p.16.
2. *Hall's Chronicle*, p.570.
3. CSPV, Vol. II, 499.
4. LPE, Vol. V, p.39.
5. LPFD, Vol. I, 3334.
6. FQL, p.66.
7. FQL, pp.67–68.
8. CSPV, Vol. II, 511.
9. CSPV, Vol. II, 511.
10. CSPV, Vol. II, 511.
11. *Hall's Chronicle*, p.570.
12. LPE, Vol. V, p.56.
13. CSPV, Vol. II, 508.
14. CSPV, Vol. II, 511.
15. CSPV, Vol. II, 511.
16. FQL, p.69.

17. The pageants are described in FQL, p.70.
18. LPFD, Vol. I, 3344.
19. LPE, Vol. V, pp.41–42.
20. CSPV, Vol. II, 511.
21. CSPV, Vol. II, 510.
22. Norris, H., *Tudor Costume and Fashion*, J. M. Dent & Sons, London (1997), p.209 and LPE, Vol. V, p.43.
23. FQL, p.70.
24. CSPV, Vol. II, 511.
25. CSPV, Vol. II, 508.
26. Norris, H., *Tudor Costume and Fashion*, J. M. Dent & Sons, London (1997), p.209.
27. CSPV, Vol. II, 508.
28. LPFD, Vol. I, 3348.
29. LPFD, Vol. I, 3348; the numbers following names refer to the number of horses each person had with him, for example, the Lord Lawarre, 30, means he had 30 horses.
30. CSPV, Vol. II, 508.
31. Turpyn R., *The Chronicles of Calais in the Reigns of Henry VII and Henry VIII, to the Year 1540*, The Camden Society (1846), pp.75–76.
32. Ives, E., *Anne Boleyn*, Basil Blackwell, London (1988), pp.34–35.
33. King's Book of Payments, LPFD, Vol. II, 1509–1515, pp.1469–1473.
34. LPE, Vol. V, pp.46–47.
35. Ellis, R., *Original Letters, Illustrative of English History: 1418–1529*, Vol. I, AMS Press, London (1824), pp.116–117.
36. Ibid., p.117.
37. Ibid., pp.117–119.
38. LPE, Vol. V, pp.48–49. The spelling has been modernised in LPE, but the original spelling can be read in Ellis, R., *Original Letters, 2nd Series*, p.244.
39. LPE, Vol. V, p.48.
40. Richardson, W., *Mary Tudor The White Queen*, Peter Owen Limited, London (1970), pp.184–185.
41. LRIL, Vol. I, p.179.
42. FQL, p.78.
43. FQL, p.170.
44. Ellis, R, *Original Letters Illustrative of English History: Including Numerous Royal Letters; from Autographs in the British Museum, and One or Two Other Collections. 2nd Series*, Harding and Lepard (1827), pp.240–241.
45. LPE, Vol. I, p.51.
46. Ibid.

Chapter Seven – Crowning a Tudor Rose

1. FQL, p.71.
2. LRIL, Vol. I, pp.175–177.
3. LPE, Vol. V, pp.52–52.
4. Ibid., p.53.
5. The date is reported by Brandon in a letter to Henry VIII. Ellis, R., *Original Letters Illustrative of English History: Including Numerous Royal Letters; from Autographs in the British Museum, and One or Two Other Collections. 2nd Series*, Harding and Lepard (1827), p.247.
6. LPFD, Vol. I, 3342.
7. LPE, Vol. V, p.56.
8. LPE, Vol. V, p.57.
9. LPFD, Vol. I, 3417. Translation is my own, any error is mine.
10. LPFD, Vol. I, 3417.
11. The illuminated copy can be seen at the British Library.
12. LPFD, Vol. I, 3417 & FQL, p.84. The quote from the archbishop is located in LPE, Vol. V, p.58.
13. FQL, p.79.
14. FQL, p. 84.
15. Ibid.
16. LPE, Vol. V, p.59.
17. LPFD, Vol. I, 3429.
18. LPE, Vol. V, p.60.
19. Ibid., p.66.
20. LPFD, Vol. I, 3434. The letter is referenced in Chapter Six, p.70.
21. LPFD, Vol. I, 3325.
22. LPFD, Vol. I, 3308.
23. LPE, Vol. V, p.61.
24. *Hall's Chronicle*, p.572.
25. CSPV, Vol. II, 518.
26. LPE, Vol. V, p.62.
27. *Hall's Chronicle*, p.572.
28. I have used the version in LPE, Vol. V, p.63 as it offers modern spelling but it can also be found in *Hall's Chronicle*, p.572.
29. LPFD, Vol. I, 3461.
30. LPFD, Vol. I, 3441.
31. LRIL, Vol. I, pp.182–183.
32. LPE, Vol. V, pp.64–65.

33. LPFD, Vol. I, 3477.
34. The copy is in the National Library of Paris, MS. 9715.
35. LPE, Vol. V, pp.67–68.
36. CSPV, Vol. II, 542.
37. LPE, Vol. V, pp.70–71.

Chapter Eight – La Reine Blanche

1. LPFD, Vol. I, 3518.
2. CSPV, Vol. II, 537.
3. CSPV, Vol. II, 575.
4. CSPV, Vol. II, 574.
5. CSPV, Vol. II, 563.
6. LPFD, Vol. II, 26.
7. FQL, p.94.
8. LPE, Vol. V, p.78.
9. FQL, p.95.
10. LPE, Vol. V, pp.76–77.
11. Ellis, R., *Original Letters, Illustrative of English History: 1418–1529*, Vol. I, AMS Press, London (1824), pp.120–121.
12. LPE, Vol. V, p.28.
13. CSPV, Vol. II, 574.
14. LPE, Vol. V, p.78.
15. Norris, H., *Tudor Costume and Fashion*, J. M. Dent & Sons, London (1997), p.355–356.
16. LPE, Vol. V, p.76.
17. LPFD, Vol. 2, Preface, Section 1.
18. LRIL, Vol. I, p.185.
19. Ibid., p.186–187.
20. FQL, p.225, note 52.
21. Ibid., p.96.
22. LPFD, Vol. II, 133.
23. FQL, p.76. Also LPFD, Vol. II, 139.
24. FQL, p.64.
25. LPFD, Vol. II, 106.
26. LPE, Vol. V, p.83.
27. LPFD, Vol. II, 113.

Chapter Nine – A Secret to die for

1. LPE, Vol. V, p.20.
2. LPFD, Vol. I, 2941.
3. Ibid.
4. LPFD, Vol. I, 2941.
5. LPFD. Vol. II, 94.
6. LPFD, Vol. II, 119.
7. LPFD, Vol. II, 134.
8. Ibid.
9. LRIL, Vol. I, pp.190–192.
10. Ibid., p.187–188.
11. Ibid., p.188–189.
12. LPFD, Vol. II, 135.
13. LPE, Vol. V, p.87.
14. Ibid., pp.88–89.
15. LRIL, Vol. I, p.201.
16. The date of marriage varies between accounts. Unfortunately, neither Mary nor Brandon refer to the date in their letters. *LPE, Vol. V, p. 90* refers to a contemporary French chronicle, *Fontanieu Portefeuille*, that gives the date as 3 March 1515. Due to lack of other evidence I have chosen to accept this date.
17. LRIL, Vol. I, p.201.
18. LPE, Vol. V, p.89.
19. LRIL, Vol. I, pp.197–198.

Chapter Ten – Favourite Sister

1. LRIL, Vol. I, pp.199–200.
2. Ibid., pp.198 & 200.
3. LPE, Vol. V, p.91.
4. This is in the letter referenced at the end of previous chapter, in response to Brandon's letter of confession. LPE, Vol. V, p.93.
5. LPE, Vol. V, p.94.
6. LPFD, Vol. II, 240.
7. FQL, p.112.
8. LPFD, Vol. II, 245–247.
9. LPFD, Vol. II, 301.
10. LPE, Vol. V, p.96.
11. LPFD, Vol. II, 237.

12. LPE, Vol. V, p.97.
13. LPFD, Vol. II, 320.
14. LPFD, Vol. II, 318 & 319.
15. LPFD, Vol. II, 327.
16. LPE, Vol. V, p.100.
17. Ferdinand would later be released, though not due to Henry's intercedence. He went on to marry Germaine de Foix whilst his mother died in poverty in 1533. LPFD, Vol. II, 257.
18. Draskau, J. K., *The Tudor Rose*, The History Press, Stroud (2013), p.102.
19. LPFD, Vol. II, 343.
20. Ibid.
21. LPE, Vol. V, p.95.
22. LRIL, Vol. I, p.204.
23. Ibid., pp.204–205.
24. Ibid, pp.205–206.

Chapter Eleven – Duchess of Suffolk

1. LPE, Vol. V, p.102.
2. Ibid., pp.107–108 and LPFD, Vol. II, 660.
3. This should be 200,000 crowns. *Recognizances for the Repayment of Loans*, LPFD, Vol. II, pp.1491–1490.
4. LPFD, Vol. II, 522.
5. LPE, Vol. V, p.108.
6. LPFD, Vol. II, 529.
7. FQL, p.123.
8. Ibid., p.143.
9. LPFD, Vol. II, 664.
10. LPFD, Vol. II, 630.
11. LPE, Vol. V, p.111.
12. LRIL, Vol. I, pp.215–218.
13. The 'bishoping' was the confirmation – a ceremony that followed the baptism. LPE, Vol. V, pp.111–112.
14. 'pounsed' meant pierced with holes so they could be used for scents, like a pomander. LPE, Vol. V, pp.112–113.
15. *Hall's Chronicle*, p.584.
16. LPE, Vol. V, p.113. The original is scribed in Latin and held at the Bodleian Library, Oxford (Tanner MS. No. 90, f. 26 b. Vol. V).
17. Gunn, S., *Charles Brandon*, Amberley, Stroud (2015), p.74.

18. LPE, Vol. V, p.114.
19. Ibid., p.115.
20. Gunn, S., *Charles Brandon*, Amberley, Stroud (2015), p.74.
21. Gunn, S., *Charles Brandon*, Amberley, Stroud (2015), p.78.
22. LPE, Vol. V, pp.117–118.
23. Gunn, S., *Charles Brandon*, Amberley, Stroud, (2015), p.74.
24. LPE, Vol. V, p.118.
25. CSPV, Vol. II, 918.
26. Ibid.
27. LPE, Vol. V, p.118.
28. CSPV, Vol. II, 918.
29. Ibid.
30. CSPV, Vol. II, 942.
31. LPE, Vol. V, p.119.
32. FQL, p.135.
33. Gunn, S., *Charles Brandon*, Amberley, Stroud (2015), p.71.
34. CSPV, Vol. II, 987.
35. King's Book of Payments, LPFD, Vol. II, 1509–1515, pp.1469–1473.
36. CSPV, Vol. II, 1018.
37. Gunn, S., *Charles Brandon*, Amberley, Stroud (2015), p.73.
38. CSPV, Vol. II, 1056.
39. *Hall's Chronicle*, p.594.
40. LPE, Vol. V, pp.119–120.
41. CSPV, Vol. II, 1085.
42. Revels, LPFD, Vol. II, pp.1490–1518.
43. Thomas, M., *The King's Pearl*, Amberley, Stroud (2017), pp.35–36.
44. *Recognizances for the Repayment of Loans*, LPFD, Vol. II, pp.1490–1491.
45. *Hall's Chronicle*, p.597.
46. LPE, Vol. V, p.121.
47. Ibid., pp.121–122.
48. LPE, Vol. V, p.122.
49. Ibid., p.123.
50. Norris, H., *Tudor Costume and Fashion*, J. M. Dent & Sons, London (1997), p.214.
51. Turpyn R., *The Chronicles of Calais in the Reigns of Henry VII and Henry VIII, to the Year 1540*, The Camden Society (1846), p.80.
52. Norris, H., *Tudor Costume and Fashion*, J. M. Dent & Sons, London (1997), p.215.
53. LPE, Vol. V, p.124.
54. Gunn, S., *Charles Brandon*, Amberley, Stroud (2015), p.75.

Chapter Twelve – Family, Friends and Friars

1. Mistress Browne and Mistress Danet are also mentioned but the eighth name is unfortunately lost. Richard Gibson's records in the Revels accounts references the ladies gowns were made of yellow satin whilst Hall refers to white. Revels, LPFD, Vol. III, pp.1548–1559; Ives, pp.47–48; Hall's Chronicle, p.631.
2. LPE, Vol. V, p.115.
3. Gunn, S. J. & Lindley, P. G., *Charles Brandon's Westhorpe: an Early Tudor Courtyard House in Suffolk*, Archaeological Journal, 145 (1988), p.272.
4. Ibid., p.273.
5. Ibid., p.274.
6. This claim was made when a survey was undertaken following Mary's death when Henry VIII was arranging a debt settlement and attempting to gain Westhorpe in the settlement. Gunn, S. J. & Lindley, P. G., *Charles Brandon's Westhorpe: An Early Tudor Courtyard House in Suffolk*, Archaeological Journal, 145 (1988), p.274.
7. Ibid., p.276.
8. Ibid., p.279.
9. Ibid., pp.282–283.
10. Ibid., p.276.
11. The full description discussing the survey and the account of the demolishment can be found in: Gunn, S. J. & Lindley, P. G., *Charles Brandon's Westhorpe: an Early Tudor Courtyard House in Suffolk*, Archaeological Journal, 145 (1988), pp.272–289.
12. This is possibly Thomas Grimston who lived to the incredible age of 92. LPE, Vol. V, p.126.
13. The dates for the birth of the second born son differ. I have chosen 1523 as he was created Earl of Lincoln in 1525, and *Hall's Chronicle*, p.707 refers to him as aged 2 at this point.
14. *Hall's Chronicle*, p.672.
15. *Hall's Chronicle*, p.674.
16. LPFD, Vol. IV, 1431.
17. Hall refers to the child as 2 years old whereas Green refers to a 9-year-old child but the latter is an error referring to Mary's firstborn who had died in 1522.
18. LPE, Vol. V, pp.128–129.
19. FQL, p.186.
20. Draskau, J. K., *The Tudor Rose*, The History Press (2013), pp.140–141.
21. Ibid., p.141.
22. FQL, p.187.

23. LPE, Vol. V, p.130.
24. LPE, Vol. V, p.132.
25. The letter is written in French in Mary's own hand but has been translated in FQL, p.188.
26. LPE, Vol. V, p.136.

Chapter Thirteen – Queen of Hearts

1. King's Book of Payments, LPFD, Vol. II, 1509–1515, pp.1469–1473.
2. FQL, p.31.
3. LRIL, Vol. I, p.202.
4. FQL, p.31.
5. LRIL, Vol. I, p.193–194.
6. LRIL, Vol. I, p.243. Unfortunately the year is not noted.
7. LPE, Vol. V, p.133.
8. Ibid., p.134.
9. Ibid., pp.134–135.
10. LPFD, Vol 4, ii, 2744.
11. LPFD, Addenda, 367.
12. LPE, Vol. V, p.136.
13. Bryson, S., *La Reine Blanche*, Amberley, Stroud (2018), p.223.
14. Cavendish, G., *Thomas Wolsey, late Cardinal in his Life and Death*, (ed. Lockyer, R), The Folio Society, London (1962), pp.125–126.
15. *Hall's Chronicle*, p.756.
16. Bryson, S., *La Reine Blanche*, Amberley, Stroud (2018), p.226.
17. LPFD, Vol. V, 340.
18. CSPV, Vol. 4, 761.
19. LRIL, Vol. II, p.87.
20. Lord Lisle was arrested on 19 May 1540 under suspicion of treason. He was not guilty but was held in prison for two years. On being advised he was to be released he allegedly suffered from a heart attack and died two days later.

Chapter Fourteen – La Volonté de Dieu Me Suffit

1. An image of what this may have looked like can be seen in St Mary's Church, Bury St Edmunds. Although I tried to obtain a picture, the images are poor quality.

2. LPE, Vol. V, p.140.
3. Ibid., p.140.
4. Ibid., p.19.
5. See Chapter Nine.
6. Bryson, S., *La Reine Blanche*, Amberley, Stroud (2018), p.235.

Chapter Fifteen – Legacy

1. The events of the succession following the death of Edward VI are too long to include here, but it is likely Henry Brandon would have succeeded Edward VI if he had lived.
2. CSPV, Vol. II, 511.
3. Mearns, R., 'Material Messages: A Reassessment of the Double Portrait of Mary Tudor and Charles Brandon' in *Textile History*, 50:2, (2019), pp.128–142.
4. This is only an excerpt from *The Justes of the Moneths of May and June*. Unfortunately there is no author recorded for the poem but it is believed to have printed by Wynkyn de Worde in 1507. The whole poem can be read in Carew Hazlitt, W. (ed.), *Remains of the Early Popular Poetry of England*, John Russell Smith, London (1866), pp.109–130.
5. LPE, Vol. V, p.105.
6. Ibid.
7. You can read more about this on the blog of Tony Riches and also read *The Mythology of the Princes in the Tower* by the late John Ashdown-Hill.
8. Sadlack, E. A., *The French Queen's Letters*, Palsgrave MacMillan (2011), p.4.

Bibliography

Online Sources

British History Online
Oxford Dictionary of National Biography
The Chamber Books of Henry VII and Henry VIII (1485–1521)
The National Archives Currency Converter

Journals/Theses

Brobeck, J. T., 'A Music Book for Mary Tudor, Queen of France', printed in *Early Music History,* (Cambridge University Press, 2016).

Fisher, C., 'The Queen and the artichoke: A study of the portraits of Mary Tudor and Charles Brandon' in *The British Art Journal*, 3(2), (2002) pp.20–27.

Gunn, S. J. & Lindley, P. G., 'Charles Brandon's Westhorpe: an Early Tudor Courtyard House in Suffolk' in *Archaeological Journal*, 145, (1988).

Harris, B. J., 'Power, Profit, and Passion: Mary Tudor, Charles Brandon, and the Arranged Marriage in Early Tudor England' in *Feminist Studies*, 15(1), (1989) pp.59–88.

Hubbard, S., *"Your Loving Sister, Mary the French Queen", The Material Culture of Mary Tudor,* (Thesis, 2023).

Mearns, R., 'Material Messages: A Reassessment of the Double Portrait of Mary Tudor and Charles Brandon' in *Textile History*, 50:2, (2019) pp.128–142.

Richards, J. M., '"To Promote a Woman to Beare Rule": Talking of Queens in Mid-Tudor England' in *The Sixteenth Century Journal*, 28(1) (1997), pp.101–121.

Sadlack, E. A., 'Epistolary Negotiations: Mary the French Queen and the Politics of Letter-Writing' in *The Sixteenth Century Journal*, 41(3) (2010) pp.691–711.

Primary Sources

Calendar of State Papers and Manuscripts in the Archives and Collections of Milan 1385–1618, Hinds, A. B. (ed.), (London, 1912).

Calendar of State Papers, Spain, Vol. 1, 1485–1509, Bergenroth, G. A. (ed.), (London, 1862).

Calendar of State Papers Relating To English Affairs in the Archives of Venice, Volume 1, 1202–1509, Brown, R. (ed.), (London, 1864).

Cavendish, G., *Thomas Wolsey late Cardinal in his Life and Death*, Lockyer, R. (ed.), (The Folio Society, London, 1962).

E101: Exchequer, King's Remembrancer, Various Accounts

Godefroy, T., *Le Ceremonial Francois*, Vol. I, (Sebastien Cramoisy, France, 1649).

Hall's Chronicle: Containing The History of England, during the reign of Henry the Fourth, and the succeeding monarchs, to the end of the reign of Henry the Eighth, (London, 1809). Originally printed in 1548.

Letters and Papers Illustrative of the Reigns of Richard III and Henry VII, 2 volumes, Gairdner, J. (ed)., (Longman, Green, Longman and Roberts, London, 1861).

Letters and Papers, Foreign and Domestic, of the Reign of Henry VIII, J. S. Brewer, J. Gairdner and R.H. Brodie (eds.), 21 vols in 32 parts, and Addenda (London, 1862–1932).

Pizan, C. de., *The Treasure of the City of Ladies or The Book of the Three Virtues*, Lawson, S. (trans.), (Penguin Books, London, 1985). Originally written in 1404/05.

Privy Purse Expenses of Elizabeth of York: Wardrobe Accounts of Edward the Fourth, with a memoir of Elizabeth of York, and Notes, Nicolas, N. H. (ed.), (William Pickering, London, 1830).

The Justes of the Moneths of May and June, Author unknown. Printed in Carew Hazlitt, W. (ed.), *Remains of the Early Popular Poetry of England*, (John Russell Smith, London, 1866). It is believed to have first been printed in 1507 by Wynkyn de Worde.

'The Spousells' of the Princess Mary. Daughter of Henry VII., to Charles Prince of Castille. A.D. 1508, Gairdner, J. (ed)., (Camden Society, London, 1893). First printed by Pynson.

The Will of King Henry VII, (Printed for *The Editor*, London, 1775).

Turpyn, R., *The Chronicles of Calais in the Reigns of Henry VII and Henry VIII, to the Year 1540*, (The Camden Society, 1846).

Secondary Sources

Amin, N., *The House of Beaufort*, (Amberley, Stroud, 2018).

Ashdown-Hill, J., *The Wars of the Roses*, (Amberley, Stroud, 2017).

Broomhall, S., *In the Orbit of the King: Women, Power, and Authority at the French Court, 1483–1563*. Published in Broomhall, S. (ed.), *Women and Power at the French Court, 1483–1563*, (pp.9–40). (Amsterdam University Press, 2018).

Bryson, S., *La Reine Blanche*, (Amberley, Stroud, 2018).

Chapman, H. W., *The Sisters of Henry VIII*, (Jonathan Cape, London, 1969).

Croom Brown, M., *Mary Tudor, Queen of France*, (Methuen & Co. Ltd, London, 1911).

Draskau, J. K., *The Tudor Rose*, (The History Press, Stroud, 2013).

Ellis, H., *Original Letters, Illustrative of English History: 1418–1529*, Vol. I, (AMS Press, London, 1824).

Ellis, R., *Original Letters Illustrative of English History: Including Numerous Royal Letters; from Autographs in the British Museum, and One or Two Other Collections, 2nd Series*, (Harding and Lepard, 1827).

Evans, V. S., *Ladies-in-Waiting: Women Who Served at the Tudor Court*, (Self-published, 2014).

Green, M. A. E., *Lives of Princesses of England from the Norman Conquest*, Vol. IV & V. (Hurst & Blackett, London, 1854).

Groag Bell, S., *The Lost Tapestries of the City of Ladies, Christine De Pizan's Renaissance Legacy*, (University of California Press Ltd., London, 2004).

Gunn, S., *Charles Brandon*, (Amberley, Stroud, 2015).

Harris, B., *English Aristocratic Women 1450–1550*, (Oxford University Press, Oxford, 2002).

Harvey, N. L., *The Rose and the Thorn*, (Collier MacMillan Publishers, London, 1975).

Hodder, S. J, *Cecily Bonville-Grey: Marchioness of Dorset*, (Chronos Books, Winchester, 2022).

Hutchinson, R., *Young Henry*, (Weidenfeld & Nicolson, London, 2012).

Ives, E., *Anne Boleyn*, (Basil Blackwell, London, 1988).

Mattingly, G., *Catherine of Aragon*, (Jonathan Cape, London, 1942).

McGrath, C., *Sex and Sexuality in Tudor England*, (Pen and Sword, Barnsley, 2022).

Mumby, F. A., *The Youth of Henry VIII*, (Houghton, Mifflin Company, Boston & New York, 1913).

Norris, H., *Tudor Costume and Fashion*, (J. M. Dent & Sons, London, 1997).

Perry, M., *Sisters to the King*, (André Deutsch, London, 2002).

Read, E., *Catherine, Duchess of Suffolk*, (Jonathan Cape, London, 1962).

Richardson, W. C., *Mary Tudor, The White Queen*, (Peter Owen Limited, London, 1970).

Sadlack, E. A., *The French Queen's Letters: Mary Tudor Brandon and the Politics of Marriage in Sixteenth-Century Europe*, (Palgrave MacMillan, 2011).

Sadlack, E. A., *"Literary Lessons in Queenship and Power: Mary Tudor Brandon and the Authority of the Ambassador-Queen."* Published in *Women and Power at the French Court, 1483–1563*, Broomhall, S. (ed.), (pp.117–138), (Amsterdam University Press, 2018).

Thomas, M., *The King's Pearl*, (Amberley, Stroud, 2017).

Watkins, S. B., *The Tudor Brandons*, (Chronos Books, Hants, 2016).

Watkins, S. B., *Margaret Tudor, Queen of Scots: The Life of King Henry VIII's Sister*, (Chronos Books, Hants, 2017).

Williams, N., *The Life and Times of Henry VII*, (Weidenfeld and Nicolson, London, 1973).

Wood, M. A. E., *Letters of Royal and Illustrious Ladies of Great Britain*, 3 vols. (Henry Colburn, London, 1846).

Index